MANAGING
THE MILITARY

SHARON K. WEINER

MANAGING
THE MILITARY

The Joint Chiefs of Staff and Civil-Military Relations

Columbia University Press / *New York*

Columbia University Press
Publishers Since 1893
New York   Chichester, West Sussex
cup.columbia.edu

Library of Congress Cataloging-in-Publication Data

Names: Weiner, Sharon K., 1963– author.
Title: Managing the military : the Joint Chiefs of Staff and civil-military
relations / Sharon K. Weiner.
Other titles: Joint Chiefs of Staff and civil-military relations
Description: New York : Columbia University Press, [2022] |
Includes bibliographical references and index.
Identifiers: LCCN 2022011786 (print) | LCCN 2022011787 (ebook) |
ISBN 9780231207348 (hardback) | ISBN 9780231207355 (trade paperback) |
ISBN 9780231556934 (ebook)
Subjects: LCSH: United States. Joint Chiefs of Staff. | United States. Office of
the Chairman of the Joint Chiefs of Staff. | Civil-military relations—United
States. | United States—Armed Forces—Appropriations and expenditures. |
United States. Department of Defense—Appropriations and expenditures.
Classification: LCC UA23.7 .W45 2022 (print) | LCC UA23.7 (ebook) |
DDC 355.0092/273—dc23/eng/20220331
LC record available at https://lccn.loc.gov/2022011786
LC ebook record available at https://lccn.loc.gov/2022011787

Cover design: Noah Arlow
Cover image: Getty Images

For Zia

CONTENTS

ABBREVIATIONS

BCA	Budget Control Act
BUR	Bottom-Up Review
CAPE	Office of Cost Assessment and Program Evaluation
CIA	Central Intelligence Agency
CINCs	commanders in chief
COCOMs	combatant commanders
FBI	Federal Bureau of Investigation
FY	fiscal year
GAO	Government Accountability Office
GWOT	Global War on Terrorism supplementals
J3	Joint Staff Directorate for Operations
J5	Joint Strategy, Policy, and Plans Directorate
J8	Joint Staff Force Structure, Resource, and Assessment Directorate
JCIDS	Joint Capabilities Integration and Development System
JCS	Joint Chiefs of Staff
JROC	Joint Requirements Oversight Council

ABBREVIATIONS

MRCs	major regional contingencies
NASA	National Aeronautics and Space Administration
NSC	National Security Council
OCO	Overseas Contingency Operations
OMB	Office of Management and Budget
OSD	Office of the Secretary of Defense
POMs	Program Objective Memoranda
PPBS	Planning, Programming, and Budgeting System
QDR	Quadrennial Defense Review
SCMR	Strategic Choices and Management Review
UFRs	unfunded requirements
UN	United Nations

1

STRUCTURE, POLITICS, AND INFLUENCE

The chairman of the Joint Chiefs of Staff (JCS) is arguably the most politically powerful military officer in the United States. Part of his influence is due to formal authority. Besides being the highest-ranking member of the armed forces, numerous laws have given him increased clout over the individual military leaders who head the army, navy, air force, and marine corps, known collectively as the JCS. He is also officially designated as the primary military adviser to the president as well as the defense secretary and the National Security Council. In these roles, his advice and recommendations have significant sway over decisions about military strategy, operations, and spending.

But part of the chairman's power comes from the broader ramifications of these policy choices. For example, Chairman Mike Mullen's strong endorsement of a troop surge in 2009 helped not only to convince President Barak Obama, but also contributed to maintaining a coalition of allied forces as well as a nation-building strategy in Afghanistan that ultimately failed.[1] The spending limits mandated by the Budget Control Act of 2011 have been repeatedly increased thanks in part to repeated arguments by senior military officers, such as Chairman Joseph Dunford, that real growth over inflation is required for national security.[2] In 2007, when Chairman Peter Pace labelled homosexuality immoral, it brought swift condemnation from Congress as well as various civil society groups because of concerns his comments would prompt discrimination in the military but also more broadly.[3]

Besides formal authority and the far-reaching consequences of choices about defense policy, the chairman's political power is also derivative of the choices he makes about how to fill his role as the most visible military officer in the United States. Mark Milley, who started a four-year term in October 2019, offers multiple examples of the chairman's influence, both intentional and inadvertent. During the 2021 presidential election, Milley became concerned that President Donald Trump's aggressive behavior, which coincided with U.S. military exercises in the South China Sea, would be interpreted by China as a precursor to military action.[4] Without informing civilian leaders or receiving direction from them, Milley called his counterpart in China to offer reassurances that the U.S. government was stable and not prone to reckless aggression. Less than a month later, Milley again sparked controversy when he suggested to Speaker of the House Nancy Pelosi that the military would override any decision by President Trump to launch nuclear weapons.[5] The year prior, in June 2020, Milley perhaps unintentionally took part in a photo op with President Trump and members of the cabinet that many interpreted as a campaign stunt with authoritarian and racist overtones.[6] Milley found it necessary to offer a public apology for "creating a perception of the military involved in domestic politics."[7]

Milley's actions certainly fueled already existing partisan disputes. He received praise, mostly from Democrats, and was labeled a traitor by Trump supporters.[8] But there was also disagreement among scholars of civil-military relations. Had Milley's actions violated long-standing norms about the proper role of the military in politics? Did they, as some argued, cross a line into inappropriately political behavior that undermines the trust Americans have in the military?[9] Or is the military's professionalism such that it can withstand temporary violations of the assumed boundaries between the military and politics?[10]

The focus on the military's role in politics has been at the core of the study of U.S. civil-military relations since the post–World War II debate between Samuel Huntington and Morris Janowitz over whether the military can ever be apolitical.[11] Yet, despite the many reasons why the position of chairman is inherently political, and the various incentives for any chairman to embrace such a role, there have been remarkably few studies of how chairmen have exercised their power.[12] This void is particularly problematic given the increased power and authority provided to the chairman by the Goldwater-Nichols Act of 1986—the most significant set of organizational changes to the defense department since the National Security Act of 1947. At the time it was being debated, there were concerns the 1986 law would create a chairman who was a danger to civilian control of the military.[13]

Colin Powell, the first person appointed chairman after the Goldwater-Nichols Act, seemed to suggest these concerns were valid. Powell assumed the role during the last days of the Cold War, when many thought a "peace dividend" would be realized as U.S. defense budgets declined in response to the demise of the Soviet threat and military force assumed a less important role in U.S. foreign policy. Not only did Powell publicly advocate for substantial military spending, but he also forcefully argued for what would become known as the "Powell Doctrine," a national security strategy based on the premise that the United States should avoid limited wars and enter combat only with overwhelming force and when there is a clear military objective. Besides being unusually public and outspoken in his support for these initiatives, in both cases Powell was advocating policies that had not been endorsed by, and in places contradicted, the commander in chief, President George H. W. Bush, and his secretary of defense, Dick Cheney.

Powell's behavior raised worries about the future of civilian control of the military. Credit was certainly given to Powell's own political prowess, but much of the concern focused on the office of chairman and the suite of new authorities given to that position by the 1986 Goldwater-Nichols Act.[14] Had the law centralized too much power in the JCS chairman? Was Powell but the first example of what would become the new norm—that of a chairman able not only to eclipse the views of the military services, but to exercise undue influence over or even dominate national security policy?

These worries proved unfounded. No chairman since Powell has played such an independent role in national security policy.[15] Moreover, the tenure of Peter Pace provides a sharp contrast. As chairman under Defense Secretary Donald Rumsfeld, Pace was seen as so deferential to Secretary Rumsfeld that he was mockingly labeled "Pete the Parrot" for his willingness to champion Rumsfeld's policy choices without challenge and regardless of how unpopular those policies were with the services.[16]

Is it Powell or Pace who best illustrates the contemporary role of the JCS chairman in defense policy? What has been the impact of the Goldwater-Nichols Act on not only the power of the chairman, but on the influence of the individual services and the clout of the military overall in policy battles with civilians? Answering these questions is important for assessing the state of civil-military relations in the United States, but also for understanding the origins of military advice and the soundness of the policy choices that are derived from it.

A MORE POWERFUL CHAIRMAN?

Since its creation during World War II, there have been numerous changes to the structure of the JCS, a senior group of military officers that is comprised of the heads of the army, navy, air force, and marine corps and that today includes a chairman who is the principal military adviser to the president. All of these changes have been aimed at increasing coordination between the services, by strengthening the authority of either the secretary of defense or the chairman. But even as these managers accrued more formal authority, the JCS became increasingly effective at protecting service interests. Chapter 3 explains how this evolution has been aided and abetted by Congress, which has sought to temper any changes to the organization of the JCS that would limit congressional access to information and advice from the services. Congress uses its connections to the services to seek parochial benefits in the form of weapons purchases and military bases, to innovate and oversee policy, and also to pick holes in the president's defense plans. This is why Congress has consistently refused to agree to presidential requests for a stronger chairman. Successive presidents, for their part, have wanted a more powerful chairman who could corral the services in support of their administrations' policies. Congress, however, has preferred independent services because they are the key to congressional power.

The exception to this trend is the 1986 Goldwater-Nichols Act, which was written by members of Congress and enacted over the objections of President Ronald Reagan and his defense secretary, Caspar Weinberger, and in spite of significant opposition from each of the services. Chapter 4 explains how the act altered the structure of the JCS by adopting changes quite similar to ones Congress had previously rejected, including providing more power and authority to the chairman and making him alone, rather than the collective service chiefs, responsible for providing military advice to the president. By finally agreeing to create a more powerful chairman, Congress hoped to accomplish something that civilians had long desired but were unable to achieve: forcing the services to prioritize national defense over their own individual interests.

The act's buzzword was and remains "jointness"—a goal discussed in detail in chapter 2. The chairman was expected to use his new authorities to offer military advice that reflects compromise and integration of individual service perspectives. Instead of the past practice of putting forward the summation of individual service preferences, the chairman would force trade-offs between those preferences in the name of national defense. The resulting advice would be "joint" because it reflected what was good for the common defense rather than parochial service preferences.

As chapter 4 explains, critics argued that the chairman's new powers would lead to less desirable effects. Some worried that service expertise would be diluted or downplayed, resulting in the loss of important capabilities or perspectives. Others argued that the chairman was given too much power and his advice would override that of the service chiefs, or, even worse, that he would become a threat to the civilian supremacy that is valued in U.S. civil-military relations.

Questions about the power of the chairman and the service chiefs after the Goldwater-Nichols Act are the empirical puzzles at the core of this book. Have subsequent chairmen followed the style suggested by Mark Milley or Colin Powell and challenged the authority of civilian leaders? Or is the example of Peter Pace, and extreme deference to civilian authority, more the norm? And, most importantly, what are the consequences and political ramifications of the chairman's new role for the relationship between civilian and military leaders? Using a combination of historical analysis and post–Cold War case studies of debates over defense spending, I argue that the chairman has indeed become more powerful and can, under certain conditions, become so influential that he requires deference and compromise from the president and secretary of defense. But there is also an important check on the exercise of this power: the service chiefs.

I argue that the chairman's power is dependent on three variables. The first is choice. Some chairmen, such as Colin Powell or Mike Mullen, choose to be more political, seeking out opportunities to influence policy in the executive branch but also among the public. Others, however, steadfastly support the president and secretary of defense, even if they personally disagree or know they are promoting a policy that the services don't like.

The second variable relates to domestic politics and the coalitions that are viable because of either partisan disagreements or battles between Congress and the executive branch. When civilians argue with each other, they seek support from military experts. Because military advice has political clout, civilians have a tradition of seeking military allies for their policy positions and of using military advice in their political battles with each other.[17] A Google search of any major presidential pronouncement on defense policy is likely to result in pictures of the president or his defense secretary flanked by the service chiefs or the chairman. Presidents since Harry S. Truman have compromised on policy so they can have the support of the military in their battles with Congress.[18] And members of

Congress have used alliances with one or more of the services in their efforts to overturn or oversee presidential policy.

Politically expedient coalitions between the service chiefs and the White House have been the norm since 1947. But the chairman is also expected to be part of the president's team. He is supposed to get the services to support administration policy or at least not challenge it publicly. The norm of civilian supremacy also often leads to the assumption that the chairman should be counted on to support the policies of the commander in chief. The Goldwater-Nichols Act reinforced these assumptions by making the chairman the principal military adviser to the president, secretary of defense, and the National Security Council.

But rather than increasing the chairman's allegiance to the White House, I argue that the act reinforced and augmented the chairman's role as a political operative. Chapter 2 provides substantial empirical evidence that the chairman is now the principal source of military advice to the president and has come to replace the service chiefs as the main military voice in policy debates. I argue that one result of the chairman's increased stature is that the president and the president's national security team must consider his preferences and political skills, and whether these will be used to support, thwart, or ignore civilian preferences. Presidents who are politically weak, or whose policy agendas face partisan or congressional opposition, may not be able to forego the chairman's support. Such circumstances also leave presidents vulnerable to a chairman who wants to propose his own policies.

Besides personal preference and political circumstance, the third variable that conditions the chairman's exercise of his authority is support from the service chiefs. A chairman who contradicts the chiefs' consensus risks losing their support and thus his influence. The services will tolerate some independence from the chairman, but only if he has a record of consulting the service chiefs and supporting the military's position in White House debates.

The service chiefs constrain the chairman because they are, ultimately, the key to a significant part of his political power. For one thing, as an agent of the president, the White House expects the chairman to help the secretary of defense keep the services in sync with presidential policy.

Disgruntled services can impede policy initiatives by refusing to provide information, slow-rolling implementation, or seeking to overturn the president's preferences by allying with members of Congress or appealing directly to the public. But the chairman's ability to control this disruptive behavior is limited because he does not command the services or their chiefs of staff. Moreover, a sufficiently unhappy service chief can usually find at least a few members of Congress who are eager to overturn White House policy decisions. If the chairman cannot wrangle the service chiefs in support of administration policy, his influence in the White House is likely to suffer.

Expertise is another reason the chairman's power is linked to the services. As his principal military adviser, the president expects the chairman to be his agent and to provide his best military advice. Although the chairman has his own staff and advisory groups, they cannot compete with the services as sources of expertise on numerous issues. A chairman who offers military advice that is divorced from the organizations that train and equip the armed forces risks being irrelevant or wrong. But the chairman is also expected to be sufficiently independent of the services that his advice is "joint"—that is, it makes trade-offs between service preferences and establishes priorities.

The result of these conflicting demands is a conundrum that every chairman must face: how to offer the advice and management expected by the White House without losing the cooperation of the services. The policy debates examined in chapters 5, 6, and 7 show that most chairmen navigate this problem by deferring to the policy preferences of the service chiefs, which are focused on building consensus between them, which is more likely if they follow the long-standing norm that all of the services should be treated equally.

Even though the chairman has gained more authority over time, the structure of the JCS has consistently treated the service chiefs as equals. As chapter 3 explains, initially this equality fueled rivalry between the services as they argued over budget shares and missions. Civilians used these arguments to make choices between service positions. Eventually, the JCS learned that consensus was a way to escape this zero-sum game. By presenting unified advice, the service chiefs made it harder for civilians to pick winners and losers.

The need to create and maintain consensus among the services led to internal JCS norms that favored equality and logrolling. Each service came to expect it could claim an equal share of resources or opportunities, and collectively the JCS would combine these preferences rather than make choices between them. The result was a lack of precisely that joint military advice that the Goldwater-Nichols Act was intended to foster by giving more power to the chairman. But as chapters 5, 6, and 7 show, the chairman's power is still linked to support from the service chiefs. A chairman who challenges consensus among the chiefs, or who uses his relationship with the White House to offer contradictory military advice, risks losing the support of the services and thus his own political agency within the White House.

It is also important to note that the chairman exercises his political power mostly within the executive branch and not in his relationships with Congress. Certainly, he testifies in support of administration policy, and he is also expected to offer his unvarnished professional advice. But there is scant evidence that chairmen have sought to create or leverage a less formal relationship with members of Congress or key committees. Since the creation of the JCS, that leverage has been and remains with the service chiefs.

In making this argument, I treat the JCS as an institution. That is, while I treat it as a collection of actors—the service chiefs, a chairman, and a vice chairman—I also pay close attention to the expectations for interactions among them that are governed by formal rules and processes as well as by precedent, informal agreement, and norms.[19] I argue that the JCS has over time evolved into an institution that is successful at protecting service interests and allows the chairman, under the right conditions, to lead rather than follow civilian policy preferences. This outcome has been enabled by past congressional choices about the formal structure of the JCS and abetted by civilians who use military expertise to gain political clout. The result is an increasingly politicized military and less civilian control.

My argument is based upon an analysis of the evolution of the JCS since 1947 as well as detailed case studies of three of the most significant debates over defense spending and resources since the Goldwater-Nichols Act of 1986. These debates include downsizing at the end of the Cold War and arguments over what would come to be called the Base Force, Secretary of Defense Donald Rumsfeld's attempts from 2001 to 2006 to transform the military into a lighter, more agile force by leveraging new technologies, and a series of budget caps and eventually cuts due to sequestration during the Obama administration. Instead of the usual incremental adjustments to the defense budget, these cases each had the potential to reduce defense budgets by 20 percent or more and to redistribute budget shares between the services. Two of the cases required responses to external events—one was the end of the Cold War, the other congressional concerns over budget deficits. The other case—Rumsfeld and transformation—has its origins in policy direction from the White House. Collectively, these cases represent the key periods since 1986 when the defense budget was the most contentious, the stakes were highest for civilians and the services, and the chairman had to make a choice about whether to exercise his power to manage the services or the White House.

I focus on defense spending for three reasons. First, the conventional wisdom is that the Goldwater-Nichols Act was a success when it came to improving military advice, clarifying the authorities and responsibilities by which military orders are executed, and coordinating military operations.[20] The exception is defense budgets, where others argue that service interests still play a preponderant role in establishing priorities.[21] It makes sense, then, to better understand if, and why, military advice has improved in some areas but not in the crucial area of resource allocation. Moreover, my analysis of defense spending calls into question the degree to which military advice in other areas is now better integrated and coordinated—in other words, "joint"—or whether that term is merely a disguise for service interests.

A second reason to focus on resources is because money and the defense budget have a significant impact on most areas of U.S. defense policy, including the ability to prepare for and wage war. If the basis for research, development, and procurement remains firmly with the services, this raises questions about efficiency, redundancy, and preparedness, as well as the quality of military advice provided about each.

Third, resource decisions are among the most complex civil-military interactions because they combine international relations with domestic politics. Even during the Cold War, when there was a general consensus over the role of the military in responding to external threats, defense budget choices were made in an environment that usually prioritized domestic political interests and dynamics.[22]

To better understand the similarities, or lack thereof, between civil-military interaction over budgets and those over other contentious military policies, to each budget debate I add a brief analysis of the role played by the chairman in other defense policy disagreements under the same administration. As explained in the next section, the literature on civil-military relations is split on whether attempts to influence the budget follow the same patterns as decisions over use of force, strategy, or other issues. My analysis suggests that the chairman's inclination and ability to exercise independent power is consistent across these policy areas.

The next section situates my claims and analysis within the study of civil-military relations. This not only makes explicit the assumptions and arguments I draw upon but provides important context for assessing this book's contributions to the scholarship on civil-military relations and national security policy.

U.S. CIVIL-MILITARY RELATIONS AS A POLITICAL INSTITUTION

People often mean different things when they talk about civil-military relations in the United States. As Mackubin Owens has explained, some scholars focus on institutions and the formal and informal relationships between different actors, while others look to culture, ideology, society, or external environments to explain interactions between civilians and the military.[23] Much of the focus on U.S. civil-military relations has been on the health or harmony of the relationship, including the degree to which civilians and the military respect each other, share or diverge on partisan preferences, and tend to obey or ignore, shirk, or redefine policy directives.[24] My purpose here is somewhat different. I share the goal of better understanding the degree to which the preferences of civilians or the military influence policy. But I also seek to describe and predict the circumstances under which different civilian and military actors are likely to be more or less influential and whether that influence is most successful as persuasion, policy entrepreneurship, or hierarchical command.

I start with two assumptions, spelled out here for purposes of clarity, not because either assumption is controversial. The first is that structure matters. The organization of the JCS influences not only the statutory power different actors can wield but the more subtle forms of give-and-take that become possible and prevalent as different actors seek to reconcile the formal boundaries of their authority with the opportunities presented by different policy problems and political contexts. The second assumption is that military expertise has political power. The services, sometimes individually but often collectively, have their own views about what it takes to secure the nation. The same is true for civilian policy makers. But how do elected officials, whose knowledge of and experience with national security may vary, differentiate between service needs and service desires? Who decides how much interservice coordination is required for national security, and the areas where service duplication, independence, and rivalry can be tolerated? Certainly, it matters who is formally vested with the authority to make these decisions, but also important is where policy makers get recommendations, how military expertise is translated into counsel, and the degree to which any adviser is beholden to subordinates but also has leverage over superiors.

These two starting assumptions combine to make the civil-military relationship a strategic game between actors with different policy preferences and differing sources of power. As Amy Zegart and Risa Brooks both argue, the formal structure of institutions such as the JCS is the product of a struggle between different political actors, each vying to create a policy process that maximizes their power and makes it more likely they will get their policy preferences.[25] In other words, changing the structure of the policy process is intended to influence power but not necessarily to produce better policy. Starting with this assumption, my goal is to better understand not only how each reorganization of the JCS changed the power dynamics between civilians and the military, but the expected, unexpected, and unintended impacts on defense spending and defense policy more broadly.

Central to this conversation is the permanence of certain enduring interests. The military and Congress both face similar collective action problems that arise from long-established preferences. They have solved these problems in quite different ways.

For the military, there is the persistent division of responsibility along service lines and the enduring influence of unique service cultures. In *The Masks of War*, Carl Builder shows the influence of service culture on the development of weapons, doctrine, and strategy, but Jeffrey Donnithorne argues culture is also an important factor in how each service interprets and responds to policy decisions and thus civilian control.[26] Because the U.S. defense structure has always been based on coequal services, it was important for the military to develop formal and informal structures to enable each service to pursue their preferences without harming the ability of the other services to do so. As explained in chapters 3 and 4, by the mid-1960s the services had learned to solve this problem by agreeing not to argue in public, offering only unified opinions, and making sure that over time resources are split more or less evenly between them.

Congress has the same problem—coequal members with individual preferences. Similar to the JCS, the structure of Congress is intended to preserve the right of each individual member to pursue their preferences; that is, to support bills and spending that benefit their district and occasionally achieve personal policy goals.[27] Collectively, however, this parochial behavior is limited in several ways.[28] Budget agreements, deficit caps, and procedures that require spending to be both authorized and appropriated all serve to limit the size of the pie that can be divided among legislators. The need to maintain the reputation and power of Congress vis-à-vis the executive branch also puts limits on parochial behavior. The same is true for delegation. Congress often lacks the expertise, resources, or time to implement its policy goals, so it delegates to agencies.[29] In turn, these agencies have discretion that can be exercised to avoid or reverse congressional direction.

There is, however, one important similarity between the JCS and Congress: the structure of both means that their members benefit from alliances with each other. Members of Congress need military expertise to support their policy preferences, and the service chiefs need support from Congress to overturn decisions made by the president. This connection isn't controversial.[30] I argue that it also doesn't depend on the chairman. The services don't need him to find congressional allies, and he has no parochial benefits to offer members of Congress. This is not to argue that the chairman can never have a constituency in Congress. In situations where Congress, or at least a significant fraction, supports a policy opposed by the president, if the chairman agrees with Congress, he will certainly find a useful ally for overturning presidential preferences. But in such cases the service chiefs would also likely favor the position of that bloc in Congress. The additional support from the chairman is redundant and likely unnecessary. Or, framed differently, the chairman is unlikely to leverage congressional support to overturn policy preferences shared by the service chiefs.

Instead of Congress, the chairman's main civilian constituency is the executive branch. The president expects the chairman to provide military advice unfettered by service parochialism and to support the president's policy objectives. The chairman is also expected to help the defense secretary by providing military advice and rallying the services in support of administration policy in front of Congress and the public, or, at the very least, to be limited in their criticisms. The president also has incentives to defer to the chairman's advice because, as Polina Beliakova argues, the public's trust in the military can translate this into support for the president's policies, or the chairman can be a useful scapegoat if things go wrong.[31]

But the chairman has another constituency: the service chiefs. The chiefs expect the chairman to persuade the administration of the wisdom of their policy preferences and to offer advice only after the JCS have collectively decided on what that advice should be.

The chairman's two constituencies, however, are not equal. In statute, the chairman directs an impressive support group: the Joint Staff. Composed of military officers from each service as well as civilian personnel, this group provides the research, analysis, and managerial support for the chairman to perform his studies. It is augmented by the CAG, or Chairman's Action Group, a set of advisers who help with everything from analysis to messaging.[32] He also gets input from the combatant commanders, the four-star military officers in charge of coordinating and using the equipment and personnel of each service in the event of war or other military operations.[33]

But the main input for military advice, and certainly on decisions about research, development, and procurement, remains firmly with the services. More importantly, part of the chairman's value to the executive branch is his ability to lead the services—something he loses if he distances himself too far from their positions. Further, the services enjoy an institutionalized channel of dissent vis-à-vis Congress. If the chairman, either acting alone or as an agent for the executive, denies any service their preference, that service can go to Congress for redress. And members of Congress have multiple incentives to encourage this behavior, including rent seeking for parochial benefit for their district, but also punching holes in any administration policy with which members disagree. For these reasons, the chairman is likely to worry more about his reputation among the services than in the White House.

This difference in constituencies matters in civil-military relations because the power dynamics in each are different.[34] When Congress is the civilian in civil-military relations, politics is distributive and collective action necessary. The president, in contrast, may need to rely on persuasion, but he enjoys more hierarchical power. Additionally, instead of distributing benefits across constituencies, his political currency is the promise of future influence. In other words, he convinces people to compromise on policy today in return for the chance that they will be consulted and thus have influence in the future.

The JCS, as an institution, has evolved specific ways to seek influence among these different types of civilians. Internal norms plus congressional action have enabled the service chiefs to maintain mutually beneficial alliances with members of Congress. Further, each service chief has the leeway to advocate for their own service as long as they don't directly attack the claims of another service in the process.

In contrast, I find no evidence that the chairman seeks similar influence with the legislature. He focuses, instead, on the White House and its representative, the secretary of defense. Some chairmen have become adept at assessing the political vulnerabilities of the president and have, in turn, leveraged their role as principal military adviser to influence and sometimes lead presidential policy. But the chairman must do so while still respecting the need for consensus and equality among the services.

Although treating the executive and Congress differently is not a novel approach, and others have applied an institutionalist framework to better understand civil-military relations, the focus of these inquiries tends to be on senior military officers, the service chiefs, or the military overall.[35] Similarly, others have written about the relationship between the structural changes made by the National Security Act of 1947 and Eisenhower's 1958 reforms.[36] My contribution is to apply this institutional lens to the chairman and, additionally, to take into account the changes made by the Goldwater-Nichols Act.[37] The result is an argument that the chairman is a unique political actor and a description of the conditions under which his political power is maximized.

Although I do not adopt a principal-agent framework, my analysis is consistent with and builds upon the research agenda introduced by Peter Feaver, with his argument that civil-military relations can be understood as a problem of delegation.[38] Augmenting Feaver's focus on preference similarities, the costs of oversight, and the likelihood of punishment, I argue that the president's ability to oversee and punish the military is exercised through the chairman and is contingent upon political circumstances, the degree of consensus among the service chiefs, and the extent to which the chiefs respect the chairman. Moreover, these variables also determine whether and to what degree the chairman can punish the president by withholding his or the military's support for presidential policy choices. In other words, sometimes the chairman acts like the principal, not the agent.

The argument in this book also contributes to an implicit debate within the literature about whether there are significant differences in the civil-military dynamics of different policy areas and especially budgetary issues versus questions of operations, strategy, or who serves. On one side is Samuel Huntington. Writing in *The Common Defense*, Huntington argues that military policy exists in two worlds.[39] One involves politics between states. Here, the president has more freedom to act. The policy outcomes are wars but also the strategy and force structure choices about how best to pursue them. Huntington's second world is the domestic political arena, where politicians and interest groups argue over resources and, in turn, make choices about end strength and procurement. Congress and its parochial political norms are the key to this world. Of course, the two worlds are related. But Huntington's point is that the president has more authority to act independently in the first world, while the second one involves the bargaining, coalitions, and persuasion that characterizes the multiple actors that have power in domestic politics.

Peter Feaver's principal-agent framework is consistent with this Huntingtonian distinction between civilian spheres of influence in that the costs and benefits of monitoring and punishment vary across different policy domains. Because Congress has parochial interests in defense spending but not necessarily in questions about strategy or military operations, and because the services have multiple avenues outside of the formal budget process for pursuing their interests with Congress, it should be more difficult and costly for the White House to punish defections from its budget requests. Certainly, the services can also complain to Congress about use of force issues, but in the case of budget matters, the back channel is routinized, something I explain in more detail in the next chapter. But all other things being equal, both the president and chairman should struggle more to control the services on budget matters.

Writing at essentially the same time as Huntington, Warner Schilling reached the opposite conclusion.[40] In *Strategy, Politics, and Defense Budgets*, Schilling argues that the question of defense is inherently a political one because reasonable people can disagree about when and how potential adversaries will threaten the United States and how best to prepare for this.

Because these disagreements can usually not be definitively resolved prior to the materialization of a specific threat, attack, or war, bargaining and politics over policy are inevitable. Although Schilling describes this push and pull in the debate over the fiscal year 1950 defense budget, the politics are essentially the same in questions of strategy, as confirmed by the other two case studies in his 1962 book. Like the mythological story about the infinite progression of turtles that support the earth, it's politics all the way down.

Both Risa Brooks and Mackubin Owens offer more contemporary arguments that civilian control faces similar political dynamics regardless of policy type. In *Shaping Strategy*, Brooks argues that the details of the political relationship matter.[41] Specifically, the degree to which preferences diverge, along with the power relationship between civilians and the military, help explain whether actors can productively air disagreements and thus vet policy ideas, or instead if actors will hide their concerns in a bureaucratic game for power. Owens similarly sees the military as engaged in a game of politics, using tools of persuasion that are similar to those of other domestic political actors. Although neither author applies their ideas to budget policy specifically, their arguments suggest that civil-military interaction over budgets is governed by the same strategic political game over persuasion and coalition building that applies to other types of policy.

Yet a third approach argues that the distinction between types of policy is not as important as service cultures. Jeffrey Donnithorne makes the case that the unique histories and culture of each service give them different preferences and thus different incentives to comply, or not, with civilian direction.[42] The argument in *Four Guardians* suggests that the key distinctions in civil-military relations are not between questions of force, strategy, or budgets, but rather between the army, air force, navy, and marine corps.

The policy disagreements assessed in chapters 5, 6, and 7 all suggest that the politics of budgets are similar to that governing other issues. Although my main focus is budget debates, in each case study I look briefly at other contentious decisions. I find that the chairman's power is transferable between policy categories and is exercised in similar ways. An ambitious chairman will exploit an administration's political weaknesses to do what he deems best for the military's interests, regardless of the policy domain. Moreover, a chairman who builds clout with the chiefs by supporting their interests in budget battles can then spend that clout in future disagreements over strategy, and vice versa. The one key difference between policy areas is that, on budgetary issues, the chairman is constrained by the preferences of the service chiefs. But on issues related to ongoing military operations, his main interlocutors are commanding officers in the field and the relevant combatant commander.

My argument also has a number of implications for U.S. defense policy. When it comes to defense spending, I argue that the Goldwater-Nichols Act failed to achieve its goal of increasing jointness—in other words, the chairman's advice is still largely derivative of the sum total of service preferences rather than trade-offs between them. As explained in detail in chapter 2, with the act Congress delegated to the chairman the responsibility for developing joint military advice. Instead, service parochialism persists, and with it, policies that may lead to unnecessary duplication, less innovation, and a suboptimal use of resources. Moreover, the act contributed to a decision-making structure that is biased toward service perspectives. This, in turn, has potentially detrimental consequences for civil-military relations.

Has civilian control of the military eroded since the Goldwater-Nichols Act? In 2021, Risa Brooks, Jim Golby, and Heidi Urben argued that, since the end of the Cold War, there has been a gradual erosion of civilian control; they cite the Goldwater-Nichols Act as one of several factors contributing to the increasing dominance of the military in policy issues.[43] While acknowledging the discord that has characterized civil-military relations under Obama and especially during and after the Trump administration, Kori Schake and Peter Feaver argue that the military remains firmly committed to the norm that it should refrain from political activity.[44] The 2021 exchange between these scholars in *Foreign Affairs* summarizes the debate over civilian control and the impact of institutional change, dissent, public attitudes, and civilian choices. The evidence presented in this book shows that the Goldwater-Nichols Act increased the chairman's political clout, but also that the men who have held this office have not consistently embraced this role or been successful in exploiting it. The reason for this variation, however, points to an erosion of civilian control because the chairman's political clout is more likely to be limited by the service chiefs than by civilians.

WHAT'S AHEAD

Chapter 2 provides a more detailed look at the notion of jointness that was so central to the Goldwater-Nichols Act. It summarizes the policy problems and provides several metrics for assessing the degree to which jointness is still largely absent. I also show that this lack of jointness persists even though the chairman has become the focal point of U.S. civil-military interaction. In other words, it is not the case that the Goldwater-Nichols Act failed to create a powerful chairman who, in turn, lacks the authority to force the services to cooperate. Instead, I argue that the chairman has become more powerful. But the structure of the JCS means even a powerful chairman will fail to impose jointness on the services.

Chapters 3 and 4 summarize the evolution of the JCS and its impact on civil-military relations and defense policy making. These chapters illustrate how institutions, and the rules and processes that govern policy making, have a significant influence over who wins and also, in the case of the JCS, the quality of the national security decisions that result.

More specifically, chapter 3 looks at the period from 1947 through the 1950s. Since the creation of the Department of Defense after World War II, civilians have repeatedly tried to force the services to cooperate and to subordinate their own individual desires to the collective common good. This was one of the main goals of the National Security Act of 1947, Truman's amendments to it in 1949, Eisenhower's Reorganization Plan No. 6 in 1953, and his Department of Defense Reorganization Act of 1958. The results were not mixed: service cooperation was consistently found to be insufficient.

Chapter 4 continues this chronology by focusing on informal and formal changes to the JCS since 1958. This is the time frame in which the architecture for a powerful chairman was established. In the 1960s, the management style of Defense Secretary Robert McNamara finally convinced the services to stop arguing in public and instead present only consensus opinions. This norm remains in place today. But to it the Goldwater-Nichols Act added additional power and responsibilities for the chairman. With that act, Congress fought for and won increased centralization of authority in the chairman. Previous Congresses had rejected such a development for fear that a strong chairman would hurt congressional power over defense policy. But by 1986, the resulting lack of coordination between the services was seen to be so detrimental to national security that Congress agreed to give the chairman many of the very same powers it had consistently refused to grant since World War II.

The contemporary case studies of defense budgets in chapters 5, 6, and 7 provide more detail about interactions between multiple chairmen, Congress, and the White House. Collectively, they show that a chairman, while he can constrain civilian policy preferences, is himself at times constrained by the services.

Chapter 5 chronicles the development of the Base Force and the Bottom-Up Review, initiatives that were intended to guide defense downsizing in response to the end of the Cold War. I argue that Chairman Colin Powell authored the Base Force in an attempt to stop the collapse of the Soviet Union from leading to significant reductions in defense spending. President George H. W. Bush was not enthusiastic about the Base Force, and his secretary of defense, Dick Cheney, was nearly hostile. But Powell was able to parlay the administration's political weaknesses into leeway for his Base Force idea. Similarly, when the Clinton administration brought pressure for additional reductions in defense spending, Powell was able to use the political vulnerabilities of both President Clinton and Secretary of Defense Les Aspin to avoid deeper cuts as a result of the administration's Bottom-Up Review.

In chapter 6, I focus on Secretary of Defense Donald Rumsfeld and his inability to transform the military by shifting resources away from traditional weapons platforms in order to embrace new technologies. Rumsfeld was never popular with the services because he was seen as condescending and, more importantly, because he excluded them from important decisions. His first chairman, Hugh Shelton, essentially ignored Rumsfeld's transformation plans and cooperated with the services to sell their existing priorities as new and transformative. Next came Chairman Richard Myers, who had a closer relationship with Rumsfeld but who lost the support of the service chiefs because he advocated for the secretary instead of the services.

The third case study, in chapter 7, analyzes the role of the JCS as the Obama administration coped with the budget reductions mandated by the Budget Control Act of 2011 and the subsequent sequestration cuts that resulted when Congress proved unable to agree on a budget. First is Chairman Mike Mullen, who led President Obama and contradicted Secretary of Defense Robert Gates in arguing that the defense budget needed to be part of deficit reduction. But when Gates was replaced by Leon Panetta and Martin Dempsey was appointed chairman, the two became a team that worked closely with the services to get increasingly deeper budget reductions.

These three cases include four presidential administrations, five defense secretaries, and five chairmen. In each case I find not only evidence of a bias toward service interests, but also that the chairman used his authority to manipulate civilian political weaknesses resulting in outcomes that favored his own, or the military's, preferences. Chapter 8 summarizes this argument and discusses its implications for debates in the study of U.S. civil-military relations.

2

THE CHAIRMAN AND JOINTNESS

Central to understanding efforts to improve the military advice provided by the Joint Chiefs of Staff (JCS) is the concept of jointness. Jointness refers to military operations, advice, or decisions that are the product of cooperation and compromise between and among the services. Jointness doesn't necessarily mean that each of the services takes part in an activity; it can also mean that all of the services agree that one of them alone should undertake a particular task. Jointness is perhaps best understood by its opposite: parochial behavior. Jointness results when the services subordinate their own individual parochial interests to the greater national defense effort. Increasing jointness was one of the reasons the JCS was created in World War II, and it was the main objective of the Goldwater-Nichols Act.

Each attempt to increase jointness has included giving more authority to the chairman. The following section provides a summary of these structural changes, as well as those made to the authorities of the service chiefs. Using an analysis of public comments by the service chiefs and the chairman, I argue that the Goldwater-Nichols Act did indeed shift the balance of power within the JCS. Prior to 1986, the service chiefs provided the most vocal military advice; after 1986, that fell to the chairman. Not only is the chairman more prominent in offering advice, the service chiefs all but disappear.

But, in spite of the increased prominence of the chairman, jointness remains elusive. In the second part of this chapter, I argue that even after the Goldwater-Nichols Act, which gave the chairman increased power and authority that can be used to force greater cooperation and integration on the services, there is considerable evidence this has not been the case. Using an analysis of service budgets, the process of building them, and roles and missions, I show that the problems with jointness that predate the Goldwater-Nichols Act not only continue, but they are also largely unchanged.

The combination of a more assertive chairman but little increase in jointness makes it especially important to better understand the impact of the Goldwater-Nichols Act. If the act led to increased service cooperation, better military advice, and a more effective national defense, then a more political chairman or less civilian control might be a price worth paying. The cases examined in chapters 5, 6, and 7, however, show that civilians made a Faustian bargain. Civilian control has become more political and problematic but military advice still appears to be firmly anchored in the service parochialism that the Goldwater-Nichols Act was intended to reduce.

THE RISE OF THE CHAIRMAN

The history of the organization of the Department of Defense is in large part the story of repeated attempts to improve military advice and increase jointness while still ensuring that the services remain largely independent. Table 2.1 provides a brief summary of the evolution of authorities and responsibilities for the secretary of defense, the service chiefs, and the chairman. The independence of the services has remained firmly intact after

TABLE 2.1 The Evolution of Authority in the Department of Defense

U.S. SECRETARY OF DEFENSE	Created to be the principal assistant to the president for all national security matters with responsibility to provide general direction for the operations and budgets of the army, navy, and air force, which collectively form the National Military Establishment (1947) and later the Department of Defense (1949).
	Authority expands from "general direction," budget formation, and eliminating duplication and overlap in select areas (1947) to "direction" (1949), and finally full responsibility for all civilian and military functions (1953).
	Authority over the military services is limited because they remain separate organizations (1947) and cannot be merged (1949), but the secretary can assign some duties (1953) and responsibility for new weapons and missions (1958). Some general tasks common to all of the services can be administered collectively (1958).
	Required to provide specific guidance to the services and chairman on budgets, contingency plans for military operations, and other functions, and for ensuring the combatant commanders have sufficient authority and control over the forces assigned to them (1986).
	The chain of command that provides orders or directions for deployed military forces runs from the president to the secretary of defense and then to the combatant commanders (1986).
JCS CHAIRMAN	Initially appointed at the discretion of the president (1947), subject to the advice and consent of the Senate, and for a two-year renewal term (1949). His term begins in October of an odd-numbered year to allow for continuity between presidents (1986).
	Authority expands from equal in rank to the service chiefs (1947), senior in rank (1949), to principal military adviser to the president, secretary of defense, and National Security Council in place of the JCS (1986).
	Role as adviser expands from passing along a summary of the advice of the service chiefs with any significant disagreements noted (1949), to providing independent advice generally but also specifically on strategy, contingency planning, military requirements, budgets, and the needs of the combatant commanders (1986). Must consult with the service chiefs and combatant commanders and present their range of opinions on issues (1986).

(continued)

TABLE 2.1 *(Continued)*

Ability to vote in JCS decisions is expressly denied (1949), then granted (1958). Is now responsible for convening JCS meetings, setting the agenda, and leading discussion (1986).

Removed from the chain of command (1949). May transmit orders but remains expressly excluded from issuing them or otherwise providing direction to deployed forces (1986).

Authority over the Joint Staff is strengthened from managing the service personnel assigned there (1949), to assigning duties and selecting personnel (1953), to having full authority over personnel and operations (1986).

A vice chairman of the JCS is created to perform duties as assigned by the chairman and with the approval of the secretary of defense (1986).

SERVICE CHIEFS As the Joint Chiefs of Staff, the service chiefs are the principal military advisers to the president, secretary of defense (1947), and National Security Council (1949), but are replaced in this role by the chairman (1986).

Reserve the right to take recommendations directly to Congress after first informing the secretary of defense (1949), and directly to the president, secretary of defense, or National Security Council when requested to do so or when they disagree with the chairman (1986).

Taken out of the chain of command with the creation of the combatant commands (1958).

each major legislative change or restructuring, but the power and authorities given to the chairman have also consistently increased.

Although the relevant details of these reorganizations are discussed in chapters 3 and 4, table 2.1 shows a clear trend toward more centralization of authority. The focus initially was the services chiefs. They began to meet routinely during World War II in order to coordinate U.S. policy with the British military.[1] After the war, the chiefs sat as equal members of the JCS, with the existence of a chairman left to the discretion of the president. The service chiefs, however, found it difficult to subordinate their service responsibilities. As a result, the 1950s saw the beginning of a trend whereby the chairman was endowed with increased authority to make decisions independent of the other services chiefs. The position of chairman was given a senior ranking, and he was allowed to vote and to manage many of the administrative functions that had initially been given to the corporate JCS. But advice and decision-making power rested firmly with the service chiefs until the Goldwater-Nichols Act. With this law, the chairman became the preeminent member of the group, with many rights and responsibilities vested in him instead of the collective JCS membership. The service chiefs still retained the right of individual dissent but control over the Joint Staff, the JCS agenda, and the ear of key civilian decision makers went to the chairman alone. Chapter 4 explains several other subsequent additions that augmented the chairman's power.

As a result of these changes, the chairman has become much more prominent in civil-military relations and has largely replaced the service chiefs as the focal point for much of U.S. defense policy. While the chairman and service chiefs each routinely testify in Congress, in other venues it is common practice for the chairman to speak for the military or to offer advice on behalf of the JCS.

Figure 2.1 provides a proxy for understanding the rise of the chairman.[2] Using the *New York Times*, I count the number of comments made by a service chief or the chairman from the period 1947 through 2016. Excluded are comments and reporting pertaining to testimony in front of Congress. Such statements are the customary way the military is expected to present its expertise and advice. For similar reasons, I exclude press releases from the Pentagon. What I tally are instances where a service chief or the chairman offered advice, or expressed an opinion, outside of such officially sanctioned channels. From 1947 through 2016 there are 1,177 examples where a service chief or the chairman wrote an editorial, provided a comment to the media, or gave a speech.[3]

Figure 2.1 shows that, over time, comments from the service chiefs have largely been replaced by comments from the chairman. Moreover, this shift happened abruptly and coincided with the passage of the Goldwater-Nichols Act.

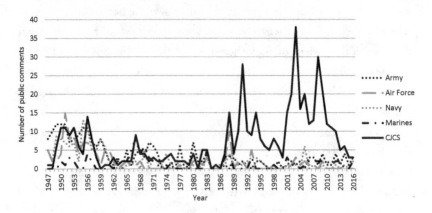

FIGURE 2.1 Public comments, per year, by members of the Joint Chiefs of Staff.

Figure 2.2 shows this same dataset but codes each comment as either about a specific service or about the military or defense effort overall. Until 1987, most comments were made by service chiefs and most of those comments pertained to a single service, usually the one represented by the speaker. From the late 1980s on, however, the reverse becomes true: service-specific comments are overwhelmingly replaced by comments about the military or overall national defense effort.

When figures 2.1 and 2.2 are combined, the story is clear: after the Goldwater-Nichols Act, the chairman becomes virtually the sole spokesperson for the military and he provides comments overwhelmingly about national security or the military overall, not a specific service.

Moreover, this focus on the chairman has political consequences for civilians. The September 11 terrorist attacks, combined with the erosion of confidence in civilian institutions, has led to increased deference to military preferences.[4] Recent scholarship shows that public support for using military force tends to fall when military leaders withhold their endorsement or speak out against the president's plans.[5] The case studies presented here show that, in addition to generals commanding troops, the chairman can leverage similar support for military preferences in internal executive branch battles over resources. As the next section explains, however, the

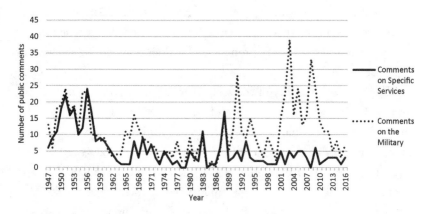

FIGURE 2.2 Public comments, per year, by members of the Joint Chiefs of Staff on service and military issues.

chairman seems to have been unable, or unwilling, to translate his prominence into increased jointness. The result is a more potent political voice for preferences that remain firmly rooted in service interests.

THE JCS AND THE PERSISTENT STRUGGLE FOR "JOINTNESS"

The problems that the Goldwater-Nichols Act attempted to rectify have a long history. Since the Spanish-American War, defense policy makers have struggled to get the services to work together.[6] The services have repeatedly proven unable or unwilling to sufficiently coordinate their efforts on their own. But forcing greater unity of effort via a powerful secretary of defense or chairman has raised several concerns. One is that a "man on horseback" would challenge civilian control of the military, or that centralized power will create a General Staff that would come to control more than just military policy. Another concern is that a powerful chairman would eventually merge the services and, in the process, do away with the single-minded focus that makes each service an expert in its area of combat. The dichotomy at the core of U.S. civil-military relations is how to centralize power such that the services are forced to cooperate when necessary while remaining strong proponents for their own individual areas of expertise.

The persistent inability of the services to act jointly should not be surprising. It is a logical consequence of widely accepted assumptions about the self-interested behavior of organizations. As organizations that want to maximize their own autonomy and resources, the military services each strive to protect their mission as it has historically been practiced and in the face of changes in technology, military requirements, and threats. U.S. national security, in the view of each service, is best supported by that service performing its mission with minimal interference from or cooperation with the other services.

Until the Goldwater-Nichols Act, the JCS was composed of the heads of the military services, each having equal power, and with no overall authority to force cooperation between them. Prior to the creation of the JCS in World War II, the heads of the army and navy cooperated even less. This JCS structure of coequal services meant that problems arising from a lack of jointness persisted even though they led to loss of life, operational failure, and excessive spending. Such problems were discussed repeatedly during consideration of the National Security Act of 1947, the Department of Defense Reorganization Act of 1958, and the 1986 Goldwater-Nichols Act.[7]

This lack of jointness has made civilian control more difficult. The mission of the defense department's civilian leadership is to coordinate the various military and civilian components into one coherent plan for protecting U.S. national security interests. That plan is supposed to reflect the policy goals of the president, as adjusted by congressional action. This means getting the services and combatant commanders to work together and to use their expertise to provide advice for decisions about resources, programs, and operations. Historically, however, the secretary of defense has struggled to force the services to see beyond their own individual interests and to subordinate these to the greater common good.

The predominance of service over joint priorities has led to several persistent problems. One set of concerns relates to the weapons the military buys and how it uses them. The services focus on developing and buying the weapons and capabilities that support their main mission. In and of itself, this is not problematic. But when multiple services need the same capabilities, the result can be duplication and excess. Another issue is orphan missions; that is, capabilities that are necessary for national security but that are not the main mission of any service. Sealift and airlift are necessary for getting troops and equipment to battle, but the navy and air force tend not to invest in these capabilities because they are not central to their fighting missions. For similar reasons, the development of joint warfighting doctrine is an orphan mission because the services prefer to focus on their own individual specialties. A related problem is interoperability, or the ability of the services to fight together. The services have tended to focus on their own specific capabilities and specifications. As a result, sometimes radios can't talk to each other, personnel are rotated according to different timetables, differences in service jargon lead to confusion, and essentially similar weapons may require completely different fuel, parts, or maintenance.

The predominance of service interests has also led to problems buying the weapons and equipment needed to win wars. The services are responsible for developing and buying weapons. They tend to emphasize missions that are central to the culture and history of each service and to focus on buying new and many weapons.[8] But when these forces are used in combat, they belong to the combatant commanders. To facilitate cooperation and efficiency during World War II, the United States gave one commander in a geographic area responsibility for all the forces assigned to that area, regardless of their service affiliation. This system of commands has remained in place, although their geographic organization has changed.[9] It is the combatant commanders in charge of these organizations that are responsible for molding the various weapons and personnel of each service into a coherent fighting unit and for that unit's training and readiness. Problems arise, however, because the services dominate the budget process, and the secretary of defense has found it difficult to force them to change their priorities because of input from the combatant commanders. The result has been an emphasis on the modernization and procurement of equipment favored by the services to the detriment of the tools and training preferred by the combatant commands.

The lack of jointness has also led to problems with strategy. The secretary of defense develops a defense strategy because this provides a road map for how to navigate threats and uncertainties in the international system, plus it allows the president to put his or her own individual policy mark on national security. The services, however, prefer their own individual versions.[10] The secretary of defense would prefer they integrate their capabilities to produce plans, strategies, and budgets for broader missions, such as the defense of NATO, countering China and Russia, or providing for nuclear deterrence.

Regardless of whether the issue is strategy, operations, budgets, or weapons choices, since the creation of the defense department, each reorganization effort has tried to convince the JCS to prioritize joint over service interests. Initially the goal was to give the secretary of defense enough power to use service inputs to reach joint decisions. It proved difficult, however, for civilians to make or enforce choices between the services. The goal then shifted to creating incentives for the service chiefs and especially the chairman to transcend service parochialism and make such choices themselves, providing the resulting joint military advice to civilians.

The JCS are responsible for providing civilian policy makers, including the president and Congress, with advice about military strategy, budgets, roles and missions, and operational plans for hypothetical future scenarios as well as in response to crises. The goal has been for this advice to reflect the expertise of each service chief, but also for the service chiefs, acting together as the JCS, to provide information, analysis, and recommendations that are cross-service or joint in perspective; address key issues even if they are controversial; and give advice in a timely manner. Historically, the JCS has had problems achieving all three of these goals.

The reason for this is "dual-hatting," a problem that arises from the structure of the JCS. Each of the four service chiefs is first and foremost the head of their service and as such is responsible for maintaining their service's budget share and missions.[11] Yet each is also responsible for the overall defense effort. It has historically proven difficult for a service chief to disregard the best interests of his own organization and support another service's claim to resources or activities.

As a result, the JCS tends to recommend spending that is higher than necessary because the chiefs prefer to add the priorities of their services together rather than make choices between them; or, their advice is the result of bargaining between service interests rather than establishing priorities. Strategy also becomes unrealistic as each service estimates what is necessary to meet threats without sufficient consideration of the capabilities of the other services. Further, strategic analysis overall is neglected because the JCS spend their time on issues that are more important to the services, such as personnel, weapons development, and dividing up the budget.

This lack of joint military advice has been reinforced by the predominance of service interests on the Joint Staff. The Joint Staff is a collection of officers from each service that is charged with helping the JCS carry out their duties. Historically, the Joint Staff has been divided into committees or directorates, each of which deals with a functional issue such as personnel, intelligence, operations, and force structure. Even after a chairman was created for the JCS, the Joint Staff provided analysis by circulating issues and decisions to the services for comment. When a service disagreed, the issue was bumped up to the next level in the hierarchy. This happened until consensus was reached, with the most controversial issues left to the JCS for resolution. This, in itself, was not a problem. The problem was that vetting every issue with each of the services took a very long time and thus the JCS was slow to offer advice on all issues, but especially on contentious ones.

In the past, the JCS adopted several survival tactics that would allow each chief to support the interests of their own service without directly confronting the other services. Avoiding such rivalry is important because at times competition between the services has invited civilians to pick winners and losers and has tended to reduce confidence in the military overall. To prevent this from happening, over time the JCS agreed to offer an opinion only when they could reach a consensus. As a result, they tended not to give advice on controversial issues and to provide input only when it was watered-down and spoke to trivial matters. Another tactic is logrolling, where decisions are made by combining positions or exchanging favors rather than making more difficult trade-offs.

The result, as articulated by James Schlesinger, defense secretary under Presidents Nixon and Ford, is that JCS advice is "generally irrelevant, normally unread, and almost always disregarded."[12] Even though over time the secretary of defense accrued the formal authority necessary to ask for joint advice, the predominance of service interests and the absence of joint ones has meant that such advice was seldom given.

JOINT ADVICE?

"Joint" has become a frequently used adjective to describe military inputs on strategy, procurement, operations, and a host of other policy choices. But just because military advice carries the label "joint" doesn't mean that it is the product of trade-offs between service perspectives and priorities. The chairman, for example, could offer advice that is his own personal opinion, and which is more or less divorced from the inputs of the services and the combatant commanders. Or the chairman could forward advice that is still largely a summation of service parochialism and logrolling but which is labeled "joint." Of course, the chairman's advice could also be somewhere in between.

Even though the chairman has the power to produce truly joint advice and decisions, he has an incentive to call advice "joint" regardless of whether that is actually the case. The Goldwater-Nichols Act mandates jointness as something desirable, required, and as clearly superior to the past history of service parochialism. Therefore, joint advice carries more political weight and is valued more by civilian decision makers. As a result, the services and the chairman have an incentive to label advice as "joint" for political reasons.[13] Indeed, there is anecdotal evidence that some civilian decision makers question the degree to which jointness is real or simply a strategic label used for political purposes.[14]

To understand the degree to which the chairman's advice is in fact joint—the product of service trade-offs—requires being privy to JCS meetings and discussions. Unfortunately, transcripts of these meetings are not available and, in many cases, are nonexistent. Having access to the services' individual budget submissions prior to their incorporation into the overall defense budget would also be useful as this would reveal the number of times each service did not get its original funding request, and thus the degree to which the defense budget makes choices between them. Outside of internal defense department circles, however, this information is also not available.

In theory, rivalry between the services would indicate jointness. If the chairman overruled a service or denied that service a desired priority, the service could appeal to members of Congress for redress or seek to overturn such a decision by exposing shortcomings in another service.[15] Chapter 4, however, explains that contesting the chairman's advice and open rivalry between the services have both been rare since the 1960s. They have remained extremely rare since the Goldwater-Nichols Act.

Given the dearth of direct measures, I use several proxies to indicate whether or not jointness has increased. These include looking at trends in how the defense budget is split between the services, the processes used to build the annual defense budget, and changes to roles and missions. Collectively, these proxies suggest that when it comes to allocating resources, jointness remains an elusive goal and service priorities remain dominant. The case studies in chapter 5, 6, and 7 reinforce this conclusion.

SERVICE BUDGET SHARES

Presumably, the budget share allocated to each service should vary over time as strategy, enemies, technology, and other variables change. Moreover, that budget share should, logically, be dictated by a service's contribution to national defense. For example, if the most likely security challenge is considered war with the Soviet Union in central Germany, then one would expect the army's share of the budget to increase. Or, if the primary concern is a challenge from China in the western Pacific, the navy's share should grow. However, since the end of World War II, service shares of the defense budget have evolved toward a remarkably stable division. Excluding spending on defense agencies and the Office of the Secretary of Defense (OSD), since the 1950s, the army, navy, and air force each have consistently received around one-third of the defense budget each fiscal year.[16] Any short-term deviation in this pattern—for example, a land war that would boost army spending—has been counterbalanced in subsequent years to restore relatively equal budget shares.

Figure 2.3 is based on the portion of the defense budget going to the services. It excludes funding for the defense agencies, OSD, and the National Nuclear Security Administration. From fiscal year 1948 through fiscal year 2016, each service share is juxtaposed with a straight line that represents one-third of the budget. Each fiscal year includes spending for ongoing

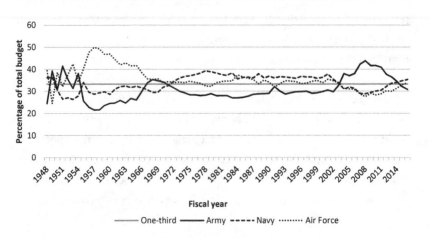

FIGURE 2.3 Service shares of the U.S. defense budget. Each service's share of the budget refers to budget authority, including spending for wars and other contingency operations, in current dollars.

Source: Derived from "Table 6-10: Department of Defense Budget Authority by Military Department," in Office of the Under Secretary of Defense (Comptroller), *National Defense Budget Estimates for FY 2017* (Washington, DC: Department of Defense, 2016), 147–153, https://comptroller.defense.gov/Portals/45/Documents /defbudget/fy2016/FY16_Green_Book.pdf.

military engagements, which, presumably, would bias the figures in favor of the service with the most involvement in current wars and military operations.

After some volatility during the 1950s and early 1960s as the services—mainly the navy and air force—fought for shares of the nuclear mission, the services settle into reasonably constant shares of the budget until the wars in Iraq and Afghanistan in the 2000s, which increase the army's share. Considering the entire period represented in figure 2.3, the army gets, on average, 31 percent of the military's budget, with 34 percent going to the navy and 35 percent to the air force.[17] Further, the Goldwater-Nichols Act seems to have ushered in an era of more equal budget splits. From 1948 to 1986, the army averaged 29 percent of the budget, with the navy getting 33 percent and the air force 38 percent. After Goldwater-Nichols—from 1987 to 2016—a more even one-third split is the norm, with the army taking on average 33 percent of the budget, the navy 34 percent, and the air force 33 percent.

Figure 2.4 looks at service base budgets since 2001 and excludes supplementals such as the Global War on Terror account and Overseas Contingency Operations, all of which tend to support ongoing military operations. The results are similar to figure 2.3, with service shares of the budget showing slightly more variation. The army averages 30 percent of the budget, the navy 36 percent, and the air force 34 percent. Keep in mind, however, that during this period the army gained significant additional resources through supplemental spending for the wars in Iraq and Afghanistan.

Others have argued that consistency in budget shares, plus the approximate division of the budget into thirds, indicates that organizational interests and collusion play a large role in determining the way the defense budget is split among the services.[18] My purpose here is much more limited. One of the paramount goals of different reorganization efforts has been to temper service parochialism by establishing priorities among service inputs and making choices between those priorities. The services have repeatedly been faulted for parochialism and organizational collusion in the defense budget. This charge was also made during debates over the Goldwater-Nichols Act. However, service shares of the budget since the law was

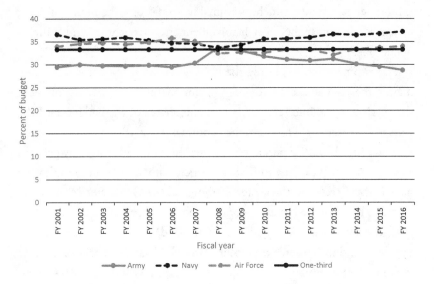

FIGURE 2.4 Service shares of the U.S. defense budget without wars and other supplementals. Each service line represents budget authority in current dollars, excluding war and supplemental funding. The straight line represents one-third of the defense budget, excluding defense agency and other non-service funding.

Source: Derived from "Table 2-1: Base Budget, War funding and Supplementals by Military Department, by Public Law Title," in Office of the Under Secretary of Defense (Comptroller), *National Defense Budget Estimates for FY 2017* (Washington, DC: Department of Defense, 2016), 24–32, https://comptroller.defense.gov/Portals/45 /Documents/defbudget/fy2016/FY16_Green_Book.pdf.

passed in 1986 strongly suggest that any influence the Goldwater-Nichols Act has had on this process has not been sufficient to reduce the tendency to split the defense budget more or less into thirds.[19] Moreover, this is true in spite of the end of the Cold War and the dissolution of the Soviet Union.

This budget data also suggests that it is total budget share that matters, an argument I take up in chapter 7. With or without spending for military operations, the army's budget share goes up after 2001. From 1948 to 1986, the army averaged 29 percent of the budget. Looking at the 1987–2001 period—which allow us to take into account the impact of the Goldwater-Nichols Act while excluding the wars in Iraq and Afghanistan—the army also averages 29 percent of the budget. In chapter 7, I argue that a refocus on Asia—a policy initially called the "Pivot to Asia" and then the "Rebalance to Asia"—serves to "correct" the budget balance between the services. After 2001, the army's traditional share of the budget increased due to the wars in Iraq and Afghanistan. With the Pivot to Asia, spending on the army is projected to decline irrespective of ongoing military operations.

PRIDE OF PLACE IN PLANNING

The Planning, Programming, and Budgeting System (PPBS) is the main process by which the defense department develops, approves, and implements its budget and thus links resources to force structure and strategy.[20] Service priorities have always dominated the PPBS process, largely as a result of the timeline for budget development and the central role given to service inputs. The Goldwater-Nichols Act did little to change this. Although mechanisms for inserting joint priorities have been developed, it remains the case that service priorities govern the PPBS process and thus the budget.[21]

Initially, PPBS was a powerful tool for the secretary because it required the services to justify their program elements. Once those elements were costed, the final figure was usually in excess of the total anticipated budget. This gave the secretary power to make choices between the services in the name of reducing the budget top line. Over time, however, the norm became for the services to be given fiscal guidance in advance. As a result, the services adjudicated between their own priorities before presenting the secretary with the result.

As defense secretary, Robert McNamara also created the civilian Office of Systems Analysis to analyze service proposals and to put forward its own priorities to compete with those of the services. Over time, the Office of Systems Analysis has evolved into various different forms and names. Since 2009, it has been known as the Office of Cost Assessment and Program Evaluation (CAPE). CAPE's primary function is to provide advice to the secretary about how to resolve differences between the services, and between the services and combatant commanders, over issues related to programming and budgeting.

Prior to the Goldwater-Nichols Act, the PPBS process for any given year started with the Defense Guidance. This was advice to the services from the JCS and OSD about the objectives necessary for national security. JCS advice was given in the form of the Joint Strategic Planning Document, which was intended to assess the difference between what was likely needed for national security objectives and what the services had been providing.

The services, in turn, were supposed to use the Defense Guidance to formulate their Program Objective Memoranda (POMs), which were the building blocks of the defense budget. POMs establish the relationship between dollars spent, planned activities and purchases, and broader national security goals. In other words, the POM recommended the activities, people, systems, and budget authority necessary to meet a given objective. Each service submitted a POM for the current budget year, plus four years into the future.

POMs were reviewed by OSD with input from the JCS. Major issues were considered by the Defense Resources Board—a body that is part of the lineage of the Office of Systems Analysis (now CAPE). The decisions that resulted were called Program Decision Memoranda; they instructed the services about what changes were necessary in the POMs in order to meet national security as well as fiscal objectives.

There were several problems inherent in the defense department's PPBS process prior to the Goldwater-Nichols Act. First, the time necessary to develop service POMs was several years, which meant that for any one given budget year, the main influence on the POM was the POM that preceded it. Because of inertia and time, POMs changed little from year to year. Second, the Defense Guidance, and indeed any strategy guidance, often came too late in the process to lead to major changes. Additionally, the guidance, as a broad strategic vision, was usually so vague that the services could easily use it to justify most of their priorities. Third, likely fiscal constraints were often inserted into the process toward the end. But by this stage, the most likely outcome was that any necessary cuts, or additional money, would be spread more or less evenly across the services. Uneven allocation of resources would likely lead to conflicts, which might upset previous consensus and agreements. Fourth, JCS input, as explained earlier in this chapter, tended overwhelmingly to reflect compromises and consensus between the services rather than choices among their preferences. JCS advice also tended to neglect the views of the combatant commanders.[22] Because of these problems, service interests were the building blocks of the budget and input from the JCS and secretary came too late in the process to make major changes. The services also had incentives to broker their own internal agreements, leaving the Defense Resources Board with what was usually a minor role.

If jointness has increased, it would be reasonable to expect the PPBS process to have changed such that service POMs are no longer the primary building blocks of the defense budget, or that nontrivial changes are routinely made to the POMs. Neither, however, appears to be the case.

First, the strategic inputs into the PPBS process are essentially the same as they were before the Goldwater-Nichols Act. The JCS works to produce a National Military Strategy that is consistent or at least does not contradict the national security strategy favored by the White House.[23] This strategy feeds into the secretary's Defense Planning Guidance (previously the Defense Guidance). This input, however, remains vague, does not clearly articulate priorities, and thus cannot serve as a robust basis for make resource decisions. As explained in more detail below, this input also comes after the services have invested considerable time developing their POMs. Concerns remain about the timeliness or usefulness of the National Military Strategy or the Quadrennial Defense Review, which is the public document that is supposed to outline objectives and threats.[24]

Second, the role of fiscal constraints has changed. Since 1974, the Congressional Budget and Impoundment Act has required Congress to identify top-line spending targets for the various components of the federal budget, including the defense department. As a result, the defense department gets fiscal guidance in the form of a ceiling, which is then translated into an expected budget share for each service. However, because the POMs are still the main building blocks of the budget, and because the POMs take several years to develop, it is still the case that the path of least resistance is to spread any cuts evenly among the services. Additionally, the National Military Strategy does not take into account fiscal constraints, and the Defense Planning Guidance, which does consider likely budgets, often focuses on top-line targets, with insufficient guidance for the services to make programmatic decisions. As a result, the services are largely free to allocate resources as long as they do not exceed overall caps.

Third, joint military inputs have also changed. As input into the secretary's Defense Planning Guidance, the chairman provides the Chairman's Program Recommendation, which is an assessment of the joint capabilities that are necessary. Inputs into the chairman's recommendation now include an Integrated Priority List from the combatant commanders. The focus of the chairman's advice, however, is readiness, doctrine, training, and warfighting that are already considered multiservice. As such, the Chairman's Program Recommendation has very limited influence on the development of service programs and priorities. Once the POMs are submitted to the secretary, they are also reviewed by the chairman to make sure they are consistent with the National Military Strategy, Defense Planning Guidance, and combatant commander priorities. The result is the Chairman's Program Assessment, which is used by the secretary to issue his Program Decision Memoranda, which provides final instructions to the services for adjusting their POMs to fit within the expected budget.

The timing of these joint inputs raises questions about their usefulness. Similar to the process prior to the Goldwater-Nichols Act, the Defense Planning Guidance is often too late to be useful for the services as they build their POMs.[25] For example, by the time the guidance is issued, the services are often one-third of the way through the POM process.[26] Similarly, by the time the chairman issues his Program Recommendation, the PPBS cycle is nearing its end, the annual budget submission is soon due, by which point service POMs can at best only be tweaked.

Since the Goldwater-Nichols Act became law, PPBS has come to include two other elements, both of which were intended to increase the clout of joint priorities. The Joint Requirements Oversight Council (JROC) was created in 1986 and Joint Capabilities Integration and Development System (JCIDS) in 2003. Neither process, however, appears to have lived up to its mandate.

The JROC is the primary forum for reconciling service and combatant commander priorities, and it is tasked with evaluating acquisition programs and joint requirements in terms of cost, timelines, performance, and alternatives. Initially, it focused mostly on specific acquisition questions, but it has evolved into the primary body for considering whether service budgets reflect the priorities of the commanders and for inserting jointness as an adjudicator for service priorities. The JROC also makes recommendations to the chairman for his inputs into the PPBS process, including both the Chairman's Program Recommendation and the Chairman's Program Assessment. The JCS vice chairman chairs the JROC and also has considerable leeway over the body's organization and management.

For its first decade of operations, the JROC largely endorsed service requests, but it eventually began to make changes to a small percentage of them.[27] It remains the case, however, that the JROC does not make significant changes to service priorities.[28] Additionally, although the combatant commanders submit their recommendations to the JROC through Integrated Priority Lists, if the services disagree they can easily wait out a commander, who has, at best, a tenure of a few years.[29] It was not until 2012 that these commanders were allowed to participate in the JROC as voting members.[30] In spite of various changes to the functioning of the JROC, it has been criticized for not leading to an emphasis on joint over service priorities.[31] As of 2017, JROC decision making was still heavily skewed toward developing consensus among the services rather than making choices between them.[32]

JCIDS came into being due to concerns that the acquisition system was not adequately meeting the warfighting needs of the combatant commands. JCIDS is supposed to use a joint perspective to identify gaps and define requirements, which are then programmed and budgeted by PPBS. All new acquisition programs also have to be approved using JCIDS, which replaces the Requirement Generation System, which was largely controlled by service interests.

As with the JROC, in spite of its emphasis on joint priorities, the JCIDS process has been criticized for advice that is too late to be useful, analysis that is ineffective or substandard, and an inability to compare requirements across programs.[33] In 2008, the U.S. Government Accountability Office (GAO) reported that the Joint Staff did not have the expertise to clearly establish priorities and that service interests were therefore predominant.[34] In a 2012 follow-up report, GAO concluded that the JCIDs process was underdeveloped and usually supported service proposals even though they were accompanied without all of the information necessary to assess them.[35] Former JCS vice chairman James Cartwright, who chaired the JROC, has argued that JCIDS is gamed by the services and requires consensus for a decision.[36]

PPBS is the main process for making decisions about defense spending. The basic building blocks of the PPBS process remain the service POMs, and control of these still rests securely with the services.[37] It remains the case that the services have overwhelming incentives to use their POMs to support requirements that correspond to their main missions. Oversight of service POMs and adjudication of disagreements and discrepancies between them not only happens too late in the PPBS process to have significant influence on the budget, but choices are made only in areas where the services themselves cannot resolve disagreements. In contrast, a joint system for determining requirements would proactively compare, contrast, and compete service POMs, make choices between them, and seek to create competition over similar missions. Or, a joint PPBS process would use POMs for major military missions such as airlift, ground combat, and air superiority rather than those based upon the services.

Instead of making choices between service POMs, the chairman's role is to assess how the military force structure produced by the POMs compares to that required by the National Military Strategy and articulated joint needs. In other words, the chairman does not mold the service POMs into a joint force, he determines the "risk" the service POM-based force poses for strategy and readiness. But that assessment of risk comes too late in the process to change the basic force structure being proposed. Moreover, the chairman's inputs into the PPBS process do not provide him with incentives to establish priorities among the service POMs unless there are significant budgetary constraints.

In a process in which joint priorities are dominant, service POMs would change as a result of the PPBS process. It is not possible to compare the original service POMs with the budget that is eventually submitted. However, others have estimated that less than 2 percent of any service's budget changes due to revision by the secretary.[38] More critically, the conclusion of a 2000 assessment of PPBS by Business Executives for National Security still rings true: PPBS is largely a ritual rather than a process intended to establish priorities.[39]

ROLES AND MISSIONS

The main functions of each service were established in a series of negotiations brokered by the first secretary of defense, James Forrestal. The resulting "Function of the Armed Forces and the Joint Chiefs of Staff," commonly known as the Key West Agreement, has governed the division of roles and missions between the services since that time. Prior to the Goldwater-Nichols Act, the dominance of service priorities led to problems with questionable duplication, but also orphan missions. For example, multiple services had their own largely independent research on unmanned vehicles, and the navy and air force tended to neglect investment in the ships and planes that transport the army. Roles and mission divisions have resource consequences, plus new technologies and security challenges have to be divided among the services. Thus, this is an important area for assessing jointness.

There have arguably been no significant changes to the division of roles and missions among the services since they were first negotiated in 1948. In the 1990s, two different studies produced little change, and since that time there have been repeated calls for additional analysis.[40] Nor has the chairman's increased authority led to significant shifts.[41] Perhaps even more telling is the recent history of the evolution of drones and unmanned aerial vehicles. Each of the services prioritizes some similar capabilities, yet there is little coordination on research, development, procurement, or training.[42]

THE JCS AND JOINTNESS

Budget shares, the budget and planning processes, and the division of roles and missions between the services all show symptoms of the same lack of jointness that prompted the Goldwater-Nichols Act. These problems have persisted even decades after the act was passed and they provide powerful evidence that jointness is still a problem, at least when it comes to defense spending. Further, this lack of jointness persists despite the chairman's increase in authority. Collectively, these metrics provide ample reason to question the impact of the Goldwater-Nichols Act and to seek to better understand the relationship between an authoritative chairman and the norms of the JCS.

3

THE ORIGINS OF NORMS FOR
THE JOINT CHIEFS OF STAFF

Initially, the Joint Chiefs of Staff (JCS) started out as a confederation of service chiefs with a weak chairman who was more of an office manager than a leader. Although the chairman became more powerful and independent, that was the outcome of a slow, gradual process that is explained in more detail in chapter 4. The norms of the JCS, however, predate its creation during World War II and were solidified during the immediate postwar period. The result was an organization that fell far below presidential expectations for providing military advice and implementing defense policy.

Presidents Harry Truman and Dwight Eisenhower both saw a strong chairman as essential for limiting rivalry among the services, improving military advice, and getting the services to cooperate to implement presidential policy. Congress, however, balked at the notion of centralized authority and repeatedly altered presidential plans in order to preserve the power of the service chiefs. The result was a JCS structure that institutionalized the primacy of service preferences and established decision-making norms that remain in use over seventy years later.

Until the 1960s, open rivalry between the services, and especially the navy and air force, gave civilian policy makers access to information and arguments that they used to assert civilian power in debates over defense budgets as well as key resource decisions such as guided missiles and navy carriers. This rivalry annoyed the president, who found it difficult to get the service chiefs to stand behind his decisions. But it empowered Congress by allowing its members to get information to challenge the president's policy agenda, occasionally make choices between the services, and maximize parochial benefits for their district.

It is this connection with Congress that gave the service chiefs incentives to collude, but the goal of this cooperation was not joint advice. It was to allow each service maximum opportunity to pursue its own preferences. Had Congress proved more interested in using service rivalry to make choices between the services, the chiefs would have had an incentive to at least keep their bickering private. But as long as some faction in Congress remained interested in their individual preferences, the service chiefs had an incentive to logroll, add together their priorities, or present them independently. Because such rivalry advantaged Congress over the president, and especially the committees in charge of military spending, there was little incentive to provide the chairman with more authority. When policy coherence did prompt Congress to agree to changes to defense organization, they gave power to the defense secretary, not the chairman. Congress also consistently made sure they had access to unfettered service inputs, a connection that remained intact after the National Security Act of 1947, amendments to that act in 1949, Eisenhower's Reorganization Plan No. 6, and the Defense Reorganization Act of 1958. But the origins of this relationship, which predates the creation of the JCS itself, was the connection between parts of Congress and the powerful bureaus within the army and navy.

CONGRESS AND THE BUREAUS

Prior to World War II, defense budgets and force structure primarily revolved around a parochial relationship between congressional committees and administrative, technical, and supply bureaus within the army and navy. This relationship dwelt on the details of military infrastructure. It was concerned with weapons and materiel purchases, the construction of military installations, and troop levels. The key interests to consider were domestic—what benefited the reelection of the chairs of various congressional committees—and organizational—what would perpetuate the role and importance of the individual bureaus within the services. With respect to resources, the president was largely a bystander.

This decentralized, congress-centered form of civil-military relations was a function of the structure of the army and navy. Both services were composed of quasi-independent bureaus that performed technical or staffing functions.[1] These bureaus dated from the early 1800s. The chief of a bureau often had a prolonged and close relationship with members of Congress responsible for war or navy department appropriations. Instead of funneling their requests through a service chief, service staff, or civilian secretary, each bureau chief was responsible for setting priorities for their own bureau and presenting the corresponding budget request directly to either the Military or Naval Affairs Committees in Congress. The chairs of these committees, in turn, had preponderant influence over who got contracts for providing supplies and services for the military.

Until World War I, promotion to bureau chief was a highly political process, with members of Congress, and specially senators, showing little reluctance to use their positions to support their "pet serving officers whose devotion had to be rewarded."[2] The civilian service secretaries were unable to control the bureaus because they lacked any means of coordinating their actions, choosing between their priorities, or intervening between the bureau chiefs and Congress. The secretaries also relied on the bureau chiefs for information about their service, and this reinforced their dependence on the military. Finally, service secretaries and service chiefs were usually in office for only a few years whereas the bureau chiefs typically served for decades and thus had more enduring relationships with members of Congress.

With the Spanish-American War, however, the power of the bureaus became increasingly problematic because it caused a de facto divorce within each service between those who were responsible for waging war and those in charge of producing and buying weapons and supplies. As a result, in times of war there were persistent problems with coordination, supply shortages, price inflation, and poor planning. Although various civilian secretaries and military chiefs in each service pressed for internal reforms, the power of the bureau chiefs remained significant until the coming of the Cold War.

In the army, Secretary of War Elihu Root proposed the first set of significant reforms in 1899. Root called for the creation of a military chief of staff to manage and coordinate the bureaus, and a General Staff to help him supervise the army but also to plan for future conflicts.[3] By establishing the General Staff, Root sought to create an alliance between the civilian secretary and the military chief of staff, at the expense of the bureaus.[4] But repeated resistance from the bureau chiefs and key members of Congress kept their alliance largely intact. By World War II, over half of all army appropriations were still controlled by largely autonomous bureaus, each of which had installations in key congressional districts.[5]

In the navy, problems in the conduct of the Spanish-American War, plus difficulties with ship construction, also led to efforts to centralize more control in a military chief of staff. But internal disagreements over the direction of reform, plus congressional investigations into the navy's conduct of World War I, delayed the navy's own attempts at internal reorganization until after World War II.[6] As with the army, Congress also preferred to maintain its traditional relationship with the navy's technical bureaus.

Problems with army-navy coordination in the Spanish-American War also led to creation of the Joint Army-Navy Board in 1903. The board was largely ineffective because it focused on mostly trivial personnel issues, met infrequently, and had only a small staff. Changes in staff size and membership allowed it to help resolve some roles and missions disputes during the interwar years, and to develop a war plan in case the United States was attacked.[7] But the president had no incentive to turn to the Joint Army-Navy Board for advice because the services placed little priority on communicating with it or on utilizing its members to resolve disputes. Instead, presidents preferred to facilitate interservice cooperation themselves on a case-by-case basis using operational commanders.

There was also a lack of coordination in Congress between army and navy issues. There were six key groups involved in defense policy: the Committee on Military Affairs and the Committee on Naval Affairs (with both the House and the Senate having one of each, for a total of four), and separate appropriations subcommittees for army and navy issues in both chambers of Congress.[8] The appropriations subcommittees focused on issues related to resource efficiency, including unnecessary overlap and duplication, while the Committees on Military and Naval Affairs concerned themselves with authorizing the purchase of real estate for military installations and the building of the installations themselves.[9] The first set of committees were by far the most influential because, until the early 1950s, less than 5 percent of military spending was subjected to authorization, whereas the entire sum had to be appropriated every year.[10] As a result, most congressional consideration of defense policy happened through a line-item review of the budget. Congress spent almost no time on questions of strategy or trying to link resources to goals.

These congressional fiefdoms had significant influence on military matters both within and outside of Congress. Internally, committee chairs had significant influence over their policy domains due to their near dictatorial powers to determine what issues their committee considered, who was involved in that consideration, and the conclusions reached by the committee. Further, both the House and Senate practiced almost complete deference to the policy decisions of their committee chairs. Externally, the influence of the committee chairs was a function of the power relationship between the president and Congress, which from the Civil War through the first decades of the twentieth century heavily favored Congress.[11] During this period Congress initiated most legislation and was usually the victor in battles with the president over policy and programs.

The alliance between the committee chairs and bureau chiefs worked as follows. A bureau chief would submit his requests to his service secretary and to the Bureau of the Budget.[12] Then, the bureau chief would appear before the appropriate congressional committee to make his case. Frequently, this included an appeal to overturn any restrictions that the president, Bureau of the Budget, or service secretary had attempted to impose on the preferences of the bureau.[13] The norm was to defer to the advice of the bureau chief, and to emphasize that the services should locate installations in, and purchase supplies from, the districts of committee members.[14] In this manner, the bureau chief got the last word about funding for his organization, and the members of the committee got first crack at allocating these funds to their own districts.

The president was usually in no position to challenge the committee-bureau alliance system. The president had almost no staff with which to oversee or guide the military. The president was further disadvantaged in that the main interaction between civilians and the military was over the details of the defense budget, and this discussion was firmly within the clutches of the congressional committee chairs. These chairs proved quite willing to change presidential requests for funding, troop levels, and weapons purchases.[15] For example, from 1933 through World War II, Congress routinely reinstated a portion of the reductions made by the Bureau of the Budget to the army's funding.[16] The president also found it difficult to unite the army and navy behind his defense requests.[17] Finally, the ability of the president to ally himself with the military was hindered by internal divisions among the services themselves, mainly a lack of coordination between the bureaus or prioritization of their requests.

PREPARING FOR THE COLD WAR

The alliance between select congressional committees and the service bureaus remained the most significant civil-military relationship until World War II. During the war, however, the JCS rose to prominence, and it remained the focal point for military decision making after 1945.[18] As a corporate body, the service chiefs met as the JCS in order to facilitate wartime cooperation with the British Chief of Staff Committee. Although their responsibilities were never officially outlined, the JCS took charge of operational planning and command for U.S. forces and reported directly to the president.[19] Modeled on the old Joint Army-Navy Board, the JCS came to replace the service bureaus as the main arena for exchange with civilians. The JCS also developed a closer relationship with the president than with Congress or its committees.

JCS decision making revolved around the desire for unanimity, as had the Joint Army-Navy Board. Like the joint board, the JCS structure was initially largely ineffective at coordinating the services. This proved particularly troublesome and embarrassing in discussions with the British during the war effort. Not only were the JCS unable to match the preparation and analysis of the British staff, they argued publicly among themselves, thereby undercutting their own suggestions for the direction of the war as well as those of the president.[20] The inability of the chiefs to agree often resulted in delays, and President Truman felt that it too often fell to him to resolve their differences.[21] Paul Hammond, in his study of interservice cooperation during the World War II, concludes that the success of the JCS is often exaggerated.[22] It was able to plan strategy and operations in Europe only for a short time and largely due to the navy's willingness to take a subordinate role in that theater. Further, service cooperation in the Pacific theater consisted largely of turning the war effort over to the navy.

The JCS, however, were very successful in two other endeavors. First, they provided a focal point for consideration of "military," as opposed to just army, navy, or air, issues. After some initial stumbling, the JCS were able to present a unified face to America's allies, and the JCS, rather than the individual service chiefs, was given a role in strategic planning, economic mobilization, and foreign policy making. By the end of the war, few questioned the role of the JCS as the logical body for service coordination.

The second endeavor in which the JCS succeeded was providing a mechanism by which the services could communicate with civilian authorities. Whereas the Joint Army-Navy Board had been routinely ignored by civilians, the JCS had direct communication with the president and National Security Council. Both Franklin Roosevelt and Harry Truman relied on the JCS to conduct the war effort as well as to provide them with information on military needs and performance. Further, the JCS had no rivals. The closest logical option, the civilian service secretaries, were not included in wartime planning or meetings with the president, and they soon found that their access to the president was no longer independent but rather channeled through the JCS.[23]

After World War II, congressional involvement in defense politics was quite different from what it had been before. In contrast to the subcommittee-bureau alliance that frequently hampered the president's policy ambitions, Congress did not seriously question the president's defense budget, nor did it debate strategy, involvement in the Cold War, or how the war should be waged. From 1945 to 1947, the only significant defense disagreements between the president and Congress were a dispute over universal military training, and a much less contentious three-way argument between the president, Congress, and the military over civilian control of nuclear weapons.[24]

Civil-military relations revolved around the rivalry between the army, navy, and the newly independent air force. Partially, this rivalry was due to the policy choices of the president. Both Truman and Eisenhower were faced with building the first substantial U.S. military to be maintained during peacetime. Both were also deeply concerned that building this military would significantly undermine the U.S. economy, an anxiety that extended to the Eisenhower years, when the president expressed his fear of a military-industrial complex and the creation of a garrison state. This military expansion under fiscal constraints led to intense rivalry between the services over budgets and missions. Competition over which service would get the nuclear mission also added to the fray.

This interservice rivalry worked to the disadvantage of the executive and the benefit of Congress. Interservice bickering over the president's policy directives was exploited by Congress, not to make choices between the services per se, but rather to upset the president's defense budget. Moreover, it was not necessarily partisan or policy differences that motivated members of Congress to challenge the president. Some legislators sought parochial benefits from defense spending and especially the construction of military installations. But others acted on the basis of a strong relationship with a particular military service. Like the relationship with the bureaus prior to World War II, some members of Congress always supported the priorities of a particular service. Representative Carl Vinson (D-GA), for example, was known as "the Admiral" for his strong support of the navy.

Most of the organizational changes to the defense department sought by Truman and then Eisenhower were aimed at ending this rivalry and at helping the secretary of defense force the military to line up behind the president's priorities. But Congress thwarted these plans. As a result of congressional action, the defense department remained largely decentralized and problems with a lack of jointness in military advice, unified command, and staff quality persisted.

THE NATIONAL SECURITY ACT

After close to three years of debate, the National Security Act's passage finally provided for some centralization of authority over the service chiefs. The act created a National Military Establishment, which included the army, navy, and the newly created air force, as well as the War Council, JCS, Joint Staff, Munitions Board, and the Research and Development Board. The services, however, remained executive-level departments.[25] According to the declaration of policy at the beginning of the law, the services were to have "authoritative coordination and unified direction under civilian control" but were not to be merged.[26] In other words, even though they would all be together in one department, each service would remain independent.

The civilian leader of the National Military Establishment was the secretary of defense. The list of authorities given to that position was impressive: the secretary was to serve as the "principal assistant" to the president for national security; establish general policies and programs for the department; exercise general direction, authority, and control; take the "appropriate steps" to eliminate unnecessary duplication or overlap in procurement, supply, transportation, storage, health, and research; and supervise and coordinate the preparation of the military's budgets. The secretary was allotted three assistant secretaries to help with these tasks.

The defense secretary's power, however, also had significant limits. One was the ability of military subordinates to appeal the secretary's decisions.

Specifically, the civilian secretaries of the services were given the right to take "any report or recommendation relating to his department which he may deem necessary" to the president or director of the budget. The second limit was even more significant: all powers not specifically given to the secretary of defense were assumed to reside with the service secretaries.

The military leaders of the National Military Establishment were the JCS. The 1947 act gave legal status to the JCS organization that had evolved during the war and that was to include each of the three service chiefs and the president's chief of staff, if there was one. There was to be no chairman, and no rules for JCS organization or decision making were given. The JCS were, however, given a small staff of no more than a hundred officers, with approximately equal numbers from each service.

The JCS were also made the principal military advisers to the president and defense secretary and were assigned specific tasks including developing strategy, establishing unified commands, preparing joint training, and reviewing weapons and personnel requirements. Notably, however, the JCS were not responsible for preparing budgets, a task that remained with the civilian service secretaries. Both before and after the act, the JCS merely responded to the president's overall budgetary ceiling and reviewed the budget requests of the services. The JCS did not recommend budgets or offer budgetary guidance based on strategy or operational plans. This was changed somewhat by the Key West Agreement, which required the JCS to provide the defense secretary with strategic and other priorities to influence the president's budget.[27] In practice, however, the JCS provided little input.

The act also created three other bodies to encourage coordination between the services. The War Council, comprised of the service secretaries and chiefs of staff, was to advise the defense secretary on broad maters of policy and whatever else was assigned to it by the secretary. The Munitions Board was to coordinate service mobilization, procurement, and distribution. And the Research and Development Board would coordinate research and development programs both among the services and between them and outside agencies. Each of these organizations was given its own military and civilian staff and a chair to be appointed by the president and with the consent of the Senate. Finally, the first section of the act dealt with the coordination of national security. To this end, it established three organizations for integrating government agencies: the National Security Council (NSC), the Central Intelligence Agency (CIA), and the National Security Resources Board.[28]

With the National Security Act, the president and Congress intended to establish a system of civil-military relations that provided for presidential leadership of national security supported and enabled by joint military advice and interagency coordination. The president, with the advice of the NSC, CIA, National Security Resources Board, and Bureau of the Budget, would determine how much money should be spent on defense. The defense secretary would then, in consultation with the JCS, determine how that budget should be split among the services. Congress would consider the budget in light of its priorities and concerns, decide on an amount, and the defense secretary would be in charge of ensuring that the services spent the amounts they were allocated in an efficient way. Additionally, the defense secretary, in consultation with the JCS, would facilitate coordination between the services for strategic and operational planning. The result was to be a more efficient military establishment, and one that worked on the basis of interservice coordination and better integration of foreign and military affairs. But, as Amy Zegart explains, the new organization was also the result of political compromise and was designed to preserve some of the prerogatives of actors, such as the navy, who did not always agree on key defense policy issues.[29]

In practice, the act did little to further jointness or service integration. The JCS came up with their recommendations without considering the president's budget and the defense secretary had to make budget decisions but without information about how this would impact military capabilities. For its part, Congress continued to focus on the details of military spending, and it paid scant attention to strategy or the relationship between military forces and foreign affairs.

In contrast to jointness, persistent and intense rivalry characterized relations between the services through the late 1940s and 1950s. This was stoked by Truman's efforts to reduce the defense budget and demobilize after World War II while maintaining the military capability necessary to counter the Soviet Union. Because the JCS worked on the basis of consensus among equals, they were able to agree to one budget only by adding up their individual requests rather than establishing priorities among them. This total was constantly over Truman's budget ceiling, in some cases by tens of billions of dollars. This funding situation was further complicated by the air force, which took advantage of its favorable public profile and undertook an aggressive campaign for funds.

This rivalry was also a consequence of the National Security Act, which left unresolved a number of disputes between the services over roles and missions. In 1947, Truman tried to help with Executive Order 9877, which contained a vague description of tasks for each service. The order was drafted by the services themselves, but the navy had strong objections to the way it seemed to impose limits on naval aviation and marine corps land operations. Also, the order did nothing to resolve old disagreements over strategic bombing or new ones about the development of nuclear weapons.

The complete inability of the services to resolve these issues resulted in a meeting at Key West, Florida, which was convened by the first secretary of defense, James Forrestal. The resulting agreement, and subsequent withdrawal of Executive Order 9877, did little to resolve the issues. The Key West Agreement stated the obvious missions for each service and continued to allow secondary missions to overlap. The only novel element to the accord was the emphasis placed on JCS responsibility for providing integrated advice rather than merely compiling service-oriented roles and missions plans.[30] A subsequent meeting at Newport, Rhode Island, ended in the same ambiguity, save for clarifying that the navy's primary mission did include strategic air operations, much to the chagrin of the air force.[31]

Rather than fostering jointness, the National Security Act complicated interservice relations because it created conflicting loyalties in the JCS. Each JCS member was faced with the need to balance loyalty to his service with allegiance to the JCS. The first was usually the winner. As a result, the JCS were repeatedly unable to provide unified advice except in areas where service interests were inconsequential. An additional conflict was created in the relationship between the services chiefs and their secretaries. According to the process established by the National Security Act, the service chiefs were to report to the defense secretary and president through their role as the JCS. Doing so, however, meant that they bypassed their own service secretaries. The result was frequent misunderstanding and poor communication between the military and civilian sides of each service.[32] A third conflict was caused by the public face the 1947 law gave to the JCS as the representative of the president's military program. On the one hand, the JCS felt obliged to support the program of their commander in chief, but on the other, they preferred to question it if they felt it was insufficient or lacking. In this manner, the chiefs were often put in the position of being disloyal either to the president or to their own service.

These conflicts on the JCS contributed to delayed decision making and logrolling, which the National Security Act did little to discourage. In fact, internal decision making in the JCS hardly changed as a result of the law, with the exception that information and requests were now routed through a defense secretary.[33] The JCS processed requests by channeling them through a system of committees that was organized along functional lines. These committees were composed of personnel from the Joint Staff, which drew equal numbers from each service. Action on the part of the committees usually consisted of a compilation of service views on the matter. Any conflicts were passed along to the service chiefs for resolution. This system was largely isolated and closed to the defense secretary and his staff, which allowed the service chiefs to shape the nature and direction of policy on important issues.[34] Further, the service chiefs guarded this privileged position, arguing that JCS deliberations and internal papers were available to the defense secretary only with the consent of the JCS.[35]

Beyond trying to keep civilians out of their internal discussions, each service quickly learned that the success of their requests depended largely on their ability to lobby Congress and to put pressure on the president and defense secretary. Samuel Huntington explains this process in *The Common Defense*:

The expansion of [the services'] political activities tended to resemble a process of castellation. Building out from the inner keep of the service itself, each service slowly constructed political, institutional, and legal defenses, coming to resemble an elaborate medieval castle with inner and outer walls, battlements and barbicans, watchtowers and moats. The services became well entrenched on the American political scene, as countless other interest groups, private and public, had done before them.[36]

As with other interest groups, the services sought to establish a privileged relationship with the committees in Congress that were important to their future.

The National Security Act intended to foster harmonious cooperation between the services. The hope was that by putting the services together in one department, they would rally to some collective identity as the "national military establishment." As a result, the JCS would offer advice on budgets, strategy, and other matters that would be the product of concern for the overall defense effort. The 1947 act, however, did little to change the independent identity and power of the services, and each service chief continued to be rewarded for his ability to pursue the interests of his own service. As a result, there was little basis for cooperation except over issues about which there was already agreement.

LEADERSHIP FROM THE SECRETARY OF DEFENSE

Prior to the National Security Act, the only official with a cross-service perspective on national defense had been the president. Although the secretary of defense was supposed to share this panoramic view, his ability to make decisions and provide advice on that basis was limited. The law denied the secretary the right to make unilateral changes in roles and missions and his budgetary authority was circumscribed by the ability of the services to take their own recommendations directly to other civilian authorities, even when these conflicted with those offered by the secretary. Additionally, the secretary's authority was limited by a lack of staff, both civilian and military. The first secretary of defense, James Forrestal, was further hindered by his relationship with Truman. Although the next secretary, Louis Johnson, had a better relationship with the president and a different management style, he still suffered from the structural deficiencies contained in the National Security Act.

Forrestal's problems with the services were twofold: the services wanted to evade control by the secretary of defense, and they were constantly bickering with each other. Initially, Forrestal took a hands-off approach; he preferred for the services and JCS to solve any disagreements. Soon, however, the president was demanding budget recommendations. Despite repeated requests for the JCS to provide advice on budgets and roles and missions, Forrestal was unable to get the chiefs to agree. One year after unification, persistent problems with the services prompted Forrestal to write in his diary that, "with regard to unification, the most substantial accomplishments are of an unspectacular character." He goes on to explain that devising a way for the JCS to participate in and take responsibility for decisions is the "greatest central problem of unification, and everything else, more or less, stems from it."[37]

Forrestal's ability to manipulate the JCS, and the rest of the defense department, was hindered by his lack of staff. The National Security Act had not authorized a staff for the secretary of defense and had provided for only three assistant secretaries. As a result, Forrestal turned to the service secretaries and War Council.[38] The secretaries, however, were frequently behind on information and decisions because they were routinely bypassed by the service chiefs, who had a direct connection to the president. The members of the War Council, although useful for discussing issues, had no authority or ability to help with implementation. Without staff, Forrestal faced two problems. First, he could not analyze service recommendations for validity, alternatives, or improvement. Second, he was overwhelmed with administrative problems that needed to be solved immediately for unification to progress. With no staff to help share this burden, Forrestal was forced to spend too much of his time on management details instead of overall planning and direction.

Forrestal's staffing problems were complicated by the unwillingness of the JCS and Joint Staff to share information. Forrestal did not attend JCS meetings, and the chiefs never developed a close working relationship with the secretary. Indeed, the workings of the JCS and Joint Staff were largely isolated and kept from the department's civilian leadership. The military used its monopoly on information as a political tool against Forrestal. Skirting his office, service chiefs often took their requests directly to Congress, the media, and the public. Forrestal thought his problems would be eased if he had a military adviser to help him interact with the JCS. General Dwight Eisenhower became Forrestal's temporary "principal military adviser and consultant" and reported to both Forrestal and the president. His duties were to help resolve differences among the services, to advise when the chiefs could not reach a decision on their own, and to monitor and expedite all JCS work. To do his job, however, Eisenhower had to rely on his own reputation because he had no formal authority with which to force consultation and compliance from the JCS.

Forrestal's inability to get the chiefs to agree on a budget annoyed Truman. This only increased when Forrestal seemed to side with the JCS is favor of higher budgets.[39] A few months into his tenure, Forrestal began to lose the support of the president and was asked to resign in the spring of 1949. Forrestal had not been Truman's first choice; indeed, he had annoyed Truman because he headed the navy's push against unification. Also, Forrestal repeatedly expressed opinions on political matters that Truman considered outside the jurisdiction of the defense secretary.[40]

Some of the management problems Forrestal experienced were eased when his successor, Louis Johnson, took over. Whereas Forrestal had been left to make decisions that he could not get the JCS to reach, Johnson forced the chiefs to reach agreement among themselves. Partly this was made possible by smaller budgets, which Johnson used more effectively to force service integration and when he refused to accept a simple division of the budget among the services. It was also facilitated by Johnson's relationship with the JCS. Johnson forced the JCS to make their discussions available to him; indeed, he even attended JCS meetings. And, when the JCS could not agree, Johnson proved willing to manipulate their differences of opinion. This "divide and conquer" tactic put considerable stress on the system and kept the JCS from functioning effectively and amicably.[41]

Johnson also benefited from a better relationship with Truman and Congress. The latter was impressed by Johnson's efforts to save money.[42] Also, Johnson was personal friends with Truman and had been the head of his campaign fundraising committee in the last election.[43] Johnson's loyalty to Truman often led him to disregard the suggestions of the services and to deny them due process in making decisions. Service morale suffered as a result.[44]

Despite the differences between Forrestal and Johnson, both shared similar problems as secretary of defense due to the structural weaknesses bestowed upon them by the National Security Act. The act made the defense secretary responsible for the leadership and functioning of the new department yet denied the office the authority it would need to accomplish this mission. Whereas the act intended for the secretary to serve as the focal point for both leadership of the department and broad policy advice to the president, in practice the president had to look elsewhere for both. Eventually, the president would turn to a military chief of staff and the NSC. As a result, the defense secretary was left to focus increasingly on matters of administration.

CONGRESS AND THE JCS

As a result of the National Security Act, the congressional Armed Services Committees and the defense appropriations subcommittees developed close relationships with the service chiefs, replicating the links members of Congress had previously had with the bureaus. This relationship was often to the detriment of the new defense secretary, who found himself faced with a service-committee alliance that proved troublesome. Although members of Congress tended, as before, to concern themselves with the particulars of the defense budget and not the details of strategy or force planning, Congress tended to band together with the services to upset the president's budget. For example, in the budget for fiscal year 1948, the appropriations subcommittees joined with the air force to support construction of a seventy-group air force over the objections of the defense secretary and the president.

Rivalry between the services proved a boon to congressional power. In areas where committee wishes differed from those of the executive, the defense committees used disagreements between the services to pick holes in the administration's program and to discover other alternatives. Forrestal found that he had difficulty forcing the services to back the president's proposals if they disagreed with them. As Paul Hammond explains in his study of the National Security Act,

> Forrestal found that with Congress looking over his shoulder in a way which was quite different from the wartime days, (now, notably, it had tight hold on the purse strings), even when he was able to negotiate mutual agreement among the services, or between his own position and the collective position of the JCS, common purposes were likely to erode away rapidly . . . time and again, Forrestal was faced with either attempting a censorship which he could never enforce or relinquishing what semblance of a common program he had been able to construct. From the beginning he was wise enough not to try the former.[45]

Without the authority to force consensus, Forrestal found that his support for the president's program was undercut by service officials who disagreed and members of the appropriations subcommittee who encouraged them. At the same time, Forrestal found that, as the face of the National Military Establishment, more and more of his time was taken up by the need to deal with Congress.[46]

Lacking authority in his defense secretary, Truman had to rely on personal persuasion to get the services to rally behind his proposals. Through the end of Truman's tenure and beyond, the chiefs were unable to agree on recommendations within the budgetary ceiling established by the president, or to agree on roles and mission changes. As a result, Congress sided with first one service and then another to upset the program proposed by the president.

The defense committees in Congress did little to encourage themselves to think about strategy or priorities or to analyze the president's budget from these perspectives. Instead, as was the case prior to the National Security

Act, members of Congress focused on their favorite service, parochial interests, or broader concerns about economy and efficiency, and used the defense budget to pursue these. The only novel aspect of the post–National Security Act era was that now the president wanted a unified military budget and the committees had to question their military witnesses, albeit only slightly, to get them to revert to offering their own service-specific recommendations.

THE 1949 AMENDMENTS

Only a few months after taking office, Forrestal recommended significant changes to both the power of the defense secretary and the structure of the JCS. Forrestal's primary concern was his own limited authority. He wanted to remove the adjective "general" that the National Security Act had applied to the secretary's direction, authority, and control over the National Military Establishment. This would give him more ability to manage the services and defense agencies. Forrestal also recommended that the secretary be given additional staff and suggested creating an undersecretary of defense to help with administrative tasks as well as to provide an ally in soliciting agreement from the JCS. To improve the ability of the JCS to reach meaningful decisions, Forrestal favored creating a chairman who would have authority to decide issues when the service chiefs were split.[47] Forrestal also felt that the JCS was understaffed, and he favored eliminating the ceiling on Joint Staff personnel.[48]

To study his suggestions, Forrestal approached the Commission on Organization of the Executive Branch of the Government, which Truman had appointed to study a broader set of changes. Referred to as the Hoover Commission, it had originally decided not to study defense because it felt the current structure was too new and untried. Forrestal, however, convinced the commission to add a study of defense to be headed by Ferdinand Eberstadt. On November 15, 1948, Eberstadt's subcommittee recommended the changes Forrestal had previously suggested to the president. It also recommended that the defense secretary be given greater control over the preparation of the military's budget, that the "reserve clause" that gave unspecified authorities to the services be repealed, that the services no longer be allowed to appeal to the president or director of the budget if they disagreed with the secretary, and that the secretary be given additional military and civilian staff.[49]

Truman modified the Hoover Commission's recommendations and sent them to Congress, where they were approved as amendments to the National Security Act in August of 1949. As a result of these changes, the National Military Establishment became the Department of Defense and the services ceased to be executive departments and were instead reduced to the status of "military departments," which were housed completely within the new cabinet-level defense department. The defense secretary's power was increased by giving him full rather than general authority and by giving him the title of principal assistant to the president on all matters relating to the defense department. The secretary also got three assistants, one of which was to be a budget comptroller.[50]

The 1949 amendments also required a chairman for the JCS, which was to be filled by presidential appointment but subject to Senate approval. The chairman's authority over the JCS was limited; he was to facilitate agreement but had no vote and no command authority. Further, the collective JCS remained the president's advisory group rather than only the chairman. The size of the Joint Staff was also increased from 100 to 210.

Most importantly, the amendments established the right of the services to bypass the defense secretary and take their recommendations directly to Congress.[51] Included at the insistence of Carl Vinson, the powerful chair of the House Armed Services Committee, this direct link between Congress and the services finally destroyed the last vestiges of the alliance between members of Congress and the technical bureaus that had characterized civil-military relations since the mid-1800s. The power of the bureaus had been reduced considerably when Congress created its Armed Services Committees in 1947, doing away with the separate Military Affairs and Naval Affairs Committees. Combined with the 1949 amendments, the merger of committees allowed members of Congress to spread particularistic relationships across all the services. In 1949, the appropriations committees in each house followed suit and created one subcommittee to handle appropriations for all the services.

The 1949 amendments, however, required that the defense budget be organized on a functional rather than a project basis. Prior to World War II, service budgets had taken the form of funding lines for individual installations, research and development of a particular weapon, and individual projects in each of the technical bureaus. Each service bureau had its own budget, and neither the service secretary nor chief of staff had the power to transfer funds between the bureaus or to exert significant input on the construction of their budgets. This decentralization meant it was difficult to relate service budgets to overall missions. Moreover, it is this budgeting system that allowed strong alliances to develop between service bureaus and the congressional committees responsible for military appropriations.

The 1949 amendments, however, gave the secretary of defense "full authority" for preparing the overall defense budget and required the services to use uniform budget categories and definitions. The services were also to shift from budgeting by project to budgeting by function—that is, by major tasks performed by each service. For example, instead of budgeting for the construction of a number of vehicles for a specific installation, the budget would instead contain a line for the procurement of vehicles for the army. These budgets were defended by the service chiefs, not the bureau heads. As a result, the power of the technical bureaus was destroyed.[52]

The new Department of Defense functioned much as its predecessor had. Service rivalry continued, as did the inability of the secretary to get the services to agree on budgets, strategy, or roles and missions. There were, however, some modest improvements to management. The chairman proved helpful in managing the services and the extra staff for the secretary helped expand the tasks he could accomplish. Also, whereas the secretary had relied on the services for information, he could now turn to his own office. None of these changes, however, meant that the secretary did not still face an uphill battle in getting the services to cooperate.

As Truman left office, his last secretary of defense, Robert Lovett, sent him a letter outlining many of the same problems that had plagued Forrestal. Lovett complained about a lack of staff resources, limited authority, and the JCS's inability to reach useful decisions. Not only was his ability to manage defense limited by his lack of power, Lovett explained that the 1949 amendments had actually created some confusion. The authority of the secretary was unclear, he explained, especially as it related to the JCS. It was ambiguous as to whether the JCS were actually under the secretary or parallel to him. Lovett wanted to clarify that the JCS were under the control of the secretary and that the secretary, not the JCS, was the president's principal assistant on defense matters. Lovett also outlined problems with the unified commands. Misunderstanding resulted from confusion about the relationship between the JCS, unified commanders, and the service secretaries.

Based upon his experience, Lovett recommended two possible courses of action. The alternative that Lovett preferred involved clarifying the authority and functions of the secretary and JCS, allowing for the JCS to delegate some of their service duties so they could concentrate more on joint matters, consolidating staff functions between civilians and the military and giving the secretary a combined civilian and military staff, and allowing the chairman to vote. The other alternative was more radical. It was to essentially eliminate the JCS and replace it with a body of officers who were divorced from their services and whose careers and thus loyalties would be determined by the president and defense secretary.

Neither of Lovett's suggestions received much attention. The country was concentrating more on the war effort in Korea and on Soviet nuclear developments. Moreover, the new president, Dwight Eisenhower, was committed to first ending the war, and then trying his own hand at managing the defense department.

CIVIL-MILITARY RELATIONS
UNDER EISENHOWER

The 1950s saw a major disagreement between the president and Congress over what became known as the bomber gap. On May Day of 1955, U.S. officials counted eleven bombers at a May Day parade in Moscow. Concerned that the Soviet Union was producing more and better bombers than the United States, President Eisenhower asked for additional funds for the production of B-52s. Congressional Democrats, however, claimed that the administration's lower defense budgets were endangering national security, not just in terms of airpower, but in other areas as well. This criticism culminated in 1956 when the Senate held hearings on the adequacy of U.S. airpower. Air force witnesses testified that within two to four years the United States would fall behind the Soviets. By the time of these hearings, however, Eisenhower believed that the intelligence estimates of the Soviet bomber program were inaccurate and that there was in fact no bomber gap. He disagreed that more funding was necessary, and when Congress appropriated more in the fiscal year 1957 defense budget, he refused to spend it. His defense secretary, Charles Wilson, said the money would "go into the bank" and be spent later as needed.[53]

Next came a different gap, this one relating to missiles. By the early 1950s, there was a widespread consensus among American foreign policy elites that the gap between U.S. security commitments and military capabilities would have to be filled by a reliance on nuclear weapons. This was fine as long as the United States was ahead in the missile race. But, on August 26, 1957, the Soviets launched their first intercontinental ballistic missile, which was followed later that autumn by a pair of satellites. These events resulted in widespread concern that U.S. national security was at risk. But based on U.S. intelligence estimates, Eisenhower soon came to believe that the missile gap was overstated and that the United States was not in a dangerous position.

Congress sharply criticized Eisenhower for his emphasis on thrift, which members claimed had resulted in inadequate defense spending, and his lack of attention to the missile gap. On several occasions, members of Congress refused to believe the revised U.S. intelligence estimates and questioned their legitimacy.[54] Peter Roman's book on Eisenhower and the missile gap explains that congressional Democrats, along with members of the defense appropriations subcommittees, used the missile gap as an excuse to criticize the president and urge increases to defense spending. The process was prone to exaggeration. For example, Roman explains that after Secretary of Defense

McElroy testified that the United States need not engage in a missile-for-missile race with the Soviets, the *New York Times* reported that "the Secretary of Defense testified today that the United States was voluntarily withdrawing from competition with the Soviet Union in the production of intercontinental ballistic missiles."[55] Congressional reaction to the missile gap served as an impetus for larger defense appropriations, more funding for science education,[56] military pay raises, the creation of NASA, and an increase in U.S.-British cooperation on the development of nuclear weapons.[57]

The president and Congress did seem to agree, however, that rivalry between the services was damaging to the U.S. security effort. Service parochialism was blamed for the inability of the United States to concentrate technology and coordinate action to develop missile and satellite capabilities. Numerous hearings to examine the issue were held, and members of the Senate Armed Services Committee claimed that they could not understand how so much money could be invested in missile technology with so few results.[58] The connection between interservice rivalry and the missile gap was expressed in a 1957 hearing:

> The Department of Defense has permitted duplication, even triplication, among the three services in the development and production of missiles; and has permitted comparable waste in the allocation of the three services of responsibilities in the missile field. The Department of Defense also delayed in giving overriding priority to the ballistic missile program. As a result, there has been a serious loss of time compared with the rapid progress of the Soviets in this field.[59]

Disagreements over the bomber and missile gaps were the most severe policy arguments between the president and Congress during the 1950s. Neither the House nor the Senate significantly questioned the wisdom of the Korean War or of Eisenhower's New Look policy. Nor did they refuse to appropriate the budgets the president wanted for either. Even Eisenhower's acceleration of the nuclear weapons program received scant comment, and Congress did little to change his requests for research and development, procurement, or nuclear sharing with allies.[60]

As for the services, their rivalry not only continued, it intensified. The service chiefs were unable to offer integrated advice on how to divide the defense budget. The services also continued to bicker over missions, with the navy and air force continuing their fight over strategic bombing and each of the services struggling to secure a role in the development of ballistic missiles. By the mid-1950s, however, the character of interservice rivalry was undergoing a change. Samuel Huntington in *The Common Defense* explains that while the services had previously quarreled mainly over the validity of missions and how best to perform them, they now argued over marginal gains and losses in resources.[61] The services still competed for shares of the budget, but this competition was over substantially similar military capabilities as well as who should have responsibility for a new program. Little attention was paid to discovering new ways of solving strategic problems. As Huntington explains, "the question of what should be done was less controversial than the questions of who should do it and how much [*sic*] resources should be allocated to it."[62]

Both the president and Congress encouraged this rivalry by refusing to choose between service programs or to assign responsibilities. Arguing that competition was efficient and innovative, civilians claimed they would allow similar programs to proceed but would eventually make a choice between them. Ongoing programs, however, soon developed a political backing. Members of Congress got parochial benefits and the services got funding and a foot in the door for future claims to that mission area. As a result, choices between duplicate programs were often never made.[63] For example, as each of the services rushed to secure a role in nuclear deterrence, they invested in ballistic missile programs. The army and air force were simultaneously building intermediate missiles, which, it was argued, would be more efficient if merged into one program. Despite assigning the air force responsibility for the use of such missiles, and the wide publicity and intense criticism of the duplicate efforts, civilians did not make a choice between them.[64] Both programs continued until they were irrelevant due to the invention of long-range missile technology.[65]

As for the president and defense secretary, they continued the habit of using the size of the budget to provide direction to the military about the development of strategy. In 1953, however, Eisenhower offered new strategic guidance in the form of the New Look.[66] The New Look stemmed from Eisenhower's concern that current defense spending would result in inflation and other economic problems. Instead, he proposed to limit military spending by relying on nuclear weapons and the threat of massive nuclear retaliation to deter the Soviet Union. To this end, the New Look called for expanding the air force at the expense of the army, navy, and marine corps. Although the New Look did shift budget shares, it did little to abate rivalry among the services or induce the JCS to submit budgets within the ceilings favored by Eisenhower.[67]

Eisenhower also made interservice rivalry seem worse than during the Truman administration because of his preference for hierarchical control and clearly defined responsibilities among his advisers and staff. Eisenhower expected his JCS to offer unified military advice and for their joint duties to take priority over their service responsibilities.[68] He also expected the JCS to stand firmly behind his policies and to stop arguing in public. When the JCS failed on both fronts, Eisenhower sought to censor their public activities and have the defense secretary impose unanimity on them. Indeed, Eisenhower's concern with the public stance of the service chiefs was so strong that early in his presidency he replaced the ones that had served during the Truman administration, claiming they were unnecessarily political and had been used to support policies with which Eisenhower disagreed.[69] Also, for part of his administration, Congress was controlled by the Democratic Party, a fact that caused Eisenhower to place an even heavier emphasis on unanimity among administration officials.[70]

Eisenhower's choices for defense secretary, first Charles Wilson and then Neil McElroy, did little to improve his relationship with the service chiefs.[71] Both men had come from business backgrounds and antagonized the military with their application of business practices and management to defense decision making.[72] Further, Wilson was often unwilling or unable to resolve trivial matters within the defense department and frequently called on Eisenhower to do so, a practice that the president resented.[73]

This defense politics routine changed slightly about six months after Eisenhower took office. On June 30, 1953, Reorganization Plan No. 6 took effect.[74] The main provisions of the plan had been inherited from the Truman administration, which had postponed action until after the Korean War.[75] The plan made three basic changes to the structure of the defense department. To improve the defense secretary's authority, he was made fully responsible for all civilian and military functions of the department, including the right to assign functions to any office or agency, and given six new assistants. To clarify lines of authority, the secretary was given the power to designate a service as the executive agent for each of the unified commands. This would indicate that the secretary, rather than the services, had predominant authority over the chain of command.[76] The other change was to increase the chairman's power by giving him the authority to direct and organize the JCS and greater control over the Joint Staff, including the ability to manage it and approve personnel changes.[77] Because the changes were submitted under the authority of the president to reorganize the executive branch, Congress had sixty days to reject the proposal.[78] Although there was considerable debate over the wisdom of increasing the chairman's power, neither house was able to rally a majority to defeat the changes.[79]

Reorganization Plan No. 6 did little to improve the functioning of the defense department. The new powers of the chairman and defense secretary were insignificant compared to the ability of the service chiefs to make their original recommendations and priorities known to Congress and the public. The year prior, in fact, the Senate Armed Services Committee had required military offices nominated to senior positions to formally promise to give their personal views to Congress, even if those contradicted administration policy.

Further, low defense budgets encouraged the services to fight for funds, and the chairman and defense secretary had few sanctions with which to force agreement. In fact, in some ways the reorganization plan made interservice rivalry worse because it reversed the order of JCS involvement in the budget process.[80] Previously, the service chiefs had been asked for their budget recommendations and then these were scaled down according to the president's overall budget. After Reorganization Plan No. 6, however, they were asked for budget recommendations only after they had been told what their share of the funding would be. This sequencing implied that military recommendations had less impact on the size of the budget. The military, as explained by army chief of staff General Matthew B. Ridgeway, found this change demoralizing. According to Ridgeway, force levels "were not based on the freely reached conclusions of the Joint Chiefs of Staff. They were squeezed between the framework of arbitrary manpower and fiscal limits, a complete inversion of the normal process."[81]

Rivalry also intensified because the reorganization plan enlarged both the staff of the defense secretary and their ability to reach into the daily operations of the military establishment. This increased the complaints the services collectively made about civilian bureaucrats meddling in their affairs.[82] At best, the changes provided some administrative assistance to the defense secretary. Regardless, Eisenhower's criticism of defense management escalated throughout his administration, finally culminating in another attempt at reform in 1958.

THE DEFENSE DEPARTMENT REORGANIZATION ACT OF 1958

The Department of Defense Reorganization Act of 1958 centralized more power in the defense secretary and made changes to the way the JCS conducted its business. The law also redefined the relationship of the combatant commanders to the rest of the military establishment in the hope that this would increase their stature and thus their ability to demand resources and attract attention to their problems.[83]

The law increased the power of the defense secretary in two ways. Overall, it replaced vague language about the power of the defense secretary versus that of the individual services with a more precise definition of their relationship to each other. Specifically, the law abandoned the requirement that the services be "separately administered," and made the defense secretary responsible for their "effective, efficient and economical administration."[84] To increase the secretary's administrative abilities, that official was allowed to delegate responsibilities over specific duties to the assistant secretaries. The law spelled out how and when these assistants can direct the services and stipulated that any delegation of authority to them must be specific and in writing. The second way the law empowered the defense secretary was by increasing the secretary's ability to make role and mission changes. Specifically, the secretary was allowed to transfer, reassign, abolish, or consolidate roles and missions, provided that any such changes be approved by the House and Senate Armed Services Committees. The law gave these committees thirty days to review any changes suggested by the secretary, with an additional forty-five days if they think longer consideration is necessary. Previously, the committees had sixty days to consider such changes.

The 1958 reorganization aimed to increase the ability and usefulness of the JCS as a source of military advice in three ways. First, the chairman was allowed to vote in JCS deliberations; this would hopefully increase his ability to force the service chiefs to make decisions. The second change involved allowing the service chiefs to delegate their "authority and duties" to the service vice chiefs in the hope that this would then allow the JCS more time to concentrate on joint matters as opposed to service-specific ones. Third, the act increased the size of the Joint Staff to four hundred members to provide the service chiefs with more research and administrative support.

The other area where the 1958 reorganization made significant changes was to the authority of the combatant commanders, who at the time were referred to as commanders in chief, or CINCs. The bill provided for the assignment, by the defense secretary, of all combat forces into unified commands—that is, geographically defined areas for military operations, such as Europe or Africa. This would leave only administrative and management personnel under the sole authority of the services. Further, the authority these commanders had over troops assigned to them was extended to all operational areas and the chain of command between the combatant commanders and civilians was standardized.[85]

But the most significant part of the 1958 Reorganization Act was that it failed to reign in the connection between Congress and the services. The 1949 amendments to the National Security Act allowed the service secretaries and chiefs to make recommendations directly to Congress. Calling this "legalized insubordination," Eisenhower argued that "it invites interservice rivalries; invites insubordination to the President and Secretary of Defense; endorses the idea of disunity and blocking of defense modernization; suggests that Congress hopes for disobedience and interservice rivalries; is bad concept, bad practice, bad influence within the Pentagon."[86]

But the Armed Services Committees insisted that the right of the services to appeal directly to Congress was fundamental to access to information and thus congressional power over defense policy.

The immediate effect of the 1958 reorganization on defense politics was negligible. The defense committees in Congress kept their relationship with the services and continued to be used by them to upset decisions of the defense secretary and president. As for the relationship between the services, the Reorganization Act did nothing to reduce interservice rivalry or to improve cooperation because it did not alter the fundamental character of the services or the JCS as organizations. The service chiefs remained unable to produce unified budget recommendations or to provide integrated advice on strategy or force planning because each service had no incentive to subordinate its concerns to the overall good of the defense effort. For the remainder of the Eisenhower administration, interservice rivalry continued as if no organizational change had taken place.

As for the defense secretary and his assistants, much of their time was spent on revising the rules and directives that governed the relationship between the Office of the Secretary of Defense (OSD) and the military. The pedantic and protracted war that took place over these changes constitutes the bulk of the efforts to implement the 1958 reorganization.[87] As explained by Alfred Goldberg in his study of defense organization, "bringing these directives into conformance with the 1958 Reorganization Act proved difficult and time-consuming because of the need for precise language that would gain the consensus of the interested parties, particularly the JCS and the services, which sought to retain as much initiative as possible and to achieve as much freedom as possible from OSD authority."[88]

Key issues were whether or not the JCS was part of OSD, rather than simply under the authority of the defense secretary, and whether or not the JCS should be treated as the military staff of the defense secretary.[89] These arguments consumed the energies of OSD to such an extent that a full year after the law was signed, a memo to the president suggested that momentum for implementation would be lost and the major goals of the act would go unrealized unless immediate corrective steps were taken.[90]

The 1958 act did make some changes that, although of seemingly little consequence during the next decade, would result in considerable problems by the time the defense department was next reorganized. One of these changes was to the combatant commands. The act gave the defense secretary the power to allocate almost all operational forces to a single combatant command, and their commanders also got increased control over the forces assigned to them. This laid the foundation for a division of responsibility that would develop between the services and the combatant commands. The former would come to concentrate on the organizational needs of each service while the latter would focus on what was required for combat regardless of which service was involved. Although this dichotomy was of little significance in the years immediately following the 1958 reorganization, over time it would serve as the foundation for a rivalry between the services and the combatant commanders that would have repercussions for combat effectiveness and jointness.

Another unintended consequence involved a change in the relationship between OSD and the military. Although the Reorganization Act did little to improve the defense secretary's ability to force the services toward jointness, it did start a process whereby OSD became more deeply involved in the military details of defense planning. By allowing the defense secretary's assistants to oversee the services, the act gave them an excuse to delve deeper into the daily machinations of the defense department. This blurred the distinction between civilian and military functions as the civilian assistants found themselves unable to monitor implementation or provide advice without involvement in areas that were previously left to the military.

This is precisely the sort of interaction that Congress had sought to limit. Fearing that OSD would come to rival Congress itself for control of the military, the Armed Services Committees had sought to restrict the ability of the defense secretary to manage by way of his assistants. These restrictions, however, required only a little paperwork to circumvent and the committees proved unwilling to keep in check or even monitor the gradual incursion of civilian staff into the details of military matters. As a result, civilian managers became militarized and military staff came to share civilian functions. Rather than overseeing the military, OSD came to be co-opted by it.[91]

Eisenhower's 1958 reforms did little to abate the interservice rivalry that was the product of the National Security Act, defense budgets, and congressional encouragement. Congress made sure the service chiefs remained independent and thus difficult for the chairman or the executive branch to control. By the mid-1960s, however, the politics of defense would be radically different, and the chiefs would have a strong incentive, not to produce joint advice, but to keep their disagreements private and confined to the JCS. The cause was not formal reorganization, but the tenure of Robert McNamara as secretary of defense.

4

CREATING A STRONGER CHAIRMAN

The structural changes to the Joint Chiefs of Staff (JCS) made under Presidents Truman and Eisenhower did little to encourage the service chiefs to make choices among the preferences of the services. Nor did advice from the chairman fill the void by offering a joint perspective. Significant change did occur, however, under the Kennedy administration. But it was not due to formal reorganization of the JCS. Instead, the catalyst was Secretary of Defense Robert McNamara and his use of systems analysis to challenge the advice given by the individual services. McNamara proved willing to privilege his own preferences over those of the services and to use systems analysis to provide an analytical underpinning for his decisions. This initially proved very persuasive to Congress. In response, the service chiefs learned to keep their disagreements private and to present a unified front to civilian policy makers. Without rivalry between the services, civil-military relations shifted from a conflict between the services that empowered civilians, to a contest between the military and the Office of the Secretary of Defense (OSD), and later between a coalition that pitted Congress and the military against the president.

Since the early 1960s, public rivalry between the services has been rare and unanimity the norm. The Goldwater-Nichols Act did not change this. It did, however, provide new authorities to the chairman that resulted in a dramatic power shift. As shown in chapter 2, the chairman became the focal point for military advice. It is unclear, however, whether that advice is joint and the product of trade-offs between the services, the traditional summation of service priorities or based on whatever consensus exists among them, or the chairman's own personal preferences. What is clear is that the Goldwater-Nichols Act gave the chairman the potential to be a powerful independent force in civil-military relations.

THE McNAMARA LEGACY

Secretary of Defense Robert McNamara was willing to use interservice rivalry to pick winners and losers among the services. He also helped civilians in the Pentagon counter military perspectives through the introduction of systems analysis, a decision-making tool through which civilians used supposedly rational analysis rather than politics to make policy choices. This management style angered the JCS and eventually also Congress. The JCS felt their expertise was being ignored, a problem that was aggravated by McNamara's tendency to make decisions about how to wage the war in Vietnam without waiting for advice from the JCS. By the mid-1960s, the service chiefs had learned to offer unanimous advice on more issues and to keep differences of opinion within the confines of the JCS.

Congress was initially welcoming of McNamara's decisive management style. But it, too, grew weary of his seeming disregard for military expertise, especially with respect to Vietnam. Congress began to side with the JCS, using the unanimous military advice they offered as a basis for upsetting President Lyndon Johnson's policy preferences.

When McNamara became President John Kennedy's secretary of defense in 1961, he declined offers from the president to legislate more authority for the defense secretary, and instead set about developing ways of controlling the services through the manipulation of information and analysis. McNamara's strategy involved two elements: he provided OSD with the tools for conducting its own analysis of defense problems, and, if it became apparent that the military would not make the decisions he wanted, McNamara overruled them with his own preferences. The focal points of McNamara's efforts were systems analysis and PPBS—the Planning, Programming, and Budgeting System.[1] Systems analysis was the name given to the idea that questions of strategy, requirements, and force structure could be divided into their component parts and then routinely reviewed and analyzed. PPBS sought to establish a process that would evaluate alternative force structures in light of strategy and budgets for both the next fiscal year and several years into the future. By comparing alternatives and relating these to U.S. defense and budgetary commitments, PPBS was able to provide a baseline for determining the priority and necessity of individual service requests.

Systems analysis and PPBS resulted in an authoritative source of information for the defense secretary that was independent of military advice. By emphasizing rationality and analysis, McNamara was able to legitimize the ability of civilians to make military decisions, and especially decisions about service priorities. According to Paul Hammond, McNamara's methods were not new. What was novel was the degree to which they were refined and integrated into the defense policy-making process.[2]

Besides providing McNamara with his own leverage, systems analysis and PPBS highlighted the shortcomings of the services' own analysis. Service advice seemed parochial, of poorer quality, and disconnected from broader questions about defense and national security. Further, service staffing procedures often resulted in political compromises. As decisions moved up the hierarchy of each service, bargains were struck between the different interests at each level; the result was service advice that was watered down by compromise at each stage in the decision-making process.[3] As a consequence, service analysis could not compete with that conducted by McNamara's civilian staff.

Further, PPBS gave McNamara power over the JCS. The service chiefs were often unable to provide military advice to the secretary because each insisted on supporting the position of their own individual service. Without consensus, the JCS could not provide a recommendation. PPBS allowed McNamara to step into this void and make recommendations to the president in the absence of JCS support or agreement.

PPBS was accompanied by an organizational change in the defense budget.[4] Since the 1949 amendments, the budget had been constructed in terms of functional categories such as operations costs for the air force or army personnel costs. To give the secretary more power, McNamara changed this to military missions, such as air defense, tactical air support, and strategic bombing. Budgeting by mission was supposed to allow the defense secretary to weigh the cost of doing one mission with different mixes of forces. Further, the new budgets also provided estimates for the expected cost of performing the mission over five years and included figures for all elements of the mission such as research and development, procurement, operations, and personnel. Budgeting based upon mission was supposed to result in increased competition between the services to perform each mission.[5] This potential, however, was short-circuited when Congress refused to adopt a similar budget structure.

McNamara's willingness to make decisions and his ability to support these with systems analysis was complemented by competition between the services. The tendency for the services to argue with each other allowed McNamara to exploit their differences of opinion as a source of power for his office. When the services could not agree, McNamara proved willing to pick winners and losers. Although service disagreements had always invited this kind of decision making, McNamara was the first defense secretary who was willing to use it on a systematic basis to manage the military. Further, McNamara could use systems analysis to question the positions taken by one service and thereby encourage the other services to pile on. In this manner, he was able to encourage service disagreement where none had previously existed, and thus to expand the range of decisions where his authority was required.

McNamara also exploited service rivalry in managing the Vietnam War. Under Kennedy and especially Johnson, the service chiefs had been unable to offer unified recommendations for U.S. military assistance to the South Vietnamese, even though the JCS strongly disagreed with the policies being followed. McNamara used this disagreement to keep the JCS out of decision making, arguing that they had no recommendations or no unanimous disagreement with his decisions.[6]

By 1965, the services had started to adapt themselves to McNamara's management style. First, they learned to play the systems analysis game. The services developed their own means of making their decision-making processes appear less parochial and more rational and comprehensive. More importantly, they learned the value of a single voice. By presenting a unified front, the services limited the ability of the defense secretary to pick and choose between them. Although McNamara could use systems analysis to question the advice of the professional military, it was a much more demanding task to confront unified military opinion on an issue. Beginning with Chairman Maxwell Taylor and accelerating under his successor, Earle Wheeler, the military made a conscious attempt to keep service disagreements within the JCS and to present a united face to the world.[7] As a result, rivalry between the services in public lessened. For example, in the early 1960s, McNamara used the split recommendations of the service chiefs as ammunition to defeat the navy's repeated bids for funding for a nuclear carrier.[8] By 1965, however, the chiefs unanimously supported requests in public about which in private they had sharp disagreements. For example, in the fiscal year 1966 budget, the JCS united behind each other's recommendations in front of Congress. As a result, McNamara was forced to agree to provisions for nuclear submarines and the Nike-X missile that he had earlier opposed.[9] According to the official history of OSD, split JCS decisions declined from about thirty per year in the early 1960s to seven in 1966, and only four by 1967.[10] The military continued to follow this strategy and public disagreements between the chiefs remained extremely rare.

Unity among the chiefs, however, began to raise concerns about the quality of JCS recommendations. Civilians increasingly became concerned that the JCS were making decisions on the basis of bargaining and trade-offs between service perspectives, rather than priorities established by consensus about the overall defense effort. The basis for this criticism was the JCS decision-making system. Favoring consensus, JCS routines and procedures worked to maximize service agreement and enable unanimity. As explained in chapter 2, issues went through a four- or five-stage review process, with each service having a veto over every aspect of any decision at each stage of the process.[11] By the end, decisions contained something for everyone. Difficult decisions that required trade-offs were either never made, made only very slowly, or watered down to the point where they were no longer useful.[12]

Problems with JCS decision-making procedures were not a new development of the McNamara era. Reaction to McNamara's tenure as defense secretary did, however, increase the consequences of these practices. McNamara and his staff were the first civilians in the defense department to routinely claim the authority to make military decisions. Certainly, previous administrations had reduced defense budgets out of concern for economy, but McNamara used systems analysis to make choices that were thought to fall within the domain of professional military expertise. McNamara also began to use the Joint Staff as a source of information and analysis for evaluating service recommendations.[13] This created animosity between his staff and the military, and this only intensified when, within two years of coming to the Pentagon, McNamara had fired all four JCS members for publicly challenging his methods and decisions.[14] McNamara's management style, plus problems with the war in Vietnam, served to demoralize the military and reduce service cooperation with OSD. Further, McNamara's willingness to make choices between service recommendations caused the main focus of rivalry to shift, from between the individual services to between the services collectively and civilians in the Pentagon.

As a result of McNamara's confrontation with the military, the defense secretaries that followed him proved less concerned with how decisions between the services were reached and more interested in a harmonious relationship between OSD and the services. These secretaries sought closer cooperation with the military and came to be prejudiced in favor of military over civilian advice. They did so by involving the JCS more in civilian decision making and deferring more to military advice. For example, Melvin Laird, who served as defense secretary under Nixon, instituted "participatory management" in an attempt to involve the JCS in downsizing after the Vietnam War. Laird continued to rely on systems analysis, but he used it within the defense department rather than to justify decisions in public. As a result, relations with the JCS improved and the secretary's staff and the services began to work together. This process was reversed during the Carter administration. Carter, along with his defense secretary, Harold Brown, once again made changes to defense policy without consulting the military, although on a much less intrusive scale than was the case during McNamara's tenure. As a result, the JCS sought a closer relationship with Congress and came to openly oppose the president on some issues. Under Reagan, however, the JCS and defense secretary resumed a close working relationship. Reagan's first defense secretary, Caspar Weinberger, brought military officers into prominent places in departmental decision making. He was often accused of paying more attention to the military than to his own civilian staff and of adopting military preferences without much critical analysis.

This lack of opposition to the military was mirrored by the Office of Management and Budget (OMB). As Aaron Wildavsky explains in his analysis of the budgetary process, OMB usually had an adversarial role vis-à-vis agencies with respect to their budgets.[15] Beginning with McNamara, however, OMB began to develop its budget guidance for defense in close consultation with the defense department. Whereas other agencies had to appeal to the president to overturn OMB funding decisions, for defense budgets OMB had to ask the president to reconsider his funding recommendations for the military. According to Wildavsky, OMB's role in defense budgeting became so minor under Reagan that many staff left because they were frustrated with their lack of influence.[16]

The relationship between Congress and the military was also affected by Robert McNamara's tenure as secretary. Initially, Congress was enamored with McNamara's mastery of data and decision-making tools. House Armed Services Committee chair Carl Vinson, who had a record of vivid opposition to any increase in the power of the defense secretary, praised McNamara's first presentation to the committee:

I want to say this. I say it from the very bottom of my heart. I have been here dealing with these problems since 1919. I want to state that this is the most comprehensive, most factual statement that it has ever been my privilege to have an opportunity to receive from any of the departments of Government. There is more information in here than any committee in Congress had ever received along the line that it is dealing with.[17]

Such comments were not isolated or infrequent.

Partly this was due to style differences between McNamara and previous defense secretaries. McNamara was the first such official who was willing to take public responsibility for his decisions and to explain the rationale behind them to the legislature. The defense committees, however, also liked McNamara because he increased congressional access to information and helped the legislature feel it was playing a role in constructing a rational, sound defense policy. As a result, Congress began to ally with the defense secretary in his attempts to overrule the services.

The services still tried to overturn McNamara's decisions by appealing to Congress. But, in cases where a service chief wished to take a dissenting opinion to Congress, McNamara required them to also present his own position on the issue.[18] Congress, however, usually found McNamara's position, backed up by systems analysis, more convincing.[19] Pressure from both McNamara and President Johnson also made the chiefs very reluctant to contradict the defense secretary on decisions concerning the Vietnam War, even when directly questioned by members of Congress.[20]

By the mid-1960s, however, opinion about McNamara began to change. Concerned that the secretary was taking over functions that rightly belonged to the military, Congress began to question not only McNamara's advice, but the role of systems analysis.[21] Members repeatedly expressed concern that professional military expertise was being subordinated to academic analysis and that the latter was inferior because it lacked a basis in experience. Additionally, Congress found fault with McNamara because of differences of opinion. In 1966, Congress repeatedly clashed with McNamara on issues such as antiballistic missiles, attack submarines, and other procurement items, as well as the war in Vietnam, and reserve and personnel policies.[22] Representative Leslie Arends (R-IL) expressed these sentiments well in 1966 when he criticized McNamara for refusing to support a congressional decision. According to Arends, "unfortunately, Secretary of

Defense McNamara has been disposed to substitute his individual judgment for the collective judgment of the Congress. He has seen fit to substitute his nonprofessional civilian judgment for the professional judgment of our Joint Chiefs of Staff . . . I sincerely hope the Secretary does not have the effrontery again to ignore our repeatedly expressed will."[23] In response, Congress reverted to its favorite means of control: it probed the services for their differences of opinion. This time, however, instead of using the services against each other, the defense committees banded together with them collectively and together they established alliances to overturn the decisions of the defense secretary.[24] For example, in 1966 the Armed Services Committees joined together with the army and forced McNamara to speed up research, development, and deployment of an antiballistic missile system.[25]

Although the services had learned under McNamara to collude, budget increases in the late 1970s and early 1980s changed the impact of this unity. Under McNamara, the services had presented a joint front to keep civilians from further cutting their budgets. With budget increases, however, the services had less reason to reduce their spending priorities and more incentive to simply add them together. The defense secretary found it difficult to discipline this process because the services had ready allies among members of Congress. For example, the navy and air force began to argue for their major weapons systems using district-by-district breakdowns of where components were produced.

Congressional micromanagement also limited the flexibility of OSD. As the undersecretary of defense for research and engineering complained, "I can hardly be held responsible if in one-third of my programs I am told by Congress what to do, not to kill a program or to add this or subtract that."[26]

Sometimes, however, this congressional activism backfired and the services found themselves forced into programs they preferred to do without. For example, in 1986, members of the House who were not on the Armed Services Committee were able to insert $3 billion into the defense budget for the T-46 jet trainer, a program that both the committee and the air force wanted to cancel.[27]

In one respect, the relationship between Congress and the JCS displayed tremendous continuity: the main mechanism for congressional oversight was still the defense budget. But in contrast to the decades after World War II, Congress no longer leveraged competition between the services in its decision making. Such rivalry had been replaced with unanimous recommendations from the JCS. Moreover, Congress was now more inclined to endorse such recommendations rather than subject them to critical analysis. But there were also members of Congress who sought to challenge Reagan's military buildup as well as the degree to which JCS recommendations were based upon strategy and a coherent force structure. Thanks to internal changes in the 1970s in Congress, these more junior members were able to convince senior congressional leadership to challenge the JCS and eventually the president. That challenge came in the form of legislation, the 1986 Goldwater-Nichols Act, that changed the structure of the JCS.[28]

LEGISLATING JOINTNESS

The overriding intent of the Goldwater-Nichols Act was to increase jointness by creating an organization in which it would have a powerful, self-motivated, institutional home. Certain offices within the U.S. defense hierarchy, and especially the chairman and combatant commanders, are naturally joint. It is the responsibility of the individuals who hold these jobs to combine the separate services, which they oversee into one integrated effort. The Goldwater-Nichols Act did not create this joint bias. It did, however, intentionally seek to prejudice defense policy-making processes in favor of joint actors and perspectives. By providing joint positions with better quality staff, more control over that staff, and increased access to information, the law sought to improve the quality of joint advice. By giving joint actors more power in decision making, the law aimed to have defense policy err on the side of jointness rather than service-based perspectives.

The intent of the law was not to eliminate or replace service parochialism. The authors of the Goldwater-Nichols Act saw nothing wrong with service advice; it was the responsibility of the services to pursue this, and the defense effort would benefit as a result. The problem was the lack of corresponding joint advice or the absence of any countervailing opinion at all.[29] Therefore, the law sought to create a contest between service and joint parochialism and to conduct that contest in an arena that was biased toward jointness. Excessive jointness was seen as "just as onerous and harmful as service parochialism."[30]

As a result of this logic, the Goldwater-Nichols Act made few changes to the power and authority of the defense secretary. Instead, the intent was to strengthen civilian leadership of the military by creating a more powerful chairman, but also to improve congressional oversight by forcing the executive branch to be more precise in its strategic and budgetary guidance. The law required the secretary of defense to give the military guidance for its program and budget recommendations, provide the chairman with policy input useful for preparing and reviewing contingency plans,[31] keep the service secretaries informed about military operations and other activities that directly affect their responsibilities,[32] and advise the president on the qualifications needed for defense department political appointees.[33] But the only formal change made to the authority of the defense secretary was to repeal his ability to reorganize defense department positions and activities that had previously been established in law.[34]

Rather than more statutory changes to the defense secretary, the Goldwater-Nichols Act focused on increasing the power of the chairman.[35] The law made the chairman the principal military adviser to the president, National Security Council, and the defense secretary. It designated that his advice was to include strategy, contingency planning, and budgets, and that the chairman alone was now responsible for the duties that were previously assigned to the JCS as a corporate body. Included in this was the transfer of the Joint Staff to the chairman, who, in place of the service chiefs, would now control its operations, including assigning duties, approving staff, and using it at his own discretion.[36] The law also required the chairman to consult with other JCS members in formulating advice, and required him to provide executive branch civilians with the range of military opinion on any given matter, along with any dissenting advice.[37] The law assigned new tasks to the chairman, including providing direction and advice on strategy, contingency planning, budgets, logistics, and net assessment.[38] Finally, the law also changed the rules governing the chairman's tenure in office to extend the number of years one chairman could serve and also to allow new presidents to appoint their own chairman rather than being stuck with the one from the previous administration.[39]

The Goldwater-Nichols Act also created the position of vice chairman of the JCS. The duties of the vice chairman were any tasks prescribed or delegated by the chairman as approved by the defense secretary, to act as chairman when he is absent or disabled, and to participate in all JCS meetings but to vote only when acting as chairman.[40]

The idea behind these changes was to balance the benefits of service-based advice with the need for jointness and more efficient decision making. As Representative Les Aspin explained in the press release that accompanied the conference report, "we aren't eliminating turf fights. You can't do that. What we are trying to do, however, is harness turf propensities to the cause of a joint or multi-service defense policy."[41] By transferring the responsibilities of the entire JCS, including the role of "principal military adviser," to only the chairman, the intent was to increase the likelihood that difficult choices would be made and that the speed and quality of all decision making would increase. Rather than relying on consensus, as had been the case with the corporate JCS, the chairman would be able to force trade-offs and take actions based upon the information and advice provided by the services, but without the need to wait for them to agree on one course of action. Also, the problem of "dual-hatting"—that is, conflicts between a service chief's joint and service responsibilities—would be eased.

The second major set of changes in the Goldwater-Nichols Act was to the combatant commanders (COCOMs). Similar to the chairman, the COCOMs were considered joint actors because their positions required them to avoid a single-service perspective on issues. The act aimed to increase their clout in both resource allocation and the conduct of military operations as a means of increasing jointness in these activities. The law changed the role of the COCOMs in several ways. The chairman was made their ombudsman so that their views would be represented in routine Pentagon decision making.[42] The chairman was also required to review the overall structure of the combatant commands and to recommend changes and to be responsible for overseeing their activities.[43] The relationship between the COCOMs and the services was also altered by clarifying the authority of the COCOMs over the service forces that make up their commands, but also by prohibiting the COCOMs from using this as an excuse to emasculate the services.[44] The COCOMs were also given small budgets of their own, which they could use to focus on activities that directly affected their missions but which were otherwise unfunded by the services.[45] Finally, the law simplified the chain of command and gave each COCOM a small staff that he could use instead of having to rely on those of the services.[46]

The longest and most detailed portion of the Goldwater-Nichols Act contained changes to the military's career and promotion system.[47] The intent of these changes was twofold. First, the goal was to ensure that officers who attained the top military positions—including the chairman, vice chairman, and COCOMs—were those most valued by their services. The services tended to send their best and brightest to service-specific, command-related positions, leaving the less capable for duty in joint positions. The Goldwater-Nichols Act intended to change this by making promotion to general or admiral contingent on some form of joint education—that is, education with a substantial cross-service component—and on previous "joint duty assignments"—that is, positions that involved working with more than one's own service. Without joint education or joint duty, a member of the military could not be promoted to the top positions in even their own service. The second goal of the law was to expose the future leadership of each service and the JCS to multiservice viewpoints and eventually to create a cadre of military leaders who had abandoned their service loyalty in favor of support for the "joint" or overall defense effort. These leaders, in turn, would help keep policy compliant with the goals of the Goldwater-Nichols Act.

Although the Goldwater-Nichols Act aimed to increase jointness through detailed and enduring organizational change, at least with respect to resource allocation, the impact appears to have been minimal. As explained in chapter 2, several key indicators suggest service preferences remain dominant. Service shares of the budget remain remarkably stable over decades, roles and missions have changed little since 1947, and the process by which the military constructs it annual budget is still dominated by service preferences. Chapters 5, 6, and 7 dig more deeply into the impact of the Goldwater-Nichols Act by focusing on three important budget-relevant decisions. In each of these cases, the policy results are characterized more by consensus and equality among the services than jointness. Despite the new power and authority given to the chairman, the preferences of the service chiefs are still quite influential.

But these cases also show that the chairman is far from irrelevant or powerless. Instead, they illustrate that in making the chairman the principal military adviser, he has become more visible as a spokesperson for the military and thus more influential. But because his power remains partially derived from, and not independent of, his relationship with the service chiefs, they, too, have benefited from the Goldwater-Nichols Act, sometimes to the detriment of civilian control over policy outcomes. In other words, the chairman has more political power, but that does not mean he uses it to further jointness.

5

LEAVING THE COLD WAR BEHIND

The collapse of the Soviet Union, and its formal end in 1991, raised expectations for changes in defense spending. In addition to widespread calls for a "peace dividend" now that the Cold War was over, it was also difficult to justify the defense spending of previous years because the main adversary had dissolved into a Russian Federation characterized by moribund defense industries, a significantly smaller military force compared to its Soviet predecessor, and a political process that seemed inclined toward, if not a healthy, high-functioning democracy, at least increased cooperation with the United States. Although many expected deeper cuts, during the first half of the 1990s, U.S. defense spending declined by approximately 30 percent.

This cut took place in two phases. First, the George H. W. Bush administration reduced spending by 25 percent. This was followed by another 5 percent reduction during the early years of the Bill Clinton presidency. Both were announced as significant changes but also as adaptations to a new global order that required fewer but more flexible military forces.[1] Critics, however, saw the result as simply smaller Cold War forces that protected the favorite weapons of each service.[2]

Regardless of whether one is inclined to think the cuts were either too deep or not deep enough, what is clear is that the process of downsizing was governed by Chairman Colin Powell. Concerned that deeper defense cuts were likely, Powell used his position to convince both the Bush and Clinton administrations to adopt spending levels, and a justification for those choices, that served to create a floor below which the military budget would not drop. Powell used his position as chairman, and the new prerogatives afforded him by the Goldwater-Nichols Act, to convince the services not to individually argue for more budget share. With united support from the military, Powell helped both the Bush and Clinton administrations overcome political problems that had little to do with defense spending.

In terms of civil-military relations, it is clear that Powell, and not civilian decision makers, had preponderant power over establishing force structure and strategy for the post–Cold War era. Moreover, in debates over downsizing during both the Bush and Clinton administrations, Powell won key arguments, with civilian officials but also with the service chiefs. Conscious of the new powers given to him by the Goldwater-Nichols Act, Powell used them to forge consensus among the service chiefs, or at least to convince them not to go public with any disagreements or complaints. He also exploited his visibility and clout to discourage key civilian decision makers, and specifically two different secretaries of defense, from challenging his advice. Although there is general agreement that Powell usurped what should have been civilian roles in responding to the end of the Cold War, at the time it wasn't clear whether Powell's personal abilities and ambition led him to exploit his position as chairman, or whether the Goldwater-Nichols Act had established a structure that would make powerful chairmen the norm.

THE BASE FORCE

The beginning of the end of the Cold War found Colin Powell serving as Reagan's national security adviser. U.S.-Soviet relations were, if not improving, at least becoming less overtly hostile in terms of both rhetoric and action. Improved relations might lead to intensified calls for reductions in

defense spending, and so Powell reasoned that the military should anticipate and control such a future by providing options. The result was a set of
ideas about force structure and strategy that became known as the Base
Force.[3]

Powell became chairman in 1989, at the height of Gorbachev's political
and economic reforms. Pressure to decrease defense spending increased further in 1990 with the passage of the Budget Enforcement Act, which set
limits for defense and domestic discretionary spending for the fiscal years
1991–1995.[4] The act put further pressure on defense budgets by requiring any
increases in federal spending to be offset by increases either in revenue collection, such as through increased taxes, or decreases in other parts of the
federal budget. Failure to produce a budget within these limits would auto-
matically trigger across-the-board budget cuts called sequestration. For
fiscal year 1991, for example, the Budget Enforcement Act limited budget
authority for defense spending to $289 billion, a 13 percent reduction.[5]

Powell inherited a Joint Staff that had been working on the implications
of multiple different future scenarios. Under the direction of Lee Butler,
the air force general who would eventually head J5, the Joint Staff Strategy,
Policy, and Plans Directorate, there was analysis of the implications of
changes in the strategic environment, including significant reductions in
the capabilities of the Soviet Union.[6] J8, the Joint Staff Force Structure,
Resource, and Assessment Directorate, was also working on the implications of different budget-reduction scenarios, including a cut of 25 percent.[7]
Powell's predecessor, Chairman Bill Crowe, asked the Joint Staff to begin
a "quiet study"—that is, a study conducted within the Joint Staff only and
the results of which are not revealed to the services. The study's goal was to
develop a military strategy to accompany a smaller defense budget. If cuts
to defense spending were likely, it would be important for the military to
determine how those cuts were distributed among the services and, if possible, develop a plan for countering any additional funding reductions. But
instead of presenting the results to the Bush administration, Crowe put
them aside for the next chairman to act on. There appear to be two reasons
for Crowe's hesitation to move forward.[8] First, Crowe was at the end of his
tenure as chairman and either lacked or was unwilling to expend the political
capital necessary to enforce force structure cuts of this magnitude. Second,

Crowe was unwilling to plan for budget cuts without an accompanying change in strategy. He reasoned that doing so would only invite further reductions from Congress or the administration.[9]

Powell adopted this analysis, including a similar focus on a 25 percent reduction in defense spending. Rather than have the services develop their own plans, which were likely to lead to three different results, Powell followed Crowe's model and used the Joint Staff to develop a common option. Throughout the course of deliberations on defense reductions, Powell continued to rely on the Joint Staff to refine his ideas and devise ways of marketing the result to the services, Office of the Secretary of Defense (OSD), and outside the Pentagon.

Powell eventually presented the plans to the service chiefs and regional combatant commanders on February 26, 1990. According to Lorna Jaffee's history of the Base Force, Powell presented a watered-down version of his ideas in the hope that the service chiefs would focus on the need for radical restructuring rather than the specific consequences that would no doubt be objectionable.[10] Additionally, Powell kept the details short for fear the service chiefs would leak them to the press in an effort to rally support for restoring cuts to their individual services.[11]

Jaffe's account of the meeting explains that the service chiefs did not necessarily agree with the Base Force or take its future predictions seriously. But instead of arguing, each chief thought their chances were better if they engaged Powell individually and in private.[12] Over the following summer, the service chiefs continued to oppose the need for radical restructuring. Similarly, the regional combatant commanders remained unconvinced that Powell's ideas were sound.

Unable to win over his military colleagues, Powell tried marketing the idea to Secretary of Defense Dick Cheney. Cheney, however, was significantly less optimistic about the changes taking place in the Soviet Union, disagreed with Powell's proposed force structure and strategy, and was opposed to reducing the defense budget. When Congress proposed cuts to defense spending, Cheney argued that their optimism about changes in the Soviet Union was premature. "It is as if they had decided to give away their overcoats on the first sunny day in January," he argued.[13]

By the end of August, changes in the Soviet Union made the services realize that significant budget cuts were coming. Powell's proposal, therefore, became less of a radical idea and more of a blueprint for how to stave off even more drastic budget reductions.[14] Reluctantly, they embraced what came to be called the Base Force. Powell's plan was premised on a 25 percent reduction in military spending and a strategy that emphasized regional threats rather than the global danger represented by the Soviet Union and its proxies. Each of the services saw reductions in force structure, with the navy faring slightly better. Army divisions were cut by 29 percent and air force fighter wings by 28 percent, but navy ships saw only a 21 percent reduction. Although the service chiefs each argued their case, the Base Force changed little as a result. The one exception is the marine corps. Powell agreed to an increase in personnel based on the argument that geography rather than threat justified its size.

One of the last converts to the Base Force was Secretary of Defense Dick Cheney. At times, this created friction between Powell and Cheney, with Powell publicly advocating for a 25 percent reduction in the defense budget while Cheney, skeptical of changes in the Soviet Union, talked about a 2 percent change.[15] President Bush also at times had to distance himself from his defense secretary.[16] Cheney was finally brought on board by Paul Wolfowitz, the undersecretary of defense for policy. Wolfowitz had his staff look at the changing security and fiscal environments. The result was three different force structures, each based upon a different outcome to the turmoil in the Soviet Union. One option was essentially the same as Powell's Base Force. With both Powell and Wolfowitz in agreement, Cheney endorsed the Base Force, and shortly thereafter, on August 2, 1990, President H. W. Bush presented the idea in a speech to the Aspen Institute. Bush explained that, while the exact force structure details were still being worked out by Cheney and Powell, the changes in the Soviet Union meant that "by 1995 our security needs can be met by an active force 25 percent smaller than today's."[17]

The Base Force, however, was soon overtaken by events. Bush lost his bid for reelection to Bill Clinton, and in December 1991 the Soviet Union ceased to exist. Both events combined to lead to increased pressure for even further reductions in defense spending.

THE BOTTOM-UP REVIEW

Soon after Bush endorsed the Base Force in early August 1990, Powell, a keen observer of the Soviet Union, began to anticipate that changes in the USSR would lead to even further downward pressure on defense budgets.[18] In January of 1992, for example, Representative Les Aspin, chair of the House Armed Services Committee, called for a much greater peace dividend and was quite critical of the Base Force. His Senate counterpart, Sam Nunn, was similarly outspoken about the need for further reductions. In early 1992, Aspin offered four force structure options, each premised on a different threat environment, and these were presented as an improvement over the Base Force. Aspin saw the Base Force as a budget-driven strategy, whereas he argued that his options put strategy and world events first.[19]

In contrast to the Base Force, which was premised on the need for forces to fight two regional contingencies at the same time, Aspin's Bottom-Up Review (BUR) options focused on a different scenario. Aspin assumed the need for forces that could prevail in one war, stop a second war from deteriorating but without necessarily providing the forces necessary for outright victory, and provide the capabilities for peacekeeping, humanitarian assistance, and what would become known as "military operations other than war."

Powell also began to question the political power of the Base Force and to see it not as a floor for future cuts, but more likely the maximum force structure and budget possible. He instructed the Joint Staff to conduct additional analysis under the assumption that further defense reductions were likely. It is unclear the degree to which Powell's thinking was influenced by Aspin and the calls of other Democrats for a peace dividend versus the prospect of even more radical change in Russia. What is clear is that Powell felt that if the military did not propose a revised budget, the services would suffer because Congress would impose its own reductions in a piecemeal fashion and with little regard for strategy.

Some sources familiar with the history of both the Base Force and the BUR claim that by September 1992, Powell and the Joint Staff had already developed "Base Force II," and that this subsequently became the BUR. No precise outline of the force structure or funding levels for this often-cited Base Force II are available to validate this claim. However, the Joint Staff almost certainly made use of previous analysis for its work on the BUR, given the speed at which events were moving. Similarly, the services complained that the pace of the BUR meant that requests for information were often filled with analysis that had previously been conducted and not sufficiently updated to take into account changes in the Soviet Union.

Regardless of whether a Base Force II became or simply informed the BUR, while the Joint Staff was undertaking its analysis, a team of senior staff in OSD were meeting informally for a similar purpose. The Clinton administration had endorsed the idea of a thorough review of military force structure in 1992 during the campaign, and Clinton's secretary of defense, Les Aspin, initially hoped that the first Clinton administration defense budget would enact further cuts to defense spending. Amid strong criticism from the military, however, the first budget was proclaimed a "holding pattern" while the new secretary of defense undertook another comprehensive review.[20] At his confirmation hearing, Aspin endorsed option C from his previous analysis, but he also instructed his civilian staff in the Pentagon to conduct an additional review with results due in July 1993. At informal biweekly meetings, they met and discussed options with the Joint Staff. Though the service chiefs were often present, the options presented at these meetings were usually well beyond the point where service input could alter them.

As part of its own analysis, the Joint Staff got input from the services and the combatant commanders and also vetted the results of their analysis with them. But, because the Joint Staff used an informal and at times ad hoc process of consultation, other stakeholders sometimes complained that they were often excluded from deliberations. Indeed, very few changes were made as a result of service input. The most significant one was the final BUR force's inclusion of an additional aircraft carrier as the result of pleas from the navy chief.

Through the summer of 1993, the Pentagon focused on force structure options for implementing the new strategy. The Joint Staff favored the forces for two major regional contingencies, whereas OSD argued that technological advances in guidance and munitions would enable U.S. forces to "hold" a second major regional war, largely by stopping an enemy advance early on and preventing future advances long enough for U.S. forces to arrive. "Win-hold-win" was criticized by the services, however, who tended to see events in the now former Soviet Union in a less positive light. Calling Aspin's construct "win-hope-win" and "win-hold-lose," the military soon forced Aspin to endorse the two major regional contingencies strategy instead.

The BUR also hit a snag with respect to cost. Once OSD and Powell had agreed on force structure, the cost was several billion dollars over the Clinton administration's anticipated defense budget. Secretary Aspin, rather than reduce the force structure or increase the budget, argued that several "enhancements," such as improvements in firepower, mobility, and precision-guided weapons, could enable the BUR force structure to carry out the strategy without significant increases in cost. Aspin officially announced the results of the BUR on September 1, 1993.

WHO WINS?

The Soviet Union ended much more quickly than most experts predicted, and the resulting security environment, and especially the future trajectory of U.S.-Russian relations, was characterized by considerable uncertainty. While it was clear that military budgets and strategy would have to change, it was by no means obvious what should replace these, or what were the appropriate analytical structures for considering how to adapt or vet the results. Both the Base Force and the BUR, however, clearly show that this process of change was governed by Colin Powell and that his views prevailed even in the face of significant disagreement.

In the case of the Base Force, Powell began to look at revisions in force structure and strategy without instruction or guidance from the president or secretary of defense.[21] In fact, Powell had the general structure and strategic rationale for the Base Force prior to becoming chairman.[22] He was thus clearly out ahead of the president and civilians in the Pentagon both in his anticipation of the need for future downsizing but also, once he became chairman, in establishing a mechanism to plan for and analyze options for future force structure and strategy. Cheney disagreed with Powell but nonetheless encouraged him to develop his ideas and present them to President Bush. Powell went further, however, and publicly lobbied for the Base Force prior to its endorsement by either Bush or Cheney, thereby forcing their hands. The Base Force that was eventually endorsed by the president was the one that Powell had developed.

Moreover, there is considerable evidence that Powell's promotion of the Base Force was also motivated by a desire to protect the military from externally imposed budget cuts.[23] The Base Force did not significantly redistribute funding between the services. This led to arguments that the Base Force was a small Cold War force rather than the radical restructuring some thought necessary. Powell also thought he was doing the service chiefs a favor by providing a force structure on which they could all agree, thus avoiding a competition between them that would most likely lead to more significant cuts overall.[24] The services had prepared their Program Objective Memorandas on the basis of annual funding increases of 2 percent over six years, which was the guidance they had been provided by the secretary of defense.[25] They disagreed with the Base Force and its budget cuts. However, as events progressed both in the Soviet Union and in Congress, it became clear that budget cuts were inevitable.[26] According to Don Snider's history of the Base Force, one of the service chiefs claimed "the planning for the defense build-down was a case of someone determining in advance what was needed, and then seeing that the result was produced."[27] The chiefs went along with Powell's design because it was clear that defense cuts were inevitable and the Base Force had established a coherent plan that just might limit those cuts. Quoting an unnamed official, Snider's writes, "we knew if Cheney offered the Congress a 40 percent reduction, it would have been pocketed while they asked for more. Therefore we supported the 25 percent number."[28]

For the BUR, the Base Force provided an obvious starting point for future analysis. This "pride of place," however, has little to do with the power of the chairman and is largely due to exogenous reasons; namely, that the BUR was the second downsizing to take place in a very short time, and Powell was one of the few senior policy officials who retained the same position during both the Base Force and the BUR processes. In the case of the BUR, it is unclear whether Powell or Aspin began their analysis first. Aspin had endorsed option C from the analysis he presented while still a member of Congress.[29] Clinton had campaigned with the promise of a peace dividend that was significantly larger than the one that would result from the Base Force. As a member of Congress, Aspin was part of a significant chorus that argued for cuts deeper than the Base Force. As secretary of defense, Aspin had proposed a range of options aiming at both more force reductions as well as a different strategy. Powell recognized that additional cuts below the Base Force were likely and had directed the Joint Staff to begin work on Base Force II while Bush was still president.[30] But while Powell thought the Base Force was no longer a floor, the details of Base Force II were never released, and it isn't clear how closely it resembled Aspin's option C or the BUR force. What is clear is that both Clinton and Aspin at one point endorsed significant changes beyond the Base Force. The BUR, however, provided more of a tweak. The Base Force reduced manpower by 25 percent; the BUR added another 5 percent cut. For fiscal years 1990–1999, the Base Force planned on a cumulative 26 percent reduction in defense spending; the BUR added another 8 percent.[31] According to Powell, the BUR was simply a "lineal ancestor" to the Base Force.[32]

Table 5.1 provides a comparison of the basic force structure proposed by the Base Force, Aspin's option C, which was his preference, and the BUR force. If one compares the BUR to option C and the Base Force, the result is clearly a compromise rather than a reassessment. Faced with a powerful and well-respected chairman, and confronting other controversies from the military, as outlined below, Aspin sought to co-opt Powell by making the Joint Staff an equal part of the BUR analysis. Or, it could be the case that the Joint Staff and Powell co-opted Aspin. What is clear is that the chairman did not organize the services to speak out against the BUR. Instead, Powell endorsed it. In terms of the BUR force structure, Powell did not enjoy the "win" he had in his disagreements with Cheney. However, Powell also didn't lose.

TABLE 5.1 Alternative Force Structures

	BASE FORCE	OPTION C	BUR
ARMY ACTIVE DIVISIONS	12	9	10
ARMY RESERVE DIVISIONS	8	6	5
MARINE CORPS ACTIVE DIVISIONS	3	2	3
MARINE CORPS RESERVE DIVISIONS	1	1	1
AIR FORCE ACTIVE FIGHTER WINGS	15	10	13
AIR FORCE RESERVE FIGHTER WINGS	11	8	7
NAVY TOTAL SHIPS	430	340	346

Source: Eric V. Larson, David T. Orletsky, and Kristin Leuschner, "The Bottom-Up Review: Redefining Post-Cold War Strategy and Forces," chap. 3 in *Defense Planning in a Decade of Change: Lessons from the Base Force, Bottom-Up Review, and Quadrennial Defense Review* (Santa Monica, CA: RAND, 2001), 44.

Note: In terms of defense dollars, the Base Force was projected to require $1,058 billion in budget authority from fiscal years 95–98. For this same period, the Clinton administration hoped to cut $105 billion from defense spending. However, the force that resulted from the BUR cost $971 billion for these fiscal years, approximately $18 billion more than the Clinton administration had desired.

Moving beyond force structure, however, Powell won three other crucial and related disagreements with Aspin. First, Powell preferred a strategy that provided the basis for forces necessary to win two major regional wars—called "major regional contingencies," or MRCs—at the same time. Aspin, in contrast, had preferred "win-hold-win." In June of 1993, Aspin announced that the BUR would assume the forces for two smaller wars, not the sequential conflicts on which option C was based. Powell won this disagreement.

The second disagreement centered on force sizing constructs. Aspin had endorsed threat-based planning. His options were all premised on the forces that were needed for Desert Storm, or its future equivalent, and assumed that external threats dictated the forces necessary. Powell, however, rejected this threat-based planning as "overly simplistic."[33] He argued that the future was too uncertain, and the best approach was to size forces on the basis of the capabilities needed. What became known as "capabilities-based planning" focused on the objectives of the state rather than defeating specific threats. Critics, however, argued that such a force-sizing construct privileges military judgment about the future because the future is inherently uncertain, and that in this case it allowed the services to retain their Cold War forces even though the Soviet threat had disappeared.[34] Regardless of one's opinion of the planning construct, threat-based planning died with Aspin's option C, while the capabilities-based approach came to be the norm at the Pentagon.

The realization of a peace dividend constitutes the third major disagreement. Over time, the planned defense spending cuts under the BUR were not completely realized. Aspin had to merge the BUR's two MRC strategy with the defense spending reductions promised by the Clinton administration. Although Aspin stated that advances in technology and efficiencies in the Pentagon would enable more force for less money, analysis by OSD showed that the BUR required about $88 billion more than was being requested.[35] Over the years after the BUR was adopted, defense spending did increase as a result of subsequent higher presidential budget requests, to which Congress added additional spending.[36] As a result, even the more modest defense cuts announced with the BUR were never implemented.

Additionally, the Clinton administration had hoped to see significant savings from major revisions in the roles and missions of the military services. Although Powell had originally planned to use a review of roles and missions as an excuse to get additional cuts from the services, the chiefs revolted. When the draft roles and mission report was first made public in December 1992, it contained only minor changes. When the final report was released on February 12, 1993, even Powell had to admit it represented the status quo.[37]

A POLITICAL CHAIRMAN

In the case of the Base Force, Powell assumed the role of chairman convinced that cuts to the defense budget were likely and with clear ideas for a smaller force structure and strategy. These ideas were refined using the Joint Staff, which under the Goldwater-Nichols Act was subordinate to the

chairman alone and not the Joint Chiefs of Staff (JCS) collectively. Powell's ability to use the Joint Staff, without the need to get buy-in or even
approval from the services, was crucial for refining and justifying the Base
Force structure. However, as Lorna Jaffee's history of the Base Force details,
some of Powell's success with the Joint Staff was also dependent upon other
senior officers. Most specifically, Powell received significant analytical help
from Lee Butler, the air force general who headed J5 and who would develop
a reputation for independent and non-traditional thinking.

Additionally, the Goldwater-Nichols Act had made the chairman the
principal military adviser to the secretary of defense and president, and Powell certainly exploited this when he pitched the Base Force to Bush and
Cheney alone and prior to its endorsement by the service chiefs. Powell was
thus clearly willing to use the powers given to him by the Goldwater-Nichols
Act. For example, in Powell's autobiography, he tells a story about Marine
Commandant Al Gray demanding that anything that goes to the president
under the name of the JCS be reviewed by all service chiefs, including the
commandant. In response, Powell cites the Goldwater-Nichols Act and
changes the heading on Joint Staff stationary from "Joint Chiefs of Staff"
to "Chairman, Joint Chiefs of Staff."[38] As shown in Figure 2.1 in chapter 2,
Powell was prescient in anticipating that the chairman would become the
primary military voice in defense policy.

But, in the case of the Base Force, Powell also won because of external
events. The collapse of the Soviet Union and calls for a peace dividend made
it clear that the 2 percent growth the chiefs hoped for was not a possibility.
Although both Nunn and Aspin had outlined plans for significant defense
cuts, the service chiefs were late to accept this fate. By the time they did,
the Base Force was the only option backed up by the detailed analysis needed
to compete with Nunn and Aspin's constructs. Plus, the secretary of defense
and president had already endorsed it.

The Bush administration, however, faced political problems that served
to reinforce the chairman's power. First, calls for even greater reductions
in the defense budget quickly followed the Base Force. Realizing that future
cuts were likely, Bush preferred to limit the extent to which they were
made by congressional Democrats. Therefore, united military advice was

important. Powell was the key to getting the chiefs onboard. Second, as the 1992 election grew nearer, the praise the president had come to enjoy in the wake of his ostensible victory in the Gulf War began to sour as the administration faced significant criticism that Bush had stopped the war short of key military and political goals. Powell, in contrast, was exceedingly popular, with some arguing he should be on the Bush ticket as vice president instead of Dan Quayle.[39] Additionally, as civil war and ethnic cleansing rose in the Balkans, the press widely reported infighting within the administration over the extent to which U.S. military forces should be used to enforce a no-fly zone over Bosnia-Herzegovina. Bush could thus ill-afford increased questions about his competence in military affairs.

The third problem stems from Powell's personal investment in the Base Force. Before either Cheney or the president had fully endorsed the Base Force, Powell began to articulate his ideas in speeches, interviews, and editorials. Amid calls for a peace dividend and floor speeches from the chairmen of both congressional Armed Services Committees outlining their ideas on defense restructuring, Powell offered his professional military advice. With Congress and some elements of the Bush administration critical of the administration's pace in responding to world changes, Bush no doubt found Powell's already tested and refined Base Force a convenient solution. Further, Powell's personal popularity with the military, Congress, and the electorate discouraged both Bush and Cheney from questioning his analysis.

For the BUR, Powell's success was also at least partially due to the speed of events and the fact that the Base Force was the obvious starting point for any future reductions. In the Aspin Pentagon, the process of considering force structure changes looked like a collaboration between the Joint Staff and OSD, in contrast to the Base Force process, which was governed by the Joint Staff. Although Aspin's civilian staff certainly played a role in the BUR analysis, it is clear that the Joint Staff governed much of the outcome and did so with modifications to the Base Force, as opposed to a new force structure, strategy, or force sizing construct.

Although it was well-known that Powell's tenure as chairman would expire in September of 1993, only the future would reveal that Aspin would also be out within a year. The reason—politics—helps explain why Powell was able to win many of the BUR disagreements. Clinton assumed office with his own set of political vulnerabilities, including the fact that he was considered by many in his own party to be weak on defense because he lacked military experience and was seen by some as a draft dodger who used college as an excuse for avoiding the Vietnam War. The Democratic Party was also split on the issue of defense spending, with some calling for more drastic cuts and others concerned that while the military appeared capable, it really lacked the equipment, maintenance, and personnel to fight capably.

This was reinforced by the vulnerabilities of Les Aspin. Concerned about bureaucratic turf battles, Aspin wanted to keep other agencies in the dark until the BUR was completed. Early in his tenure as secretary, Aspin had been surprised when a briefing on future defense restructuring had been given by the Office of Management and Budget, with little input from the defense department. Additionally, the National Security Council was engaged in its own effort to develop a new strategy. Determined to avoid such interference, Aspin conducted the BUR in private and gave little standing to the analysis of others. After the defense department determined the appropriate results, he reasoned, other agencies would have little choice but to accept the work of the experts. In order to keep a close hold over the BUR process, Aspin could not afford the service chiefs offering their own advice independent of Powell. In other words, the service rivalry that would have been useful for coming up with alternatives and vetting them was not encouraged by Aspin. Instead, Aspin opted to allow Powell to develop a military consensus and then use that to bolster his own process.

Aspin and the appointees he brought with him to the Pentagon were seen as outsiders by the military. As a group, they were considered too liberal, too willing to privilege their own analysis over military expertise, and too focused on the promise of technology as the basis for a smaller and cheaper military.[40] Aspin was also not known for his interpersonal skills, and he did little to repair the damage caused by repeated clashes with military officers. As Aspin's respect among those in the Pentagon dwindled, the White House began to distance itself from a cabinet secretary who did not seem able to control his own agency. In September 1993, Aspin turned down a request for additional gunships from a commander in Somalia on a mission to capture a warlord in Mogadishu. Aspin was blamed for the resulting deaths of eighteen U.S. soldiers, and he was eventually forced to resign as secretary in December 1993.

Both Clinton and Aspin had political problems for which they needed support, or at least a lack of opposition, from Colin Powell. Powell had repeatedly proven he was willing to publicly disagree with presidential policy. As was the case with Bush and the Base Force, the Clinton administration couldn't afford to challenge Powell on the details for defense downsizing. For these reasons, neither president tried to cultivate critiques or input from the service chiefs, and they eventually agreed to results that were closer to Powell's preferences than their own.

MISSING ACTORS

The Base Force and the BUR illustrate the chairman's abilities to leverage his position and power within the executive branch to get the president to endorse policy options favored by the military. Powell skillfully exploited Bush's political vulnerabilities and his own resources in the Joint Staff to corral the services and the White House in favor of his defense downsizing plan. This is almost exclusively a story about the chairman's relationship with the service chiefs, the president, and the secretary of defense. Missing are Congress and the combatant commanders.

Congress, and especially pressure from key Democrats for a peace dividend, provided plenty of motivation for Powell to engineer the Base Force and the BUR. But there is little evidence that Powell worked behind the scenes with members of Congress to build support for his ideas. Certainly, Powell testified in support of the Base Force and the BUR at the annual authorization and appropriations hearings. But he did not lobby members of Congress to try and convince the president, secretary of defense, or the service chiefs to get behind his ideas. In other words, Powell was much more of an independent political player within the administration than he was with Congress. The members of Congress even complained about Powell's lack of candor. After the publication in 1991 of *The Commanders*, Bob Woodward's history of the war with Iraq, a number of members of Congress were annoyed at Powell because the book showed he had shared his private advice about Desert Shield with Woodward, but not with them.[41]

The one exception to this lack of involvement with Congress is an ill-fated secret deal between Powell and Senator Sam Nunn, the chair of the Senate Armed Services Committee. As the Bush Pentagon was preparing to announce the Base Force in August 1992, Nunn became increasingly vocal in calling for changes in roles and missions with the aim of reducing redundancies and duplication between the services. Powell reviewed the draft of a major speech on the subject that Nunn was scheduled to give on July 2. According to reporting by the *Washington Post*, Nunn sought to give a fiery speech about the need for a review of roles and missions that would scare the service chiefs into action, while Congress would refrain from making changes and instead defer to an internal military effort led by Powell.[42] But the plan backfired when the service chiefs refused to agree to even the modest changes Powell proposed in a draft roles and missions report that was made public in December 1992.

The other missing actors in this story are the combatant commanders— also called commanders in chief, or CINCs, before the title was changed in 2002 by Secretary of Defense Donald Rumsfeld. One of the main goals of the Goldwater-Nichols Act was to increase the role of these commanders in defense policy because they were seen as inherently joint. Despite modest increases in their formal powers, however, they played little role in the Base Force and the BUR. Although Powell briefed his ideas to them, the chairman was more concerned about possible dissent from the service chiefs. He worried the chiefs might seek redress from Congress, and after initially keeping them in the dark about the details of the Base Force, he later took steps to brief them and listen to their concerns. Both the Base Force and the BUR were premised on the need to share the pain of budget cuts evenly between the services, not the combatant commanders. Although several of these commanders disagreed with the Base Force, both as a budget request and as a force-sizing guide, Powell does not seem to have worried that they would complain to Congress or that they had the political clout to derail his policy plans.[43] The changes Powell made to the Base Force were the result of complaints from the service chiefs, not the combatant commanders.

BEYOND BUDGETS

In budget battles, Powell proved to be an adept political actor who used his skill and prestige to lead defense downsizing. He repeatedly argued publicly for the Base Force prior to its endorsement by either Bush or Cheney, and his support from the chiefs made it difficult for Clinton or Aspin to challenge the BUR. Additionally, Powell's budgets preserved equality among the services rather than picking winners or losers. Thus, when it became clear to the service chiefs that budgets were going down, they supported Powell's ideas.

Powell's role in other disagreements shows significant similarities. In the next two sections, I briefly examine five cases where Powell had major disagreements or concerns with civilian authorities. Four relate to the use of military force. The remaining case is the Clinton-era policy debate over allowing gay men and lesbians to serve openly in the military. These cases suggest that in other policy disagreements beyond the budget, Powell was more likely to publicly air his disagreement with the president if the latter was politically vulnerable, and that Powell never argued for a policy that was not fully supported by the service chiefs. Further, these cases reinforce the conclusion that a skillful political chairman can force the president to delay, amend, or change his policy preferences.

USING FORCE

Operation Just Cause, conducted from December 1989 through January 1990, ended with the capture and extradition to the United States of Manuel Noriega, the military dictator of Panama. Besides drug trafficking, racketeering, and pro-Soviet inclinations, Noriega allowed his Panamanian Defense Forces to increasingly harass U.S. service members and their dependents stationed in Panama. After the detainment and harassment of a navy officer and his wife, President Bush authorized an invasion. Bush initially preferred either a small military footprint or simply abducting Noriega. Powell, however, argued that another dictator would likely replace Noriega and that U.S. interests would be better served by defeating the Panamanian Defense Forces that propped up Noriega and returning a democratically elected leader to power.[44] Doing so, according to Powell, would require a large-scale military deployment. A legacy of his view of the errors of the Vietnam War, Powell, in keeping with what was originally called the Weinberger Doctrine, believed that the United States should only commit troops when the objective is clear and with the force necessary to quickly win before U.S. public support erodes.[45]

In close consultation with Powell, General Maxwell Thurman, the commander with jurisdiction over Panama, put together plans for a large military operation using mostly U.S. Army forces rather than allowing each service to play a role, as was the usual practice. Although Bush and Vice President Dan Quayle preferred a smaller force, the plan outlined by Powell and Thurman was quickly endorsed by the administration.

Although Powell deferred to Thurman and his staff during planning, he became more involved as the operation unfolded. According to the official JCS history, Powell was concerned that the military operations not jeopardize Bush's political objectives—namely, avoiding American casualties and capturing Noriega.[46] This led Powell to pressure Thurman to send troops to occupy a particular target—a Marriot hotel in Panama City where some U.S. citizens were hiding—and to cease attempts to get Noriega to surrender by playing loud rock music at the Nunciatura, the Vatican mission to Panama where he had sought refuge.

The second use-of-force case under Bush involved Iraq. When Iraqi leader Saddam Hussein invaded and occupied Kuwait on August 2, 1990, the United States became concerned that his next target was Saudi Arabia. As the United States was sending troops under Operation Desert Shield to defend Saudi Arabia from possible invasion, the Bush administration turned to the idea of liberating Kuwait and ousting Saddam from power. Cheney wanted options for invading Iraq and bringing about a change in regime. Bush also wanted an aggressive defense of Saudi Arabia, and he, too, came to endorse regime change. Powell, however, strongly favored economic sanctions and containment of Iraq, rather than war. According to Powell, Saudi Arabia's defense was a vital interest, but Kuwait's was not.[47] The chairman also worried that after the war the United States would get bogged down in trying to occupy and govern Iraq. Both went against the principles of the Weinberger Doctrine. Frustrated with Powell's repeated reluctance to use force or develop military options, Cheney angrily confronted him on multiple occasions, including during a National Security Council meeting at which he reminded Powell, "You're not secretary of state. You're not the national security adviser. And you're not secretary of defense. So stick to military matters."[48]

Plans for the defense of Saudi Arabia were developed under the direction of Norman Schwarzkopf, the general in charge of the military command that includes the Middle East. Both Schwarzkopf and Powell favored sanctions and avoiding a ground war, and their briefings to the president reflected this restraint. Several senior members of the Bush administration felt Powell was dragging his heels on providing military options. Cheney in particular thought the chairman was not following the president's guidance. Avoiding Powell, Schwarzkopf, and the Joint Staff, Cheney went directly to his allies on the services staffs to develop more robust military options. Powell was snubbed again when President Bush, somewhat inadvertently, announced to the press that he was inclined to commit ground troops to a war against Iraq. Powell was incensed that Bush made his announcement without consulting him.

On January 17, 1991, the United States began Operation Desert Storm, a month-long war that ousted Iraq from Kuwait but stopped short of pushing further into Iraq and ousting Saddam Hussein from power. The military operation itself was seen as evidence that service parochialism was alive and well. There was limited cooperation between the services, and each fought for a specific role.[49] The air force, in particular, was vocal about the ability of air power alone to achieve U.S. objectives. This culminated on

September 17, 1990, when Cheney fired air force chief of staff Michael Dugan for boasting to reporters that air power was the best option for ousting Iraqi forces and, in the process, revealed sensitive information about battle plans.[50] The marine corps also advocated for and was eventually given a larger role.[51]

The last two cases are the U.S. interventions in Bosnia and Somalia. During the summer of 1992, the Bush administration actively debated whether to intervene in what would become a civil war in the Balkans. Powell and the service chiefs were strongly opposed. They argued that the widening war and associated humanitarian crisis had no military solution. When asked for military options, either for protecting relief supplies or enforcing a no-fly zone, the military inflated the number of troops needed in order to make the options seem unattractive.[52]

As the Bush administration was agonizing over what to do in the Balkans, conflict in Somalia intensified, with various rival warlords fighting for control of the government. In August 1992, the United States sent food aid to Somalia, but Powell and the service chiefs were all opposed to any broader use of the military. Initially, the U.S. objective was to establish order, restore the delivery of aid, and then hand over the mission to a multinational force of the United Nations (UN). But one of the warlords, Mohamed Farah Aidid, began to attack UN forces and prevent the delivery of aid. As pressure mounted for the United States to play a more active role, the Joint Staff and Central Command—the combatant command in charge of the Middle East—provided Bush with military options, including a small contingent of special operations forces as well as a larger deployment of ground troops.[53]

Powell and the service chiefs were strongly opposed to the use of the military in either Bosnia or Somalia. But as the summer wore on, public support for humanitarian intervention grew, partially because presidential candidate Bill Clinton challenged Bush on his administration's inaction. According to Jon Western, Powell and the service chiefs became concerned that public pressure would soon lead to military intervention in both Bosnia and Somalia.[54] This concern only intensified after November, when Clinton was elected. Reasoning that Somalia was the least likely to lead to prolonged conflict and a Vietnam-type quagmire, the military embraced Somalia while amplifying its opposition to involvement in Bosnia. Powell requested an interview with Michael Gordon of the *New York Times* in which he argued against the use of military options in Bosnia and the perils of "limited military force." Although the Bush administration was still weighing the pros and cons of various options, Powell vividly took sides: "As soon as they tell me it is limited, it means they do not care whether you achieve a result or not. As soon as they tell me 'surgical'; I head for the bunker."[55] Next, Powell published an essay for *Foreign Affairs* in which he reiterated the rules of what would become known as the Powell Doctrine: commit troops only when vital interests are at stake and objectives are clear, and then use overwhelming force.[56] Meanwhile, the service chiefs did an about-face and, instead of arguing that Somalia was a "bottomless pit," put forward a plan for the limited use of force.[57]

Consistent with Powell's advice, and with support from the service chiefs, in November Bush eventually opted for a large deployment of U.S. troops to Somalia but expressly limited the mission to providing security for the UN's humanitarian efforts.[58] In December, almost thirty thousand U.S. forces were deployed. Bush rejected efforts by UN secretary-general Boutros Boutros-Ghali to expand the mission to disarming the warlords and pursuing nation building in Somalia.[59]

For multiple reasons, soon after the inauguration of Bill Clinton in January 1992, the U.S. and UN forces had moved beyond humanitarian assistance and were increasingly involved in battles with Aidid.[60] Clinton, along with Secretary of State Warren Christopher and Madeleine Albright, the U.S. ambassador to the UN, endorsed the expanded mission. It was opposed by Secretary of Defense Les Aspin, Powell, and the service chiefs. But when Aidid's forces attacked and killed UN peacekeepers in June 1993, Albright put the United States squarely in favor of disarming the warlords and pursuing nation building. That summer, the White House weighed a request from the U.S. special representative for Somalia to the United Nations for special operations forces to capture Aidid. Although Powell and General Joseph Hoar, the combatant commander in charge of the area, both advised against this, they were outweighed by Aspin and National Security Adviser

Anthony Lake, among others.[61] In September, just before his retirement, Powell tried one last time to convince Clinton to either provide significantly more troops to Somalia or withdraw.[62] The next week, in an attempt to capture some of Aidid's lieutenants, eighteen U.S. Army Rangers were killed, with the press reporting widely on the desecration of their bodies as they were dragged through the streets of Mogadishu. The "Black Hawk Down" incident ended the career of Aspin, who had denied a request from the field for additional armor without consulting the president.

Panama, Iraq, Bosnia, and Somalia illustrate patterns of interaction between the chairman, senior civilian officials, and the service chiefs that appear at first glance to be significantly different than those that led to the Base Force and the BUR. In selling the Base Force, Powell frequently advocated in public for a policy that had not been endorsed by Bush and that contradicted the views of the secretary of defense. Yet in the case of Iraq, and to a lesser extent in Panama, Powell did not reach out to the public, the media, or Congress in an attempt to sway administration policy. Moreover, he had multiple excuses to do so. In the run-up to Desert Storm, key Democrats in Congress were openly critical of the administration's policy and Powell's predecessor, Admiral William Crowe, testified to the Senate in favor of sanctions and containment and against war. Yet Powell kept his dissent largely within the confines of the executive branch.

Upon closer examination, however, Powell's reluctance to publicly advocate for his position shows the same pattern as his advocacy for the Base Force and the BUR. During the summer of 1992, Powell kept his dissent on Bosnia and Somalia within the confines of the executive branch until he went public in September. At that point, not only did Bush appear poised to endorse limited intervention, but his polling numbers had slipped. Starting in mid-July, it seemed increasingly likely that Clinton would be the next president.[63] In other words, Powell was more willing to publicly contradict a politically vulnerable commander in chief. Additionally, under President Clinton, Powell did not shy away from publicizing his dissent vis-à-vis a president who was considered weak on national security policy. Although Clinton favored intervention in the Balkans, he did not authorize the use of military force until after Powell retired. Powell's successor,

General John Shalikashvili, was much less dogmatic about adherence to what was now called the Powell Doctrine and more inclined to defer to the president and his civilian advisers.

In the Base Force and the BUR decisions, Powell never offered advice that contradicted the collective advice of the service chiefs or that challenged the equal division of resources among the services. A similar dynamic was also at work in these decisions about military operations. In each case, Powell offered advice that was supported by the service chiefs, who were actively consulted, partially because Powell learned from the Base Force experience that consultation would lead to better relationships.[64] There was also a tendency to reinforce equality among the services, illustrated by the fate of air force chief of staff Michael Dugan and, to a lesser extent, that of John Loh, the commander of the air force's Air Combat Command. During the conflict with Iraq, both generals at times claimed that air power alone could push Iraq out of Kuwait or defeat the Iraqi military. Powell consistently contradicted them, reminding the president that air power alone would not save the day and that each of the services had a role to play. The other service chiefs agreed.

INTEGRATING GAY MEN AND LESBIANS INTO THE MILITARY

The prediction that the chairman will be more outspoken when the president is politically vulnerable is clearly correct in the case of Clinton's efforts to integrate gay men and lesbians more fully into the military. Candidate Clinton had pledged to end the military's ban on gay men and lesbians serving in the military. Under military policy at that time, anyone who admitted to being gay was dismissed from the military, usually dishonorably. Clinton, however, was ahead of many, even in his own party, and was forced to retreat to a position that became known as "Don't Ask, Don't Tell."

Aspin had to broker the compromise and then implement a policy that satisfied few. Under "Don't Ask, Don't Tell," the military was not allowed to ask people about their identity and was required to allow gay men and lesbians to continue to serve as long as they were not open about their sexual orientation. Advocates of gay rights saw the policy as a form of big-otry. Within the military, some saw the policy as an invitation to harass and blackmail gay service members. Powell repeatedly voiced his opposi-tion to any change in policy, eventually prompting concern that he and the chiefs was being insubordinate and fueling a debate about whether U.S. civilian control was being compromised.[65] As with the Base Force and the BUR, Powell's criticism showed that he could mobilize opposition to the policies of the president and force the president to compromise even on his strongly held beliefs.

A NEW ERA OF CIVIL-MILITARY RELATIONS?

It is clear from figures 2.1 and 2.2 in chapter 2 that 1986 represented a water-shed. In years prior, the norm had been for the service chiefs, speaking pre-dominantly about their own service interests, to be the public voice of the military. After 1986, the norm quickly became the chairman speaking for "the military." The history of the Base Force and the BUR both reinforce this notion of a powerful chairman post-Goldwater-Nichols Act. But while the changes made by the act clearly contributed to Powell's power, there are also reasons to see Powell as an exception. It is not clear from the Base Force and the BUR cases that subsequent chairmen would be politically powerful actors capable of ushering in a new era of civil-military relations.

One reason why Powell's tenure did not lead to a new normal is that he had considerable experience serving in inherently political positions. By the time Powell became chairman, he was well versed in the ways of Wash-ington.[66] Powell was also outspoken, and often ahead of the curve, in antic-ipating the need to respond to the collapse of the Soviet Union. Moreover, both Bush and Clinton lacked the political clout to challenge or prevail in a battle with Congress over defense restructuring. In other words, both presidents needed Powell as a political ally. This context—a politically astute chairman combined with politically vulnerable presidents—was not a con-sequence of the Goldwater-Nichols Act.

Additionally, the way Powell sought buy-in from the service chiefs was similar to routines that predate the Goldwater-Nichols Act. During the Cold War, various secretaries of defense sought to avoid public challenges from the service chiefs by seeking their input in private. Powell did the same. As a result, the service chiefs felt they had the chance to make their individual cases and, having made the case for their service, could afford to endorse Powell's recommendations. The fact that any dissent would likely have given members of Congress ammunition with which to argue for deeper budget cuts made it even easier to agree to Powell's force structure. But the policy debates examined here also show that Powell's advocacy was never for a position with which the service chiefs collectively disagreed or that contradicted a consensus among them. In other words, even at his most ambitious, Powell showed deference to the JCS.

The Base Force and the BUR were smaller force structures that preserved the division of resources among the services. Rather than being the result of joint military advice about how to adapt to the post-Soviet era, they are more consistent with the historical logrolling and service biases that the Goldwater-Nichols Act had sought to remedy. But the political clout given to Powell's advice was new because he was now officially the principal military adviser to the secretary of defense. But to understand whether Powell's exercise of that power was exceptional, or whether it was indeed the beginning of a new era in civil-military relations, requires an understanding of how subsequent chairmen exercised their roles.

6

TRANSFORMATION

When Donald Rumsfeld became secretary of defense for the second time, in January 2001, he shared a sense of mission with his boss, President George W. Bush. Both men felt that the United States needed to move away from preparing for traditional war against other states and instead leverage emerging technologies to defeat insurgents, terrorists, and other nontraditional threats. Rumsfeld assumed office with a mandate from Bush to transform the military from service-specific Cold War platforms into a joint force that focused on networked systems, precision munitions, and flexibility. Rumsfeld tried twice to achieve this transformation—once during the months right after he assumed office, and then again from 2002 to 2006. He failed both times.

Hugh Shelton was the chairman when Rumsfeld took office. Shelton disliked Rumsfeld, did not agree with Rumsfeld's emphasis on transformation, and did little to help achieve it. Although Shelton had the reputation and skills to help Rumsfeld further his goals, he chose not to in the case of transformation. His replacement, Richard Myers, tried to champion Rumsfeld's transformation agenda, but lacked the abilities to corral the increasingly dissident service chiefs. From the start, Myers was handicapped because he was seen as too closely allied with the secretary.

Rumsfeld's inability to get transformation done illustrates the limited impact of the Goldwater-Nichols Act. Transformation embraced nontraditional weapons and joint operations. It was supported by a secretary of defense who aimed to take charge of the Pentagon and who had the full backing of the president. But twenty years after the act, service parochialism and attachment to Cold War platforms remained powerful enough to thwart civilian direction. Further, Rumsfeld's attempts at transformation show that the chairman can choose whether or not to ally with the secretary, but that, in doing so, he disregards the wishes of the service chiefs at his own peril.

TRANSFORMATION IN 2001

In the 2000 presidential election, both Al Gore and George W. Bush campaigned on platforms that included increased defense spending and shifting the military to a more responsive and agile force. When Bush was elected, his secretary of defense, Donald Rumsfeld, embraced this mandate and very quickly announced plans to move the services away from Cold War legacy systems and to use technical advances to transform them into a more coherent, flexible, and rapid-response force.[1] "Transformation" meant embracing precision-guided munitions, unmanned platforms, special operations forces, joint operations, transportation capabilities, and space capabilities.[2] It also meant moving away from some of the weapons the services valued most: heavy tanks and vehicles, single-role aircraft, and big naval formations. Rumsfeld's plan was to cut force structure, and especially army end strength, and shift procurement spending. If implemented, transformation would have a significant impact on future service budgets, especially in the areas of research, development, and procurement.

In February 2001, Rumsfeld organized working groups to review strategy and force structure and make recommendations. Led by Andrew

Marshall, the review groups largely excluded the military and career Pentagon civilians. Instead, they relied on political appointees, some of whom were openly dismissive of senior military leaders.[3] Both Rumsfeld and Bush had felt that the military had gained too much power during the Clinton administration, and they referred to "Clinton generals" as the problem when differences arose between Rumsfeld and senior military leaders. Rumsfeld sought to replace the senior military leadership with more junior officers, and also to reassert strong civilian leadership in the Pentagon.

Rumsfeld was also under no illusions about the challenge transformation posed to business as usual in the Pentagon. Concerned that the services would appeal to Congress to save their favorite weapons, Rumsfeld told the Joint Chiefs of Staff (JCS) to stop providing Congress with their list of unfunded requirements, or "UFRs"—that is, items that were cut from the president's final budget request to Congress. It was standard practice for the service chiefs to provide these UFR lists to Congress in the hopes that some programs would be restored, either through amendments or earmarks.[4] The secretary also instructed the various civilian transformation working groups to keep their conclusions secret for as long as possible, including from the service chiefs.[5] These working groups also took over planning for the upcoming Quadrennial Defense Review (QDR)—an assessment of the adequacy of U.S. strategy and force structure that Congress required be undertaken every four years. Both the Joint Staff and services had organized groups to focus on specific QDR topics, but these working groups were put on hold, their analyzes never completed.[6] This, in turn, increased frustration with the secretary because the services felt that the considerable work that had already gone into the QDR was for naught. The combatant commanders were also excluded from substantive deliberations.

The Marshall group completed its review in March 2001. Systems identified for potential cuts, reduced purchases, or delays included the navy's Zumwalt-class destroyer as well as plans for a next-generation aircraft carrier, the army's Crusader artillery system, Comanche attack helicopter, and planned upgrades to tanks and other vehicles, and a variety of air force planes, including the F-22, F-35, B-52, and B-1.[7] Later, Rumsfeld also called for personnel cuts in the army, navy, and air force to pay for the new weapons needed for transformation.[8] As the Marshall group's recommendations began to be leaked, the services made it clear they did not approve of either the results or the fact that they were excluded from the process. In response, the services turned to delay and obfuscation. As explained by Thomas K. Adams in his study of the army during these years,

> Within certain senior circles at the Pentagon the transformation initiatives sparked an unspoken rebellion accompanied by bureaucratic resistance and general foot dragging. The major visible effect was the sudden inclusion of the magic word "transformation" in hundreds of Pentagon planning and procurement documents. Weapons and other systems that had been planned and programmed for years were suddenly portrayed as "transformational."[9]

By May, tensions between Rumsfeld and the service chiefs forced the secretary and other senior political appointees to meet more frequently with the chiefs and to share details about the plans for transformation and their implications for strategy and force structure. By all accounts, these meetings were not collegial.[10] The chiefs complained that the transformation initiative was focused too much on buying high-tech weapons for the future while discounting the need to maintain current capabilities.[11] This concern was reinforced when the Bush administration pushed for tax cuts but also smaller-than-expected increases in military spending. The chiefs also complained that they could not recommend cuts in force structure without prior guidance about strategy and risk.[12]

Members of the Senate Armed Services Committee joined the fray. Some Republicans disliked being excluded from Pentagon decisions during an administration that was led by their own party. Both sides of the aisle objected to cuts to their favorite weapons systems, and they also complained that they were not being briefed on the review and its budget implications.[13] Tensions increased further in May 2001 when Vermont senator James Jeffords switched party affiliation, giving the Democratic Party control of the Senate and making Carl Levin chair of the Armed Services

Committee. As a result, Rumsfeld was subsequently forced to include members of the committee in the Marshall group's review.

Rumsfeld was also dissatisfied with the advice he was getting from the JCS. Bradley Graham in his biography of the secretary quotes Rumsfeld as complaining that the services colluded and refused to comment on or contradict each other's positions.[14] Rumsfeld reportedly justified relying on studies by outside groups because the Joint Staff was "essentially useless."[15]

As the transformation initiatives merged with work for the 2001 QDR, Rumsfeld complained that his meetings with the service chiefs were leaked to the press and Congress. The chiefs, for their part, complained that Rumsfeld doctored the minutes of these meetings to reinforce his own conclusions.[16]

By late summer, Rumsfeld had replaced his semi-private meetings with the service chiefs with Senior Level Review Groups, whose expanded membership included other military officers and more political appointees. The Senior Level Review Groups were supposed to focus on the QDR, but the service chiefs found decisions were often made elsewhere and that the larger body was not a good forum for airing ideas and making decisions.[17] The service chiefs eventually became quite vocal about their exclusion. Their complaints to the press and Congress led to increased collaboration in the review process. But the cost, as explained below, was continuity rather than the transformation Rumsfeld sought.[18]

In August, relations between Rumsfeld and the service chiefs got even worse. Instead of increased purchases or accelerated development of long-planned systems, Rumsfeld announced that budget increases would instead fund a missile defense system. The secretary then floated the idea of paying for transformation by reducing the size of all of the services, but especially the army.[19] That same month, the Joint Staff released the results of its own internal review, which concluded that the personnel and weapons cuts being championed by Rumsfeld were unwise and that the administration's upcoming budget request was too small.[20]

The situation reached its nadir by late summer. The transformation initiative was dead in the water. The service chiefs identified everything as "transformational" and refused to back key elements of Rumsfeld's plans.

The JCS was in near open revolt, some in Congress were opposed to the cuts implied by transformation, and members of Rumsfeld's own party were upset that the president's defense budget request was too small. The president was forced to amend his defense spending request for fiscal year 2002 by adding an additional $18.4 billion. But even then, Rumsfeld lost; he had asked for twice that amount.[21] The conventional wisdom was that Rumsfeld's days were numbered, and it was rumored that he would either quit or be fired.[22]

When the results of the QDR were released in September 2001, transformation was embraced verbally but backed up by few changes in force structure or planned investment. The most significant shift was the Pentagon's force-planning construct—that is, the guidance for the threats that military forces should be planned and sized to defeat. The previous requirement to be able to fight two major wars simultaneously was replaced by "1-4-2-1"—that is, to be able to defend the United States, be prepared to respond to conflicts in four specific regions, significantly engage in two of those conflicts at the same time, and have the ability to "win decisively" in one. The shift was supported by the service chiefs. In fact, Chairman Shelton had endorsed just such a plan in a previous study dating from 1997.[23]

One particularly contentious part of the QDR review involved the army. It would be the first in a series of public disagreements between Army Chief of Staff Eric Shinseki and Secretary Rumsfeld. Later disputes would lead to the resignation of Army Secretary Thomas White and expand to include the conduct of the wars in Afghanistan and Iraq. The rift would become so wide that eventually it would lead to charges that Rumsfeld "hates the army" and was their "enemy."[24]

As army chief of staff, Shinseki had led the charge to transform the army by modernizing its organization and investing in networked systems that incorporated advanced technologies. The Future Combat System, for example, involved using information technology and wireless networks to connect ground troops to vehicles, unmanned systems, and the data that were seen as necessary for successful ground combat. Shinseki had introduced the idea in the late 1990s. It was the core of the army's future acquisition plans and was estimated to cost at least $160 billion.[25]

Rumsfeld, however, had a different view of transformation. He agreed with Shinseki that ground forces needed to be more flexible and mobile, but Rumsfeld thought they also needed to be smaller. In the secretary's view, future combat would rely less on ground troops, and the savings from personnel reductions could be used to pay for transformation. When Rumsfeld proposed to cut four army divisions, Shinseki fought back. Although the army chief eventually prevailed, Rumsfeld took this as evidence that the army was unwilling to change.[26] Shinseki also appealed to army supporters in Congress, and in August 2001, eighty-three members sent a letter to Rumsfeld warning him not to cut army end strength.[27] The result was a very public feud between Shinseki and Rumsfeld that would continue until the general's retirement in June 2003.[28]

THE SHELTON-RUMSFELD RIFT

From the start of Rumsfeld's transformation initiative in February 2001 until its seeming demise in the fall of 2001, there was little evidence that Hugh Shelton supported the secretary. Instead, it appears that Shelton sided with the service chiefs and, if anything, used his authority to avoid helping Rumsfeld with transformation.

Rumsfeld's relations with Shelton were problematic from the start. The secretary distrusted Shelton because he was a holdover from the Clinton administration. Additionally, Rumsfeld felt the position of chairman had been given too much power by the Goldwater-Nichols Act. According to Bradly Graham's biography of Rumsfeld, the secretary felt he and not the chairman should be the principal national security adviser to the White House, and he also preferred to bypass the JCS entirely and get advice directly from the combatant commanders.[29] Rumsfeld also sought to control and limit the engagement of the service chiefs and the chairman with both Congress and other federal agencies, arguing that the defense department needed to speak with one voice.[30]

Further, Rumsfeld felt the Pentagon was out of touch with reality and that the Joint Staff, service chiefs, and Chairman Shelton were apparently not exceptions. In a September 20, 2001, speech delivered at the Pentagon,

Rumsfeld was explicit in his disdain when he compared the Pentagon bureaucracy to the Soviet Union, finding both guilty of "central planning," "brutal consistency," "stifl[ing] free thought and crush[ing] new ideas."[31] He went on to call the Pentagon bureaucracy a "serious threat" to the national security of the United States.

Shelton also had a strong dislike for Rumsfeld. In his autobiography, Shelton speaks in glowing terms about the respect he felt from people in the Clinton administration. In contrast, Shelton found that the political appointees under Bush focused on a predetermined agenda. Shelton explains that from day one Rumsfeld distrusted him, and that like McNamara, Rumsfeld worked by "deception, deceit, working political agendas, and trying to get the Joint Chiefs to support an action that might not be the right thing to do for the country but would work well for the President from a political standpoint."[32] In his book about the Bush administration's response to the September 11 terrorist attacks, Bob Woodward writes that Shelton grew "despondent" under Rumsfeld.[33]

In September 2001, Shelton retired and was replaced by JCS vice chairman Richard Myers. Shelton had recommended a different successor, Admiral Vern Clark, then chief of naval operations. Arguing that the JCS needed a strong chairman who would stand up to Rumsfeld, Shelton worried that Myers, and the new vice chairman, Peter Pace, would be too reluctant to do so.[34] At the time, a widely shared concern was that Rumsfeld had selected Myers precisely because he did not want a chairman who would challenge him.[35]

Shelton certainly understood the political potential of the position of chairman. In a post-retirement interview in 2010 with the *Daily Beast*, Shelton spoke with pride about his behind-the-scenes political maneuvering during the Clinton administration. He explained that "it was playing one party off against the other. It was taking advantage of a Democratic president and a Republican-controlled Congress, and weaving in and out to get what you needed for the Department of Defense."[36]

In the case of transformation, Shelton could have similarly used his position to help the White House appeal to Congress to further transformation. Although many key members of Congress opposed cuts to traditional service priorities, there were also some who favored budget increases, investing in the revolution in military affairs, and transformation.[37] Shelton could have used his military advice to help support an alliance between Rumsfeld and these members of Congress. But supporting Rumsfeld on transformation would have required Shelton to directly oppose the unified position of the service chiefs, not to mention support someone he despised. The chairman chose to let Rumsfeld fight the uphill battle for transformation without his support.

TRANSFORMATION 2.0

Rumsfeld had a second go at transformation in late 2001. Writing in *Foreign Affairs*, he used the war in Afghanistan and 9/11 to call for more lethal, mobile, and joint operations.[38] When Bush announced increases in defense spending in the fiscal year 2003 budget request, Rumsfeld explained that these would go toward power projection, information warfare, leverage and defending assets in space, and information technology. He also argued for innovations in doctrine and Pentagon business practices. In announcing the appointment of Richard Myers as JCS chairman, Bush explained that transformation was once again a priority.[39]

In October, Rumsfeld established the Office of Force Transformation and appointed Arthur Cebrowski its director. Rumsfeld was buoyed by the seeming success of light, mobile forces in the initial weeks of the war in Afghanistan. Plus, the 9/11 terrorist attacks had secured supplemental funding for the Pentagon, some of which Rumsfeld used for his transformation priorities, including unmanned platforms, precision weapons, and special operations forces. By October, the office was rumored to be considering canceling the F-22, the navy's next-generation aircraft carrier, and eighteen army programs, including the Comanche attack helicopter, the Stryker armored vehicle, and the Army's Future Combat System.

For his first salvo, Rumsfeld cancelled the army's Crusader—a tracked artillery vehicle originally expected to be used in 2005. The $11 billion program had been delayed and restructured due to technical problems, and the army had attempted to improve its mobility by decreasing its weight. But in early 2002, Rumsfeld once again argued that the Crusader was not mobile or precise enough for future battlefield needs. The army disagreed, and rallied supporters in Congress as well as the defense industry. Part of this effort inadvertently led to an internal army memo in support of the Crusader being leaked to Congress, a move Rumsfeld viewed as a challenge to his authority. In May 2002, Senator Carl Levin held a hearing on the program before the Senate Armed Services Committee. The hearing reinforced the already ongoing battle between Shinseki and Rumsfeld over the army's future. Although Shinseki and the army lost—the Crusader program was terminated—the episode reinforced the bad blood between all of the service chiefs and Rumsfeld. Additionally, although Rumsfeld had planned to shift the Crusader funding to transformation priorities, it instead went toward other army artillery programs.[40]

The Crusader skirmish was followed in February 2004 by the termination of the army's Comanche attack helicopter program. Dating from the late 1980s, the Comanche was supposed to be a stealthy helicopter for a variety of missions, including intelligence, surveillance, and support of ground troops. Originally, the army planned to buy twelve hundred of the helicopters. But, after spending $6.9 billion, it cancelled the program in 2004. The rationale for this decision included technological problems related to the engine, the demise of the Soviet Union—the very enemy the Comanche was supposed to defend against—plus concern over mounting federal deficits. Collectively, these realities made it difficult for congressional supporters to save the program. Although the Comanche's demise seemed to reinforce Rumsfeld's push for transformation, the program was actually cancelled by the army, with funding redirected to other army helicopter programs.[41] Nonetheless, the episode reinforced the conclusion that Rumsfeld hated the army.

In April 2003, the Office of Force Transformation issued its "Transformation Planning Guidance" to the services. "Transformation" now included a shift from an "industrial age" to an "information age military," but also more efficient bureaucratic and business practices at the Pentagon.[42] Central to transformation were better joint operations, improved intelligence, iterative development, competition between the services, and road maps for how the services were supposed to develop certain joint operations.

The guidance had been delayed almost a year because of objections from the services. Whereas Rumsfeld had wanted precise budget priorities, the services eventually succeeded in watering these down.[43] The result was a collection of road maps that involved little coordination between the services, and which continued the trend of calling current service plans "transformational."

The Office of Force Transformation had little authority to force the services to take the process seriously. In January 2005, Cebrowski, the driving force behind the initiative, retired due to ill-health. In August of that year, the Pentagon suspended the road map process, and the office itself was closed in September 2006.

The 2005 QDR, released in February 2006, certified the failure of transformation for a second time. Written amid the mounting costs of the wars in Afghanistan and Iraq, plus personnel and equipment shortages, the QDR talked once again about the need for transformation and emphasized counterterrorism, fighting insurgencies, and capabilities for dealing with failed states. Rumsfeld himself is thought to have written the terms of reference for the QDR, which emphasized the 1-4-2-1 strategy, irregular warfare, and nontraditional threats.[44]

Initially, the 2005 QDR process looked like it would result in open warfare between the services. The army was optimistic that the process, in combination with the wars in Afghanistan and Iraq, would validate the need for more ground troops, counterinsurgency operations, and army modernization budgets. The navy and air force worried that their priorities would be cut in order to fund the army.[45] But, as with previous QDRs, the process did not impose resource constraints. Also, Rumsfeld did not take an active interest in the process, and it was widely seen as something on the Pentagon's "to do list" and not a major examination of strategy or force structure. As a consequence, the document contained something for everyone but also, as explained by the *Washington Post*, allowed Rumsfeld to "dodge almost all the hard decisions."[46] In the end, although the QDR emphasized counterterrorism, homeland defense, and nation building, it also endorsed the current force structure.

The president's budget request for fiscal year (FY) 2007 was released at the same time as the QDR. Although it increased funding for special forces by almost 15 percent, it also continued to fund the previous priorities of the services rather than transformation. Rumsfeld argued that efficiencies and better management practices would be used to free resources for transformation in the coming years.

But money turned out not to be a problem. According to the U.S. Government Accountability Office, from FY 2001 to FY 2006, the defense department's base budget grew by 21 percent.[47] Additionally, starting in FY 2001, funding for the wars in Afghanistan and Iraq, as well as some devoted to homeland security, was provided through a series of supplemental spending measures through what became known as Global War on Terrorism, or GWOT, supplementals. According to analysis by the defense department, from FY 2001 through FY 2006, it obligated $332.4 billion to the costs of ongoing wars.[48] But its budget authority through the corresponding supplementals exceeded $412 billion.[49] Certainly, obligating the money granted by budget authority often takes time. But given that the supplementals were supposed to go toward ongoing military operations that were too pressing to wait for the regular appropriations process, the $80 billion difference seems excessive. In fact, after 2001, supplemental budget requests increased and also quickly came to include a variety of programs that might have supported, in theory, a global "War on Terrorism," but one that had little to do with ongoing military operations.[50] Most of the money that eventually went toward the force structure envisioned by Rumsfeld came from the supplements and not cuts to the traditionally favored weapons of the services.

With the exception of the army's Crusader and Comanche programs, the same weapons planned under the Clinton administration continued throughout the two George W. Bush administrations. As explained by Thomas K. Adams in his study of the army during these years, "transformation had been introduced as a revolution, but over $100 billion later it had turned into business as usual."[51]

A TEAM PLAYER

Unlike Rumsfeld's first attempt at transformation, which received little support from Shelton, Chairman Richard Myers publicly supported Rumsfeld. He not only endorsed many of the force-structure changes proposed as part of transformation, he also argued that the services needed to change their mind-set and embrace innovation and new technologies.[52] Unlike Shelton, Myers was a frequent public advocate for the transformation agenda, even though the service chiefs still strongly opposed Rumsfeld's vision. Throughout his tenure as chairman, the chiefs found Myers too closely allied with the secretary and either unwilling or unable to stand up for service interests.

By all accounts, Myers and Rumsfeld had a strong working relationship. But this is likely because the chairman clearly saw himself in a subservient role. Two examples illustrate the degree to which Myers deferred to the secretary; these also provide a sharp contrast to similar experiences under Shelton.

First, soon after becoming chairman, Myers identified the officer he wanted to head the Joint Staff's J3 Directorate for Operations. The Joint Staff works for the chairman, who is given wide latitude over its operations. Moreover, the norm is for the service chiefs to determine who is promoted to three- and four-star positions. Rumsfeld, however, insisted that he approve all nominees for these higher ranks. In 2002, Rumsfeld rejected Myers's choice to head J3, and instead of pushing for his own handpicked officer, Myers found someone else who met with Rumsfeld's approval.[53]

In contrast, Shelton dealt with a similar situation in a very different way. Early in his tenure, Rumsfeld argued to Shelton that the Joint Staff offices for protocol, legislative liaison, and legal affairs should either be eliminated or merged with those in the Office of the Secretary of Defense. Shelton, however, forcefully disagreed. At first, he explained that the military and civilian offices had different perspectives and therefore complemented each other. When that didn't seem to convince Rumsfeld, Shelton pointed out that the military offices for these functions totaled 19 people. In the Office of the Secretary of Defense, the total came to 190. Realizing that Shelton was not going to back down, Rumsfeld gave up on the idea.[54]

The post-9/11 war in Afghanistan and invasion of Iraq provide another illustration of the difference between Shelton and Myers. As the Afghanistan operation was being planned, Shelton became concerned that Rumsfeld would use the promise of transformation to argue that only a small force was necessary for the invasion of Afghanistan. In the days before he retired, Shelton warned senior military officers to watch out for any attempt by Rumsfeld to circumvent military advice and argue for fewer troops.[55]

This appears to have been exactly Rumsfeld's strategy in planning the Iraq war, and it was a strategy that was supported by Myers. In planning for the Iraq war as well as the postwar stability operations, Rumsfeld relied on a handful of political appointees and General Tommy Franks, the head of Central Command—the combatant command with responsibility for the Middle East. Such a pivotal role for the regional combatant commander was not unusual, given that Central Command's area of responsibility included both Afghanistan and Iraq. What was unusual was Rumsfeld's exclusion of the service chiefs. Although not formally in the chain of command, the chiefs were used to being closely consulted about all ongoing military operations. They resented being excluded from what they considered to be their proper role. Similarly, Franks and Rumsfeld excluded the chairman.

Risa Brooks, in her study of the relationship between civil-military relations and strategic assessment, argues that differences of preference between military and civilian leaders can lead the latter to limit consultation or to improperly vet plans.[56] This can in turn lead to ill-considered military operations or, in Rumsfeld's case, the neglect of key variables in post-conflict stabilization and recovery. Rumsfeld's earlier efforts at transformation convinced him that the service chiefs were still wedded to Cold War weapons, claiming equal shares of the resource pie, and using overwhelming military force. Rather than argue with the JCS, or attempt to persuade them, he excluded them from planning. The result was a postwar stabilization effort that was underdeveloped, based on a variety of false assumptions, and that relied on too few U.S. forces to fight what would quickly become a growing and formidable insurgency.[57] Unfortunately, Franks shared Rumsfeld's view that the service chiefs were parochial and unhelpful. Rather than create a back channel to get their input, he reinforced their exclusion.[58]

With one exception, the service chiefs raised few concerns about plans for Iraq. When Rumsfeld insisted that a small force was sufficient for the occupation of the country, the army disagreed strongly and in public. On February 25, 2003, General Shinseki told the Senate Armed Services Committee that "several hundred thousand soldiers" would be needed for stabilization efforts.[59] The Bush administration soon denounced Shinseki's estimate; it eventually sent 145,000 troops, which proved woefully inadequate. When Franks supported the administration's plans, the army turned on him, calling him "Rumsfeld's general."[60] In what became known as the "revolt of the retired generals," several prominent and recently retired military officers called for Rumsfeld's resignation, claiming that he had ignored military advice, both in planning the war but also in running the Pentagon.[61] Among these officers was retired army general Paul Eaton, who had served in Iraq. In an op-ed in the *New York Times*, Eaton called Rumsfeld "incompetent strategically, operationally and tactically."[62] Myers, however, continued to stand by Rumsfeld and the Iraq war plans.

These examples illustrate Shelton's willingness to contradict the secretary and to protect the prerogatives of the JCS. As a result, Shelton enjoyed the respect of the service chiefs. Myers, by contrast, was viewed with skepticism because he did not seem a strong advocate for the JCS, colluded with the secretary to exclude them from decisions, and appeared too willing to concede to Rumsfeld.

Myers defended his support for Rumsfeld by arguing that he was not deterred from speaking his mind and had stood up to the secretary when they disagreed, but that he felt it was only appropriate to do so in private. In a 2003 interview, he also explained how he felt it was his responsibility to provide the opinions of all members of the JCS, even if he disagreed with them.[63]

The service chiefs, however, apparently remained unconvinced of Myers's leadership abilities. From day one until he was replaced in September 2005 by Vice Chairman Peter Pace, the chiefs were frequently critical of Myers, claiming that he did not adequately represent their concerns and that he failed to keep the chiefs sufficiently informed about Rumsfeld's plans and decisions.[64] In his biography of Rumsfeld, Andrew Cockburn makes it clear who the military thought was in charge: "Under Rumsfeld's contemptuous bullying he [Myers] came to be viewed as 'an abused puppy,' the 'sycophant to end all sycophants' who shrank from facing up to his master."[65]

Pace was similarly criticized for allying himself with Rumsfeld and not with the chiefs. In *State of Denial*, Bob Woodward explains that when Pace was offered the job of chairman, he was advised not to take it because Rumsfeld was looking for a "parrot on the secretary's shoulder"—someone to unquestioningly follow his lead.[66] And indeed, during his tenure as chairman, Pace was sometimes referred to disparagingly as "Pete the Parrot."[67]

TRANSFORMATION AND CIVIL-MILITARY RELATIONS

Rumsfeld's two attempts at transformation show the limits of civilian control. Rumsfeld arrived in the Pentagon with the full backing of President George W. Bush for his transformation agenda and lacking any inclination to be timid in asserting what he considered appropriate civilian control of the Pentagon. The president's support was subsequently reiterated in the fall of 2001 and the spring of 2002 when Rumsfeld established the Office of Force Transformation. Moreover, success in Afghanistan and Iraq seemed, at least initially, to validate Rumsfeld's argument about a smaller, more flexible mobile force.

Yet after five budgets and two QDRs, most of the service's favored weapons remained. The battles Rumsfeld won, such as those concerning increased funding for missile defense and drones, were due to budget increases and supplements, not cuts to service priorities. The one exception was the army, which lost the Crusader, Comanche, and eventually the Future Combat System. But, with the exception of the Crusader, the army supported canceling or restructuring these platforms. Moreover, Rumsfeld failed to reduce the size of the army. The active-duty army was at 481,000 members when Rumsfeld arrived at the Pentagon. It was 482,000 when he left in 2006.[68]

Certainly, part of the failure of transformation lies with Rumsfeld's management style. His dismissive and authoritarian tactics annoyed not only the service chiefs, but many of the career people working in the Pentagon. The service chiefs distrusted Rumsfeld and felt he was dismissive of their expertise. They were not about to unquestioningly follow his direction to eliminate many of their long-standing investment priorities.

Congress did not offer a counterweight to the unified opposition of the service chiefs. Not only did the services' weapon preferences have congressional supporters, but Rumsfeld also gained more enemies when he proposed significant cuts to one of the mainstays of congressional pork: military construction projects. Some Republicans disliked him because they felt defense budgets were too low. Democrats opposed the administration in general, and especially after questions about the war in Iraq mounted. Even when the 2002 midterm elections returned control of both houses to the Republicans, Rumsfeld's support in Congress was meager.

The chairman played a minor role in the failure of transformation. Even if Shelton had supported Rumsfeld's agenda, in the face of opposition from the service chiefs and with only a few allies in Congress, even a politically savvy military officer would have faced an uphill battle. But Shelton's and Myers's roles do provide important clues about the changed nature of civil-military relations. Like Powell before him, Shelton's experience makes it clear that the chairman can successfully stake out a position independent of and in contradiction to the defense secretary. Moreover, early in his tenure Shelton asserted his right to provide advice to the president independent of the secretary. In his autobiography, Shelton recounts an early exchange with the Rumsfeld:

Finally he [Rumsfeld] asked me, "How do you view your job?"

That was easy because it's specifically delineated by federal statute.

"Mr. Secretary, I am the principal military adviser to you, the President, and the National Security Council, and also—"

"No, you are *not* the adviser to the National Security Council."

"Well, I beg your pardon, but according to Title Ten of the U.S. Code, it states very clearly that—"

"But not the staff, not the staff."

"No sir," I answered, allowing him to save face when he realized that I had him by the balls since I knew exactly how the law defined my job . . . I thought to myself, *We're going to need some heavy-duty cleaning supplies if all we're going to do is waste time having pissing contests like this.*[69]

But with respect to transformation, there is no evidence that Shelton asserted his role to provide independent military advice to the president and National Security Council. To stop transformation, he didn't have to.

Moreover, there is no evidence that Shelton attempted to create common cause with members of Congress who were opposed to Rumsfeld's agenda, or to Bush administration policy in general. Aside from his formal testimony, Shelton did not seek to provide back-channel advice to members of Congress or to create alliances with them.

Rumsfeld had no more success when he received Chairman Myers's consistent support. In fact, the secretary's position may have become even more precarious because the service chiefs did not consider Myers their advocate. Shut out of key decisions about war planning as well as resources, the service chiefs more frequently sought external allies in Congress because they did not trust Myers to advocate for them vis-à-vis the secretary or the White House, or to accurately relay their policy advice. Myers's experience illustrates the limits of the Goldwater-Nichols Act. Even twenty years after its passage, the power of the chairman can still be severely limited if he does not have the support of the JCS.

7

SEQUESTRATION

The election of Barack Obama coincided with increasing pressure to control federal spending. In an echo of the budgetary response to the collapse of the Soviet Union, which eventually resulted in a 30 percent reduction in defense spending, the military was faced with the specter of significant budget cuts, either through congressional action or as the result of the automatic deficit-reduction mechanism known as sequestration. Unlike the early 1990s, however, the catalyst for budget cuts wasn't a radically different security environment. Instead, pressure came from what at the time seemed a realignment of the Republican Party, combined with opposition to public financing of health care. Like other federal agencies, the defense department was caught in the middle of bipartisan squabbling that led to an ongoing inability to agree to appropriations, a series of budget caps, and eventually, when Congress proved unable to agree to specific reductions, the imposition of across-the-board budget cuts through sequestration.

This budget drama unfolded at a time when the military was reconsidering its future focus. Although Obama's first year in office found him emphasizing counterinsurgency, stability operations, and other strategies to overcome setbacks in the war in Afghanistan, at the end of his two terms he had personally disowned such approaches.[1] Instead, he settled on the "Pivot to Asia," which allowed the services to return to their preferred emphasis on traditional warfare against other states. With the decline in war funding, service shares of the budget shifted back toward their traditional split after a decade's worth of ongoing military operations had favored the army and marine corps.

As for the service chiefs, they consistently supported Obama's budget choices even though the president was eventually forced to adopt significant cuts to defense spending as part of a budget-reduction strategy. This support from the chiefs is surprising. One common criticism of the Obama White House is that it centralized decision making among a small group of advisers who often ignored, or did not sufficiently value, the advice of cabinet members or the expertise of agencies. This was particularly true with respect to national security. It was therefore surprising that a president who had presided over significant changes and reductions to the defense budget managed to avoid active service squabbling, disapproval, or interference. Instead, by all indications the service chiefs played an active role in making the necessary choices to implement multiple cuts to the defense budget and then supported the president's choices, even amid indications from Republicans in Congress that they were willing to provide some relief.

Further, unlike Colin Powell's role in formulating the Base Force, there is scant evidence that Chairman Mike Mullen or his successor, Martin Dempsey, played a predominant role in determining the size or structure of the decreasing defense budget requests that came between fiscal years 2010 and 2015, or the various strategic reviews that supported those budgets. Instead, two different secretaries of defense—first Robert Gates and then Leon Panetta—led the services through repeated reviews that culminated in budget recommendations that the service chiefs endorsed. Although some Republicans in Congress were in favor of more defense spending, and some Democrats favored less, the military stood behind the Obama results for two reasons: budget politics were uncertain and it was by no means clear that further reductions could be avoided, and even though budgets were smaller, they returned the military to its traditional preferences for equal budget shares and preparing for major conventional war against other great powers.

What role was played by the chairman? Here the tenures of Mullen and Dempsey are different. Dempsey served under a secretary of defense who was committed to implementing budget reductions. He helped Panetta lead the services to consensus in support of these smaller budgets. Mullen, however, served under Robert Gates, who wanted to maintain defense budgets. Gates also thought he had secured Obama's agreement for modest growth. In contrast, Mullen articulated a connection between national security and budget deficits, seemingly endorsing defense budget cuts in contradiction to Gates and in advance of Obama. Although neither chairman played as prominent a role as Colin Powell in the Base Force, the years surrounding the threat of sequestration illustrate an important shift in civil-military relations: rather than assuming the chairman can be counted on to assist with the president's agenda, the chairman's support is his choice, not an obligation to the commander in chief.

BUDGET POLITICS

Barack Obama's presidential campaign focused mainly on domestic issues. With respect to national security, Obama's key message concerned ending the "bad war" in Iraq and shifting resources to win the "good war" in Afghanistan. Obama did highlight the dangers to the economy of increasing deficits, arguing that "we cannot afford to mortgage our children's future on another mountain of debt."[2] But his solutions were job creation and reforms to health care and taxes, not reductions in spending. Obama's first budget, for fiscal year (FY) 2010, came in at over \$3.5 trillion and included significant increases for health care, education, and climate change initiatives, as well as a 12 percent increase in defense spending.

But pressure to control the deficit was building. Key factions in Congress, and in both parties, expressed concerns about the size of the U.S. deficit—estimated at over \$1 trillion for 2010—and its overall effect on the country's economic health. In his 2010 State of the Union speech, Obama called for a three-year freeze in some government spending. Exempted were defense as well as Medicare, Medicaid, and Social Security. Then, in February, concerns from Republicans led the Senate to reject Obama's request for the creation of a bipartisan commission to focus on ways of reducing the national debt. In April 2010, the president struck out on his own and created the National Commission on Fiscal Responsibility and Reform. Chaired by former senator Alan Simpson and former Clinton chief of staff Erskine Bowles, the bipartisan commission released its recommendations in late 2010, but it lacked enough support from its own members to forward those recommendations to Congress. The commission recommended spending cuts that were shared equally between defense and non-defense agencies. In November 2010, Obama released a draft deficit-reduction plan that included cuts to defense, largely at the insistence of liberals in Congress who argued that defense spending should not be exempt from deficit-reduction efforts. The plan called for cuts to be shared equally by domestic and defense discretionary spending. Also, in November 2010, a private bipartisan group of budget experts, led by former senator Pete Domenici and former White House budget director Alice Rivlin, called for tackling the deficit with tax increases and budget cuts, including a five-year freeze in defense spending.

Although Obama did not champion cuts to defense, his health and education priorities would swell the federal deficit in the absence of offsets from other parts of the budget. Some congressional Republicans shared Obama's concern about ballooning deficits, but most were united by a preference for defense over domestic spending priorities, with less concern for the overall size of the budget. But the success of the Tea Party movement put many Republicans on notice. The Tea Party began as a grassroots movement, partially in opposition to Obama, but it later gave voice to the backlash against Obama's increased spending to stabilize the economy and deal with the mortgage-lending crisis that began in 2007. Special elections and primaries in 2009 and 2010 foreshadowed the 2010 midterm elections, which left Republicans in control of the House and reduced the Democratic majority in the Senate. Tea Party candidates proved willing to challenge incumbent Republicans, and, as a result, Republicans in Congress shifted priorities to focus on the deficit, even if that meant less money for defense.[3]

Democrats were more splintered. Some factions within the party worried about the deficit, while others were less concerned and favored increased spending on a variety of domestic issues. More liberal Democrats in the House balked at the notion of spending more for ongoing military operations. The president, largely enabled by the work of Vice President Joe Biden, who sought to gather support for Obama's agenda among his former congressional colleagues, was able to bring together a coalition that would tackle the deficit without sacrificing the president's domestic priorities or the support of liberals in Congress.[4] The winning formula was based on a strategy from the 1990s for sharing budget surpluses: parity. Except this time, budget cuts, in the name of deficit reduction, would be shared equally among defense and domestic spending.

The result was the Budget Control Act (BCA), signed into law in August 2011. The BCA mandated caps on the appropriation of budget authority for discretionary spending for a ten-year period from FY 2012 through FY 2021. Any new increases in spending during these years would have to be fully offset by either increases in revenue or spending cuts in other areas. The BCA set separate caps for security and non-security appropriations for FYs 2012 and 2013 but one overall cap for 2014 and beyond. "Security" included spending for the Departments of Defense, Homeland Security, and Veterans Affairs, as well as the National Nuclear Security Administration and other specific defense- and international affairs–related funding accounts at the Departments of State, Energy, and Justice. As of FY 2013, however, "security" came to be defined more narrowly as "defense-related," meaning the federal government's 050 budget account, which includes the defense department, the atomic energy activities of the National Nuclear Security Administration as well as other of defense-related activities, the FBI and CIA, and some programs in Homeland Security.[5]

If enforced, the BCA caps would require a $1 trillion reduction in defense-related spending over a ten-year period.[6] But this pressure on the defense budget was amplified for two other reasons. First, of the 050 budget, approximately 96 percent concerned military activities in the defense department.[7]

Second, procurement was likely to bear the brunt of any reductions because Obama announced that personnel, salaries, and benefits would be exempted. Combined, these additional pressures meant that the services' priority programs were likely to be hit especially hard.

The BCA postponed enforcement of its spending caps until January 2013 and created a bipartisan joint committee, which came to be known as the Super Committee, tasked with recommending an additional $1.5 trillion in cuts by the end of 2012. If the committee was unable to agree on recommendations, or Congress did not approve them, all nonexempt discretionary spending would see across-the-board cuts to below BCA spending levels. The cuts would be divided equally between defense (defined then as the 050 account, and not broader security spending) and non-defense spending.

By late summer 2012, it was clear that the Super Committee was in trouble. Thanks to the last-minute passage of the American Taxpayer Relief Act of 2012, the deadline for avoiding sequestration was pushed back to March 1, 2013. Once again, however, Congress proved unable to reach agreement, and sequestration took effect on March 1, 2013.

Sequestration was never meant to happen. The provision was included in the BCA because congressional Democrats as well as the White House thought that if they included defense in the sequestration cuts, this would force Republicans to compromise in order to avoid what was overwhelmingly thought to be a terrible outcome.[8] But the 2010 midterm elections had created a schism in the Republican Party by strengthening the hand of deficit hawks who thought debt reduction without tax increases trumped the need to protect the defense budget.

Table 7.1 shows the impact of the BCA and sequestration on defense spending. For FY 2010, the Obama administration requested $538 billion for the defense department's base budget; it asked for $553 billion for FY 2011. Under the cuts imposed by sequestration, however, it would take eight years for defense spending to reach these levels. Congress subsequently amended the BCA four times—in 2012, 2013, 2015, and 2018—and increased the spending caps for two years at a time, leaving the out-years at previously specified levels. This resulted in increases to the 050 caps of up to

TABLE 7.1 Defense Budget Authority, Budget Caps, and the 050 Defense Account (Excludes Overseas Contingency Operations; in Billions of Dollars)

	2010	2011	2012	2013	2014	2015	2016	2017	2018	2019	2020	2021
FY 2010 PBR*	534											
FY 2011 PBR*		553	570	586	602	620						
BCA LIMITS			555	546	556	566	577	590	603	616	630	644
SEQUESTRATION				492	501	511	522	535	548	561	575	589
AMERICAN TAXPAYER RELIEF ACT OF 2012			555	518	497	511	522	535	548	561	575	589
BIPARTISAN BUDGET ACT OF 2013			555	518	520	521	523	536	549	562	576	590
BIPARTISAN BUDGET ACT OF 2015			555	518	520	521	548	551	549	562	576	590
BIPARTISAN BUDGET ACT OF 2018			555	518	520	521	548	551	629	647	576	591

Source: Brendan W. McGarry, *The Defense Budget and the Budget Control Act: Frequently Asked Questions*, CRS Report No. R44039 (Washington, DC: Congressional Research Service, 2018), 5, https://sgp.fas.org/crs/natsec/R44039.pdf.

Note: The FY 2010 presidential budget request did not include spending projections for the five-year Future Years Defense Program.

*PBR: Presidential Budget Request for the base defense department budget (051 account). This excludes overseas contingency operations.

15 percent per year over the original BCA levels.[9] Although the caps increased, they were still significantly below what the defense department expected prior to the BCA. The president's FY 2011 budget request, which was put together before caps were an issue, projected the need for $620 billion in budget authority in FY 2015 for the defense department's base budget alone. By FY 2015, however, the entire 050 account was capped at $521 billion by the Bipartisan Budget Act of 2013, a 16 percent reduction.

The defense budget normally enjoys strong support among Republican members of Congress, and they did make attempts to shift budget caps and sequestration cuts more toward domestic programs. In negotiations leading up to the BCA, for example, Republicans tried to limit both the caps on defense spending but also the degree to which sequestration would include defense spending.[10] For example, the initial budget firewalls were broadened from "defense/non-defense" to "security/non-security" in an effort to get Republican agreement to the BCA.[11] During deliberations on the Super Committee, Republican senator Jon Kyl threatened to walk out and thus end any chance of avoiding sequestration if the committee recommended additional defense cuts.[12] House Armed Services Committee chair Buck McKeon argued that defense should be exempt from sequestration, as did Senator John McCain, ranking minority member on the Senate Armed Service Committee. But the Tea Party had created a split between traditional defense hawks and fiscal conservatives. As Senator Rand Paul asked in a 2015 Republican presidential debate, "How is it conservative to add a trillion dollars in military expenditures? You cannot be a conservative if you're going to keep promoting programs that you're not paying for."[13]

This split within the Republican Party would hold until the election of Donald Trump in 2016. Under Trump, most budget hawks abandoned concern about deficit spending in order to embrace Trump administration priorities for large tax cuts, curbing immigration, enhanced border security, and increased defense spending. But under Obama, the Tea Party movement made budget politics volatile. On October 1, 2013, the government shut down for sixteen days because Congress was unable to pass a budget for FY 2014. Congress also continued the practice of using continuing resolutions when agreement could not be reached on a budget prior to the start of the fiscal year. But in contrast to past practice, it took longer to agree to these resolutions, they more often included riders or other unrelated additions, and they were contentious and thus brought into question whether an agreement would be reached in time to avoid a partial or complete government shutdown.

The battle over the size of the federal budget and the spending caps was primarily about resistance to Obama. But it was acted out as conflict over raising taxes, deficit reduction, and paying for new initiatives in domestic programs. Although defense spending was necessarily part of this equation, it was less a primary driver for the White House than a casualty of the coalition needed to protect the president's domestic priorities. Pentagon officials, either military or civilian, were largely absent from the negotiations over caps. Relegated to the sidelines, they provided pithy sound bites about the impact of sequestration on national security. The secretary of defense, chairman, and service chiefs all argued that cuts from sequestration were harmful, but they did not break ranks with the White House by calling for an end to the parity between cuts in defense and non-defense spending. But, as the next sections illustrate, the Pentagon was involved in budget battles of a different nature.

FROM "EFFICIENCIES" TO SEQUESTRATION

The Pentagon's first budget battle preceded the BCA and was well underway when Obama took office on January 20, 2009. Secretary of Defense Robert Gates, who initially served under George W. Bush and who agreed to stay on under Obama, faced a bloated budget. The president is supposed to submit a budget request on the first Monday in February, although since the 1990s incoming administrations have usually provided only top-level details in February, with budget specifics coming later in the spring.[14] This schedule means the incoming administration usually has only enough time to tweak the budget inherited from their predecessor. The Bush administration had encouraged the services to be less constrained in their FY 2010 budget build and proposed a top line with a larger percentage increase in defense spending than any passed by Congress during the previous eight years. Plus, Gates had transferred a number of items into the base budget that had gravitated into the supplemental war funding requests.[15] The result was a $581 billion base budget. The Obama White House told Gates to plan on $534 billion for the base budget, with an additional $130 billion for what is known as the Overseas Contingency Operations (OCO) account—the funding mechanism that is supposed to be reserved for the cost of ongoing wars and military operations.

Secretary Gates spent the next two months working with the services to identify cuts, but also to continue his effort to get the services to translate the lessons from Iraq and Afghanistan into strategy, budgets, and planning for nontraditional operations such as counterinsurgency. In his autobiography, Gates explains that he was willing to take more risks in preparing for traditional wars in order to do this.[16] While the combatant commanders agreed with this focus, Chairman Mullen and the service chiefs did not. Gates describes this in a section of his autobiography entitled "The War about War":

> In the spring of 2008, the vital issue of the military services' preoccupation with planning, equipping, and training for future major wars with other nation-states, while assigning lesser priority to current conflicts and all other forms of conflict, such as irregular or asymmetric war, came to a head. It went to the heart of every other fight with the Pentagon I have described. In my four and a half years as secretary, this was one of the few issues where I had to take on the chairman and the entire Joint Chiefs of Staff.[17]

Obama agreed with Gates; he had campaigned on shifting defense resources to win the "good" or "necessary" war in Afghanistan. On February 1, 2010, the Pentagon released the 2010 Quadrennial Defense Review (QDR), which reflected this shift. The QDR emphasized nontraditional war and counterterrorism and moved away from some of the favorite weapons of the services, especially high-tech weapons for fighting more traditional state-to-state wars.

The FY 2010 budget foreshadowed this emphasis. On April 6, 2009, Gates previewed the FY 2010 request that would be submitted in May. It included significant cuts in missile defense, ended the navy's plans for a new stealth destroyer, restructured the army's Future Combat Systems program, and delayed air force plans for a new bomber while limiting production of the F-22 fighter. The budget prioritized unmanned aerial vehicles, special operation forces, and increased the size of the army and marines. In total, the request canceled or limited almost twenty programs that over their lifetimes would have cost at least $300 billion.[18] Congress would haggle over the budget past the October 1 start of the FY 2010 fiscal year, eventually agreeing on a budget in December 2009. Instead of the $534 billion requested for the base budget, defense got $528 billion. Congress increased the president's supplemental request for ongoing military operations—the OCO account—from $130 billion to $163 billion.

Although the service chiefs did not necessarily agree with the size or composition of the budget, they supported it publicly. Gates credits this to a series of collaborative meetings held between the services and the Office of the Secretary of Defense during February and March of 2009.[19] Additionally, at the suggestion of Mullen, Gates had the participants sign non-disclosure agreements, which he credits with stopping the services from leaking information to Congress in an attempt to undermine cuts with which they disagreed.[20] Also, for the FY 2010 budget, Gates required the services to submit to him their lists of unfunded requirements (UFRs)—items that had not been included in the president's budget request. As a result, the amount dropped from just over $30 billion to $3.5 billion for FY 2010.[21] The services were also told to make it clear to Congress that they endorsed the formal budget submission and that any UFRs were not intended to suggest that the president's budget was inadequate or that a UFR was a higher priority.

In mid-July 2009, Gates began negotiations with the White House on the size of the FY 2011 budget. Prior to agreeing to serve under Obama, Gates had sought and received assurance that there were no plans for significant cuts to the defense budget.[22] But when he asked for $558 billion for the base budget for FY 2011, the White House offered $16 billion less. Eventually, they settled on $550 billion, with only modest increases in the out-years.[23] When the FY 2011 budget was submitted, it called for a freeze on non-security discretionary spending and continued the emphasis on the wars in Iraq and Afghanistan, but made few changes to major procurement programs. Compared to the changes requested in the FY 2010 budget, however, the FY 2011 budget discussion was ho-hum.

Throughout 2010, pressure was building in Washington to address the federal debt, and Gates worried that the defense budget would be a tempting target for deficit reduction.[24] Rather than cuts, Gates hoped for modest increases, or at least a continuation of current defense spending. But even under these scenarios, some procurement programs would have to be curtailed. To avoid this and preserve military capabilities in the absence of budget growth, Gates announced "efficiencies initiatives" aimed at eliminating waste, reducing duplication, and "instill[ing] a culture of savings and restraint in America's defense institutions."[25] The savings from these efforts could then be redistributed internally to preserve certain priorities even if the budget did not continue to grow. In his autobiography, Gates argues that there is a "daily 'river of money' running through the building [Pentagon]," a phrase he attributes to Gordon England, the deputy secretary of defense under George W. Bush.[26] On August 9, 2010, Gates followed up on his previous program cuts by announcing a series of initiatives aimed at streamlining Pentagon practices and reducing overhead and duplication.[27] The goal was $150 billion in "efficiencies."[28]

Although it takes the Pentagon two to three years to build a budget for any one fiscal year, that process is guided by assumptions about the overall size of the budget. Then, in the fall, before the president submits a budget request in February, the Office of Management and Budget (OMB) and the Pentagon negotiate the specific budget top line. For the FY 2012 budget, this process brought some surprises. Gates argues that Obama promised there would be no significant reductions in defense spending. But in the fall of 2011, OMB proposed $20 billion less for FY 2012, plus slower growth in the out-years.[29] Eventually, the FY 2012 budget would flatline defense, asking for $553 billion, the same as in FY 2011.

The "efficiencies" initiatives cut or reduced programs to meet these lower budget targets. Casualties centered on the ground forces. Cancelled were the army's Future Combat System and the Marine's Expeditionary Fighting Vehicle.[30] The marine's version of the Joint Strike Fighter program was also delayed for two years, pending proof of technical viability. The budget also reduced funding for the wars in Iraq and Afghanistan to their lowest levels since FY 2005, and Gates said he would support cutting the size of both the army and the marines starting in FY 2015.[31] Relative winners were the navy and air force.[32]

But finding efficiencies was in itself insufficient. On April 12, 2011, the White House informed Gates that the next day Obama would announce that the defense budget would be cut by $400 billion over the next ten years. Gates explains in his autobiography that he was angry at both the size of the reduction as well as the fact that the president had broken his promise not to cut the defense budget.[33] At the Pentagon, Gates nonetheless initiated an internal review of missions and capabilities that would culminate in recommendations for the necessary cuts. This review would be completed by Leon Panetta, who would become secretary of defense in July.

Gates then embarked on what was essentially a farewell speaking tour in which he warned about the impact of such cuts on national security. Gates claimed that his "efficiencies initiatives" had resulted in the termination of more than thirty programs that would have cost, over time, $300 billion. Gates continued this theme in a speech to the American Enterprise Institute on May 24, 2011:

> When it comes to military modernization accounts, the proverbial "low hanging fruit"—those weapons and other programs considered most questionable—have not only been plucked, they have been stomped on and crushed. What remains are much-needed capabilities . . . that our nation's civilian and military leadership deem absolutely critical . . . That is why I launched a comprehensive review last week to ensure that future

spending decisions are focused on priorities, strategy, and risks, and are not simply a math and accounting exercise. In the end, this process must be about identifying options for the President and the Congress, to ensure that the nation consciously acknowledges and accepts additional risk in exchange for reduced investment in the military.[34]

Gates acknowledged that cuts to the defense budget would have to be part of the solution to the national debt problem, but he also warned they would only come at the cost of higher national security risks.

On July 1, 2011, Leon Panetta succeeded Gates as secretary of defense. Unlike his predecessor, Panetta knew from the start that defense budgets were likely to decline. Moreover, Panetta did not argue that defense should be immune from cuts. Instead, he focused on denouncing sequestration. Soon after the BCA was signed in August 2011, Panetta began referring to sequestration as a "doomsday mechanism" because it would impose automatic across-the-board cuts rather than allow the defense department—or any agency, for that matter—to determine which programs are cut and by how much.[35] Panetta even went so far as to suggest to the White House that he offer Congress an additional $100 billion cut in the defense budget as an incentive for the Super Committee and Congress to avoid sequestration.[36] Mullen backed Panetta, both on further cuts to the defense budget— Mullen went so far as to call the BCA cuts to defense "reasonable and fair"—and on sequestration, which he argued would have a "devasting impact."[37]

The BCA required the Pentagon to take an additional $87 billion in cuts over ten years, on top of the $400 billion in reductions Obama had ordered in April. Gates had set up a strategic review to consider choices about priorities and strategy in light of the required cuts. Panetta embraced this review. In contrast to Gates's efficiencies initiatives, which were the result of collaborative meetings inside the Pentagon, this Defense Strategic Review culminated in a series of meetings in the White House. Led by National Security Adviser Thomas Donilon, these meetings involved Mullen and then Dempsey, Panetta, senior military leaders, and other members of the president's national security team. The goal was to make choices about budgets, national security priorities, and how to sell those choices to Congress and the public—the last point being especially crucial as Obama was hoping to be reelected in November.[38] Similar to claims made about the Gates meetings two years prior, this process was described as collaborative and as a way to build consensus among the services.[39]

Obama went to the Pentagon on January 5, 2012, to announce the new Defense Strategic Guidance that resulted from the review, along with the implications for the FY 2013 defense budget.[40] The guidance took into account the $487 billion in reductions required by the BCA, but it did not include plans for any additional cuts required by sequestration. At the time, the defense department argued that if sequestration happened, it would mean abandoning the guidance as well as "missions and commitments and capabilities that we believe are necessary to protect core U.S. national security interests."[41]

Flanked by the service chiefs, the secretary of defense, and the new chairman of the Joint Chiefs of Staff (JCS), Martin Dempsey, Obama called for a peace dividend and a rebalancing of U.S. forces toward preparing for traditional warfare and projecting power in the Pacific region and away from stability and counterinsurgency operations like those in Iraq and Afghanistan. The guidance shifted from sizing forces based on the need to succeed in two simultaneous major contingencies to, instead, prevailing in one major war while denying an adversary their goals in a second one.[42] What was initially called the "Pivot to Asia," and later the "Rebalance to Asia," included steep reductions in army and marine corps personnel, and delays and possible termination of the Joint Strike Fighter. The winners included budget support for the next air force bomber, navy carriers and attack submarines, special operations forces, and drones. At $525 billion for the base budget plus $89 billion for ongoing military operations, the FY 2013 request was the first in ten years to propose a decline in defense spending. Although congressional Republicans attacked the changes, the chairman and service chiefs all stood behind it.

Obama's speech reflected the White House's view that ground troops would be less important in the future because the United States would not be fighting wars similar to those in Iraq and Afghanistan. And, because ground troops require significant budget support, defense spending could be reduced by a pivot to the naval and air forces that would dominate in conflicts in Asia. Dempsey disagreed, arguing it was unwise not to plan on future ground operations, but Obama decided to take this risk. During 2011, the Pentagon debated the role of ground troops in future warfare, and the resulting strategic risks and budget implications, eventually leading to the Pivot to Asia and the 2012 Defense Strategic Guidance.

During the fall of 2011, many analysts noted that the Pentagon seemed to be assuming that sequestration would not happen. In December of that year, Dempsey argued that at the Pentagon "we just literally have not had the intellectual bandwidth to think about and to do any of the analytics relating to sequester."[43] Additionally, the Pentagon was concerned that any items they proposed to cut would then become targets for later congressional budget reductions.[44] The 2012 presidential election also contributed to delays as many thought negotiations would be different if Mitt Romney were elected. The Pentagon finally began planning for sequestration in January 2013.[45]

Certainly, senior Pentagon officials were frequently quoted as predicting very dire consequences if sequestration happened.[46] There was support from key defense hawks in Congress, and particularly John McCain, to exempt defense from sequestration, and the White House worried that this might happen.[47] But the services did not lobby for an exemption. Instead, the service chiefs, Chairman Dempsey, and Secretaries Panetta and then Chuck Hagel (Panetta's successor) all followed the White House script, arguing that sequestration itself would be catastrophic for national security. But they all refrained from siding with the members of Congress who wanted to treat the defense budget differently.

Sequestration took effect on March 1, 2013. Of the $1.1 trillion in across-the-board cuts to discretionary spending that were required by FY 2021, defense was responsible for $454 billion. Originally, $55 billion had to come in FY 2013, which, by March, was already half over. The Pentagon's delays in planning meant it had only six months to absorb the cuts. But the American Taxpayer Relief Act of January 2013 not only delayed the onset of sequestration by three months, it reduced to $37 billion the reductions needed for FY 2013.[48] It also allowed the Pentagon to use prior year unobligated balances to absorb some of the cuts. As a result of these changes, sequestration meant a 5.7 percent reduction in the defense spending for that year.[49] Obama had previously exempted military pay from sequestration, meaning that a larger proportion of the cuts would have to be absorbed by procurement. But the rest of the cuts had to be spread equally across all programs and activities.

One month later, Obama requested $527 billion in the base defense budget for FY 2014. This budget request had been put together under the assumption that sequestration would not happen and thus it did not include the necessary reductions. The request did, however, include cuts to a number of items that members of Congress had traditionally opposed, including base closures, reductions in health benefits, and the elimination of certain weapons.[50]

The Pentagon also announced another strategic review in light of the likelihood of additional budget cuts. Chuck Hagel, who had taken over as secretary of defense on February 27, 2013, ordered the Strategic Choices and Management Review, or what became known as the "SCMR" (pronounced "skimmer"). Originally, this review was expected not to redefine the strategy but to tweak it in light of the decreased budget.[51] But soon everything was on the table.[52] Led by Deputy Secretary of Defense Ash Carter and Chairman Dempsey, the review was tasked with considering the feasibility of executing the current defense strategic guidance under multiple budget scenarios, including sequestration, as well as the more optimistic FY 2014 budget request.

The review began with the assumption that the cuts mandated by the BCA would remain in place; it then considered scenarios involving additional budget reductions over the next ten years: $150 billion (the FY 2014 budget request), $500 billion (the sequestration level), and $250 billion (the in-between scenario).[53] When the results were released in July 2013, they showed that the military could cope with the FY 2014 budget, would need to "bend" the strategic guidance if budgets came in at the in-between levels, and that cuts on the order mandated by sequestration would "break" the strategy and result in a smaller and force and a "modernization holiday."[54]

In October 2013, the government shut down for sixteen days because of partisan disagreement over budget cuts. Eventually, in December, another two-year budget agreement was reached that increased the BCA spending caps but maintained a firewall between "defense" and "non-defense" discretionary spending. Budget caps would increase through two subsequent additional budget agreements in 2015 and 2018. In March 2014, the Pentagon released the results of its QDR as well as the FY 2015 budget. The QDR reinforced the choices and narrative of the SCMR and of the Defense Strategic Guidance, including the need to make hard choices due to the constrained fiscal environment.[55] It retained the "win-spoil" force-planning construct, the shift from insurgency and stability operations to confronting traditional adversaries, especially in the Pacific Rim, and the reductions in end strength for the ground forces.[56] The FY 2015 budget request abided by the necessary budget caps, but for FY 2015 only; it requested $115 billion more over the five-year Future Years Defense Program than allowed by the budget caps, and was accompanied by a separate "Opportunity Growth and Security Initiative" that asked for an additional $26 billion in FY 2015.[57] The FY 2016 budget request exceeded the budget cap for all years, and subsequent budget requests continued this pattern into the Trump administration.

LEADERSHIP FROM THE CHAIRMEN

The period from 2009, when budget reductions were beginning to become a possibility, through sequestration in March 2013 spans three secretaries of defense—Gates, Panetta, and Hagel—and two JCS chairmen. The first chairman, Mullen, agreed to stay on after the Bush administration. When Mullen's second term expired, he was replaced by Martin Dempsey on October 1, 2011. Both Mullen and Dempsey had strong working relationships with their respective secretaries of defense. Mullen, however, was much more willing to offer advice that was independent of, and sometimes contradicted, that of the secretary. He also had a strained relationship with the White House, a legacy of debates over the war in Afghanistan, as explained in more detail below. Dempsey, by contrast, had a much less contentious relationship, in spite of the fact that he was opposed to defense budget cuts and thought the military had much less of a responsibility for solving the federal deficit problem. Besides disagreeing about the role of defense cuts in the budget crisis, Mullen and Dempsey also played very different roles in navigating the political dynamics of this budget environment.

From the available evidence, it appears that Mullen was not an entrepreneur in helping the services adapt their priorities to increasingly smaller budgets. Mullen was not a significant figure in Gate's efficiencies initiative, nor did he play a prominent role in finding the $400 billion in cuts Obama called for in April 2011. As explained in more detail below, it was JCS vice chairman James Cartwright who was most involved in the meetings between the Office of the Secretary of Defense and the services at which budget details and choices were hashed out.

Mullen did, however, play an important role in the larger question of how to address the federal deficit—namely, by establishing the link between deficits and defense. In late August 2010, Mullen told CNN that "the single most significant threat to our national security is our debt . . . The strength and the support and the resources that our military uses are directly related to the health of our economy over time."[58] Mullen did not directly call for cuts to the defense budget, although when he met then president-elect Obama, Mullen did indicate that if he stayed on as chairman he understood and accepted that defense would not be exempted.[59] But Mullen's argument offered a much more explicit rationale for why cuts to defense spending should be included in deficit-reduction efforts. Moreover, Mullen made this argument six months before Obama called for cuts to the defense budget and in direct opposition to Gates, who thought he had secured a promise from Obama not to cut military spending. Although Mullen frequently appeared with Gates as the secretary discussed program cuts and the dangers of further reductions, Mullen did not provide a strong endorsement of the results. Instead, Mullen was a much more forceful advocate for deficit reduction. Obama only proposed defense cuts in November 2010 due to pressure from liberals in Congress, and he remained concerned that his endorsement of defense cuts would fuel Republican arguments that he was weak on defense.[60] Mullen, by contrast, was out in front of both. However, he played no other role in the negotiations that led to the BCA. That agreement was a product of Congress and direct negotiations with the White House.

Dempsey enters the picture in the fall of 2011, after the BCA was in place and during the period when the defense department was grappling with additional budget reductions but also avoiding plans for how to cope with sequestration. In his confirmation hearing in July 2011, then Army Chief of Staff Dempsey told the Senate Armed Services Committee that he did not agree with Mullen. Instead, he explained that "national security didn't cause the debt crisis nor will it solve it. I agree that the national debt is a grave concern. Our national power is the aggregate of our diplomatic, military and economic influence. We have to address our economic stature, but that doesn't mean we can neglect the other instruments of national power."[61]

Dempsey did not publicly back the White House in the campaign to maintain parity between cuts to defense and non-defense spending, but neither did he campaign in favor of exempting defense from sequestration, even though there were willing Republican allies in Congress. And, although Dempsey was more involved than Mullen in the reviews that led to the division of budget cuts among the services, he did not cultivate a close or independent relationship with civilians in the Obama administration in an attempt to influence the outcome of budget decisions.

TWO PUZZLES

From 2009 through sequestration, the service chiefs were repeatedly forced to reconsider their budget priorities in the face of funding limitations they saw as increasingly dire and that proved to be resilient. Although the service chiefs, and especially the heads of the army and marine corps, did voice some dissent, this period is characterized more by consensus among the service chiefs and support for President Obama's policy. This history, however, presents two puzzles.

The first has to do with why the service chiefs didn't break with the president and collude with the Republican members of Congress who offered to exempt the defense department from most of the impacts of sequestration. Such an exemption was no doubt preferred by each of the service chiefs as well as by Secretary Panetta. Moreover, historically such collusion is not uncommon. But even though Obama was considered by many in the military to be weak on national security, the service chiefs stood behind his insistence on parity between defense and non-defense spending.

The second puzzle is why the army and marine corps accepted their reduced shares in forthcoming budgets as well the strategic shift toward Asia. Historically, budget reductions have been shared relatively equally among the services. But this time, the air force and navy were the clear winners. The army and marine corps both lost the bonuses that wartime supplementals had been providing for years. Plus, in FY 2008 the army's share of the base budget began to decline, eventually decreasing by almost 5 percent by FY 2016. Answering both questions provides important insights into the impact of the Goldwater-Nichols Act on interservice as well as civil-military relations.

Several Republican members of Congress publicly argued that the defense department should be exempt from sequestration, and they continued to do so up until sequestration took effect in March 2013. And while Secretaries Panetta and Hagel, the chairman, and service chiefs all predicted dire consequences for national security if sequestration were to occur, there is no evidence of any effort to create a coalition with Republicans. Secretary Panetta explains in his autobiography that he offered to put forward additional cuts to the Pentagon's budget if that would help encourage a budget deal and thus avoid sequestration. But the White House discouraged this out of concern that it might lead Congress to exempt defense but apply sequestration to the rest of the government.[62]

Why didn't the service chiefs or chairman independently pursue such a deal with members of Congress? Although Dempsey was opposed to sequestration, his tenure shows little evidence that he was willing to defy both the secretary of defense and the White House. Mullen, however, had done both. But he also had a reputation for being a budget hawk and had argued that the debt crisis had serious implications for national security. Further, the negotiations for what would become the BCA were conducted by high-level White House officials and congressional leaders. The defense department, and, indeed, most other cabinet officials, were excluded. As for the service chiefs, one possible explanation is that they assumed sequestration would be averted. But this doesn't explain why they didn't object to the inclusion of defense spending in the BCA.

The Tea Party movement offers what is perhaps a persuasive answer to this puzzle. Since the Reagan era, the service chiefs could count on the Republican Party's strong support for military budgets. But the Tea Party brought to Congress a number of budget hawks. Although those budget hawks subsequently proved willing to support increases in both the deficit and military spending, during the Obama administration they were a powerful force for budget reduction. They also proved willing to challenge incumbents within their own party. As a consequence, support for increases in military spending was at best uncertain and the potential for additional and more significant cuts a clear concern.

The second puzzle is why the army and marine corps did not more strenuously argue against budget cuts that had a greater impact on ground troops. During 2011, Secretary Gates's efficiencies initiative cut key army and marine corps modernization programs. Gates also signaled he would support cutting the end strength in both services. The budget share issue became more significant during the summer and fall of 2011 as it became clear that finding "efficiencies" was not enough. Then, in January 2012 the secretary announced a rebalancing of strategy toward Asia, and with it, long-term implications for procurement and modernization funding that favored the navy and the air force. Subsequently, this was reinforced by the SCMR.

Prior to the 2011 Defense Strategic Review, the army intended to reduce its personnel levels as the wars in Iraq and Afghanistan were expected to wind down. Plans called for the army to go from 569,000 to 520,000 by 2015 and for the Marine Corps to reduce from 202,000 to 186,800.[63] But the strategic review led by Panetta considered cutting the army to 482,000 and potentially even lower, and the marine corps to 175,000.[64] Eventually, the FY 2013 budget would put the army at 480,000 and the marine corps at 182,000.[65] If the cuts from sequestration became permanent, all of the services would have to shrink, but, again, the plan in the SCMR hurt the ground services more, with the army potentially going as low as 380,000 and the marine corps between 150,000 and 175,000.[66] Given the strategic rebalance toward Asia, the SCMR prioritized investments aimed at countering anti-access and area-denial threats, to the benefit of the navy and air force.[67]

Initially, both the army and marine corps pushed back. When Gates instructed the services to find $28 billion in savings, the army instead submitted a budget consistent with the lower level but did not specify what it would cut to get there, only promising it would find the necessary savings later.[68] Then, in October 2011, one month into his tenure as chief of staff of the army, Ray Odierno argued that the army's budget had not grown as much as the other services and thus could not absorb as many reductions.[69] He dismissed the increases due to Iraq and Afghanistan as ongoing operations, not additional funding for procurement or modernization. Army secretary John McHugh went further, telling an Association of the United States Army news conference that any reductions should be shared among the services: "I'm operating under one-third, one-third, one-third . . . If that changes, it won't be because I suggested it."[70] Marine corps commandant Jim Amos also argued that the marines and navy deserved a larger share of the budget.[71]

Initially, Mullen worried that budget cuts would mean an open competition between the services for money.[72] Early in his tenure in the Bush administration, Mullen testified that equal budget shares among the services had been good for national security and did not need to change significantly.[73] But shortly before leaving office, he changed his mind and argued that equal budget shares were no longer appropriate.[74] Dempsey was more inclined to continue the traditional one-third split, but by his tenure the groundwork had already been set for the Asia rebalance as well as downsizing in Iraq and Afghanistan. As explained by JCS vice chairman Winnefeld in August 2011, when Mullen was still chairman, "We made a very conscious decision . . . that we were not going to do what the department traditionally has done in a time when we were drawing down, and that is just hand out proportional cuts to the services."[75]

Why didn't the army and marine corps gain more traction for their arguments, especially after Dempsey became chairman? There are several possible explanations. First, Secretary Panetta had presided over a strategic review that justified unequal budget shares. Further, both Mullen and Dempsey backed President Obama's budget and strategy choices. It would have been politically difficult for the army and marines to gain traction in such circumstances.

A second possible explanation involves the army's view of the future.[76] Of all of the services, the army was in the greatest crisis. Exhausted from more than a decade of ground war, it was faced with twin budget problems: making the investments necessary to avoid a hollow army and paying for one of the most expensive "weapons" in the arsenal—personnel.[77] Budget cuts exacerbated these problems. Given the rise of the Tea Party, advocating for more defense spending would have been risky. A safer bet would be to allow a reduction in end strength through the voluntary separations that would go with the drawdowns in Iraq and Afghanistan. Then the army would wait. Eventually, either congressional alignments would shift, or the international situation would once again make ground troops seem a good investment. This bet proved prescient. By 2016, it seemed likely that defense budgets would increase significantly under the Trump administration.

Yet a third explanation is the "Pivot" or "Rebalance" to Asia. Over time, the services tend toward remarkably stable budget shares. The ongoing military operations since 2001 had upset this, to the benefit of the army. From FY 2001 through FY 2013, various supplemental budgets—but most specifically the Global War on Terror and then Overseas Contingency Operations—served to increase the army's base budget by 56 percent. Initially, supplementals accounted for only a small fraction of army budget authority, but by FY 2004, supplements were 57 percent of the army's base budget, and they grew to an almost equal portion by FY 2007.[78] In contrast, during this same period, supplements added 12 percent to the air force budget and less than 10 percent to the navy's. The Pivot to Asia promised to reverse this trend by emphasizing navy and air force investments. Viewed within the context of this budget history, reducing the army's budget share would seem a course correction. Odierno alludes to this logic in 2011 when he argues, briefly, that ongoing military operations have not increased the army's share of the *base* budget.[79] The other service chiefs, however, were not persuaded by Odierno's argument; they did not object to reductions in army spending.

The Pivot to Asia underscores that two budget battles matter for the defense department. One battle is over the top line. The service chiefs, however, were unlikely to be successful in lobbying for increased defense spending because both liberal Democrats and the Tea Party movement made concern over the federal deficit preeminent. The navy and the air force won the second battle over how to divide up the defense budget within this overall top line. The efficiencies initiatives, Defense Strategic Review, and SCMR each made cuts that would enable a larger budget share for the navy and air force, even without significant top-line growth. These cuts, in turn, gave the navy and air force incentives to support the president's budget requests.

The notion of a Pivot to Asia is usually credited to Secretary of State Hillary Clinton's October 2011 article in *Foreign Policy* magazine.[80] But the implications for the military's strategy and force structure began to appear almost a decade earlier, in the form of AirSea Battle, a plan to focus on countering anti-access and area-denial threats in the Pacific, specially from China.[81] In 2008 and during the time when army supplemental budgets were at their peak, Gates announced, as secretary of defense under George W. Bush, a focus on the Pacific Rim. This shift was emphasized even more in the 2010 QDR. Mullen was a strong proponent of this shift in strategy. And, although Dempsey as chairman questioned the wisdom of assuming stability operations would be less necessary in the future, he supported the rebalance strategy, concentrating his ire on the dangers of sequestration-level budgets.[82] The Pivot to Asia provided the services chiefs with a strategic guide for making budget cuts and a rationale for returning to normal budget shares.

OTHER ACTORS

Three other actors are central to this story about the role of the chairman in budget politics. Two of them—Congress and the combatant commanders (COCOMs)—are important because of their absence. The third actor, the vice chairman of the JCS, is important because of his ability to wield influence independent of the services and the chairman. But, similar to the chairman, this influence also comes at a cost if it neglects the service chiefs.

In their testimonies before Congress, both Mullen and Dempsey were willing to provide their own opinion, even if it contradicted administration policy. But neither chairman attempted to cultivate a relationship with members of Congress or pursue a back channel in an attempt to pursue service interests or increase defense spending.

Similarly, the influence of the COCOMs was quite limited. In his autobiography, *Duty*, Bob Gates explains that he held some forty meetings in his search for efficiencies and budget cuts.[83] Most of those meetings included Mullen, frequently they included the services chiefs, but only twice did they include the COCOMs. There is no evidence these senior military officers were more involved in budget drills under Panetta or Hagel. Moreover, as explained in chapter 2, the Joint Requirements Oversight Council and other bodies that were intended to increase the budget clout of the COCOMs remained captured by service interests. As explained in the next section of this chapter, this is in sharp contrast to the role of COCOM David Petraeus of Central Command, who was central to internal White House debates over strategy in Afghanistan.

Instead of the COCOMs, two other senior military leaders are important to understanding sequestration: JCS vice chairman James "Hoss" Cartwright and his successor, James "Sandy" Winnefeld. In 1986, the position of vice chairman was created partially so the services couldn't game the system to consider business only when the chairman was absent and a service chief would temporarily act as chairman.[84] During the sequestration saga, both vice chairmen played important roles in forging consensus among the services about how to implement a series of budget cuts and the resulting implications for strategy. Again, however, the roles they played were different. Although both had a strong relationship with the White House, Cartwright used this to assert his own independent advice and, in the process, lost the trust of the service chiefs.

Both Cartwright and Winnefeld had a much closer relationship to the White House than either Chairmen Mullen and Dempsey, or Secretaries Gates, Panetta, or Hagel. Cartwright also proved willing to contradict the chairman and secretary of defense and provide his own independent advice to the White House. Explained in more detail in the next section, a particularly sore spot for the Pentagon came during the review of strategy for Afghanistan. Critical of the options being offered by the military, Vice President Biden asked for an option focused on a robust counterterrorism strategy. When Cartwright developed this option, Mullen refused to provide it to the White House. Cartwright, however, argued that he was also an adviser to the White House and would not withhold the requested option.[85] He then defied Mullen to offer the White House an alternative view for a more limited troop surge.[86] Cartwright cultivated a back channel to the White House, informally providing information and analysis that increased his clout and made him Obama's first choice for a successor to Mullen.[87] But it also cost Cartwright the support of the service chiefs, who felt that he was not keeping them sufficiently informed and that he tended to offer his own advice rather than theirs. Cartwright's independence cost him the trust of the service chiefs. Because he could not be counted on to maintain their cohesion and support for administration policies, Obama took the advice of Gates and appointed Dempsey chairman instead of Cartwright.[88]

Cartwright was central to Gates's efficiencies initiatives. He cochaired the effort, along with Deputy Secretary of Defense William Lynn. In announcing the initiatives, Gates focused on finding waste and duplication and increasing efficiency within the department, and he argued that the savings could be shifted to pay for more military capability.[89] Cartwright, however, contradicted both claims. Making clear his feeling that "it's not a question of people being wasteful as much as a question of rebalancing the force," Cartwright saw this as an opportunity to shift military capabilities more in the direction of low-intensity conflict.[90] He also argued that he had "zero" confidence that any resulting savings could be captured by the Pentagon and reallocated within the defense budget.[91] Cartwright again charted his own path by stating, during the summer of 2011, that Obama's request for $400 billion in additional cuts to defense were likely not sufficient. As Gates was retiring, he argued against additional cuts, but, at the same time, Cartwright stated that "on his own" he was looking at how to make significant cuts to the defense budget beyond the $400 billion requested by Obama.[92] Cartwright also criticized the self-interested culture of the services and made changes to the Joint Requirements Oversight Council in an effort to increase the clout of joint recommendations from the COCOMs and also the degree to which choices would be made between service priorities.[93]

Winnefeld shared Cartwright's more sober predictions about future budgets. Rather than wait and hope for relief, Winnefeld thought budget pressures and debates would be around for a long time, and that the military should therefore begin to make some tough choices.[94] But Winnefeld's tenure was served under two secretaries of defense—Panetta and Hagel—both of whom shared this assessment. Even though Winnefeld was deeply involved in both the Defense Strategic Review and the SCMR and was thought to have a close relationship with the White House, there is scant evidence that he used his information and access to contradict the secretary, Chairman Dempsey, or the service chiefs. As a consequence, he maintained a productive and cooperative relationship with all of them, but especially the service chiefs.

AFGHANISTAN AND OTHER ISSUES

To what extent did the chairman play a similar role in other contentious issues? During the Obama administration, two key disagreements between civilians and the military were strategy and troop levels for the war in Afghanistan and the repeal of Don't Ask, Don't Tell. In both cases, Mullen displayed a willingness to contradict the president's preferences. Because Mullen had the respect of the service chiefs, he was able to force the president to compromise on both issues, and, in the case of Don't Ask, Don't Tell, advocate for a policy that was contrary to the chiefs' views.

AFGHANISTAN

Months of debate over issues related to the war in Afghanistan set the tone for, and heavily influenced, the administration's relationship with the chairman and the military. The process found the administration with a growing sense that most senior military officers, including Mullen, were attempting to force the president to agree to their preferred options. Repeated interviews, public statements, and leaks also led the White House to distrust these same officers. For Mullen, and for senior commanders in charge of the war, the experience left them feeling disrespected and that the White House was preferencing political concerns over strategic ones. Although the chiefs were not directly involved in the debate, Mullen's reputation was enhanced because he was seen as willing to back the commander in the field, even when confronted with the prospect of being fired by the president. This is in sharp contrast to Vice Chairman Cartwright, who was condemned for being too closely allied with the White House.

Obama came into office committed to shifting focus from Iraq to the "necessary" or "good" war in Afghanistan. The president immediately ordered what was supposed to be a quick review of strategy, progress, and options. The results led him to authorize an additional seventeen thousand troops—just over half of a pending military request that was inherited from the Bush administration. The review of Afghan policy would eventually consume months and lead to multiple high-level meetings among cabinet officials and military leaders. It culminated in Obama's December 1, 2009, announcement of a surge of thirty thousand additional troops to be deployed by the summer of 2020. It also included a shift in strategy from attacks aimed at killing terrorists to a counterinsurgency strategy aimed at stabilizing Afghanistan just enough so that U.S. forces could withdraw.

The Afghan review was inherently contentious for several reasons. For one, it had become increasingly clear that the United States could not win the war against the Taliban without a massive financial and political commitment over many years. Moreover, the outcome of the war in Afghanistan depended heavily on cooperation with unreliable and often corrupt or double-dealing allies in the government in Kabul, as well as in Pakistan. Combined, these issues led to a host of options, all with significant drawbacks. On top of this was the intense disagreement between Obama's advisers. Although some shifted positions during the course of the review, the debate tended to pit Vice President Joe Biden, National Security Adviser Jim Jones, and Cartwright against Gates, Mullen, and Secretary of State Hillary Clinton.

Mullen consistently sided with army generals David Petraeus and Stanley McChrystal, key actors in the debate who bore primary responsibility for crafting options. McChrystal, the commanding general in Afghanistan, had been Mullen's pick to replace David McKiernan, whose counterterrorism focus and lack of progress led to him being essentially fired in May 2009.[95] McChrystal, too, would eventually be fired in June 2010. The catalyst was an article in *Rolling Stone* in which McChrystal and some of his staff were quoted making derisive comments about the administration, especially Vice President Biden. But, as explained below, the article was but the latest in a series of public statements in which McChrystal seemed to contradict administration policy. McChrystal was replaced by army general David Petraeus, the head of Central Command. As COCOM, Petraeus was already involved in the review because his area of responsibility included Afghanistan.

During the nearly year-long period in which the administration debated Afghan policy, three interrelated themes consistently reemerged. One focused on quantity: the number of troops to be deployed, how quickly, and when they would begin to be withdrawn. Jones, others on Obama's national security team, and Cartwright were skeptical of the analysis that underpinned the Pentagon's unfulfilled request, inherited from the Bush administration, for 30,000 more troops. Although Mullen backed the Pentagon's math and argued that civilians should leave such matters to the military, Gates intervened.[96] The result was a revised request for 17,000 troops, which Obama authorized in February 2009. Soon after taking over from McKiernan, McChrystal told Gates that the situation in Afghanistan was much worse than he anticipated, and that an additional 40,000 troops might be necessary.[97] Until December, the administration would debate various options for a troop "surge." Although the Mullen-McChrystal-Petraeus team consistently presented multiple options for consideration, they were also consistent in their strong endorsement of the one that called for 40,000 additional troops. Biden, Jones, and Cartwright, as well as key civilian political advisers, felt the military repeatedly made 40,000 the "goldilocks option" by pairing it with alternatives that were clearly too big, too small, or too unlikely to succeed.

The second theme in the debate related to strategy. The military wanted to shift to counterinsurgency, which would require a much larger commitment of troops. But Biden supported a hybrid option focused on targeted counterterrorism attacks plus troops to train the Afghan police and military to fight the Taliban. This, in turn, would free up U.S. forces to focus more on counterinsurgency. When Mullen and McChrystal repeatedly failed to provide this option, Biden asked Vice Chairman Cartwright to develop it. The result was an option that totaled 20,000 troops—half for counterterrorism and half to train the Afghan police and military.

But fulfilling Biden's request came at the expense of Cartwright's already deteriorating relationship with Mullen. Opposed to any strategy except the one endorsed by McChrystal, Mullen told Cartwright not to present this option to the White House.[98] But the vice chairman insisted that he was also a political adviser and that the president and vice president deserved options when they requested them. The Biden-Cartwright option was endorsed by the White House national security staff in November.[99]

On December 1, 2009, Obama announced his decision during a speech at West Point. But the option he chose was a compromise developed by Gates. The plan called for 30,000 additional troops, plus potentially up to 10 percent more, to meet unforeseen developments, a focus on degrading the Taliban enough to turn the war over to Afghan forces, and asking the allies to provide an additional 5,000–7,000 troops.[100]

The third theme that runs throughout the debate over Afghanistan is mistrust between the White House and Petraeus, McChrystal, and Mullen. Key Obama advisers, but especially National Security Adviser Jim Jones, his deputy and then successor Thomas Donilon, and Chief of Staff Rahm Emanuel, thought the military was trying to box in the president so it would be difficult for him not to agree to the 40,000-troop increase. Obama had authorized an additional 17,000 troops in February and the military had committed to a review and assessment of progress before asking for additional increases. But before the review was complete, senior military leaders began to make the push for additional troops.

It began as early as McChrystal's June 2 confirmation hearing, at which he told the Senate Armed Services Committee that future troop increases might be necessary.[101] Later that fall, he used a speech to the International Institute for Strategic Studies to argue for a counterinsurgency strategy before the White House had made such a decision.[102] When McChrystal finally did his assessment and concluded that additional troops were crucial, a copy of his report was leaked to the *Washington Post* prior to an administration decision.[103] McChrystal's fate was sealed when *Rolling Stone* published the extended interview with the general and his staff in which they derided numerous civilian political appointees, questioned Obama's understanding of Afghanistan, and mocked Vice President Biden, calling him "Bite Me."[104] Soon thereafter, Obama fired McChrystal and replaced him with Petraeus.

Petraeus and Mullen created similar problems. In September 2009, Petraeus told the *Washington Post* that current troop levels in Afghanistan were inadequate.[105] He then convinced several leading Republican senators to question Obama's strategy and troop levels.[106] He also made use of interviews with journalists to create concerns about the president's strategy and plans for a drawdown in Afghanistan.

Mullen, too, leveraged Congress and the press to advocate for more troops. At his confirmation hearing for reappointment as chairman, he stated that additional troops would likely be necessary.[107] Similarly, he used his numerous interviews with reporters to question the adequacy of current troop levels through statements about the "deteriorating" situation in Afghanistan and references to a "tough fight" that will require additional troops.[108]

Although one could argue that McChrystal, Petraeus, and Mullen had a responsibility to give candid advice in their congressional testimonies even if this contradicted presidential policy, less excusable are the frequent comments to the media. Moreover, it is clear that the Obama White House, the president included, felt the military was trying to generate pressure that would force Obama to agree to forty thousand additional troops and a counterinsurgency strategy. In *Obama's Wars*, Bob Woodward provides numerous instances where the administration felt "boxed in" by the military, assumed they were the source of media leaks, or that they were willfully not providing the president with additional options.[109] In his memoirs, Gates explains that the relationship between the White House and senior military officers became "poisonous" and that key advisers saw Mullen as "insubordinate."[110] National Security Adviser Jones hinted that Mullen could be fired for not reining in McChrystal, and at one point Mullen offered to resign because the president no longer had confidence in him.[111] In December, when Obama reached his decision to send thirty thousand additional troops, the president threatened that if the military did not stop asking for additional troops, he would revert to an option that authorized only ten thousand.[112]

Throughout this process, the service chiefs played little role. There is scant evidence that Mullen or Petraeus consulted them. In an attempt to generate new thinking on Afghan strategy, Obama convened a meeting with the chiefs on October 30, 2009, but it did not lead to new options or their increased involvement.[113] In his book, Woodward states that Cartwright did consult the chiefs when he prepared the option preferred by Biden and that the chiefs supported Cartwright's option rather than that preferred by Mullen.[114] Why, then, did the chiefs continue to support Mullen but dislike Cartwright? Part of the answer can be found in the debate over allowing gay men and lesbians to serve openly in the military.

DON'T ASK, DON'T TELL

The service chiefs' continued backing for Mullen is even more surprising given the chairman's role in the repeal of Don't Ask, Don't Tell. President Clinton failed to get agreement that lesbians and gay men could serve openly in the military, and instead allowed a compromise whereby they could serve as long as they were not open about their sexual orientation. Obama came into office determined to quickly repeal the policy to allow gay men and lesbians to serve openly. The chiefs were all strongly opposed to such a policy shift. Mullen, in testimony on February 2, 2010, surprised many when he told the Senate Armed Services Committee that "allowing gays and lesbians to serve openly would be the right thing to do."[115] But he sided with Secretary Gates in asking for time to better understand how to implement this change with the least disruption.

Some in the White House continued to push for immediate repeal, which Congress legislated in July 2011. But because of intervention by Gates and Mullen, both Congress and the president agreed to postpone implementation for two months, pending the results of the internal military review.

The repeal of Don't Ask, Don't Tell and the debate over Afghanistan illustrate the willingness of an activist chairman to use his position to advocate publicly for policies that contradict those of the commander in chief. But these two examples also show that the chairman's power and influence is still largely derivative of support from the service chiefs. Although they were excluded from discussions about the surge, and Mullen contradicted their consensus on Don't Ask, Don't Tell, he was still seen as an advocate for the services. With respect to Afghanistan, he consistently backed the commanders in the field. On Don't Ask, Don't Tell, it was clear that Congress was going to legislate a repeal. Mullen's actions created space for the services to implement the change with less disruption.

In contrast, Vice Chairman Cartwright was seen as an advocate for the White House and too willing to offer his own advice regardless of service positions. Even though Cartwright was Obama's "favorite general," his independence cost him the support of the chiefs, and ultimately that of Obama.[116] The president appointed Dempsey to replace Mullen even though Cartwright had been his first pick.

SEQUESTRATION AND CIVIL-MILITARY RELATIONS

Obama entered the Oval Office at a time when concern for the federal deficit was mounting. This culminated on March 1, 2013, when sequestration was triggered by the inability of Congress to agree on budget cuts. The resulting budget reductions, plus the repeated use of continuing resolutions instead of new appropriations, forced the service chiefs to individually prioritize their spending recommendations and then revise those prioritizes downward. Congress did agree to raise defense spending caps in 2012, and again in 2013, 2015, and 2018. But it was only after the Obama administration left office that it became clear that deficit reduction, and parity between defense and non-defense budget cuts, were no longer politically salient.

The Obama administration was considered politically vulnerable on national security issues, tended to centralize decision making in the White House, and did not initially have strong opinions about defense spending and its role in deficit reduction. The addition of defense cuts was done to placate more liberal members of the Democratic Party and subsequently in an attempt to incentivize the Republicans in Congress to agree to fund some of Obama's domestic priorities and to avoid sequestration. In one sense, the president's priorities won out, as he was able to avoid deeper cuts in domestic priorities. But it would be incorrect to argue that Obama was also committed to reducing defense spending. Smaller defense budgets were a consequence of the strategy used to achieve other priorities.

The service chiefs, chairmen, and vice chairmen supported the commander in chief but in different ways. Dempsey followed the lead of the secretary of defense, who championed the administration's priorities both with Congress but also inside the Pentagon. Overall, the service chiefs also mostly cooperated, even though they had a chance to avoid budget cuts if they allied with some factions in Congress. The fact that the service chiefs didn't take this gamble is due more to the uncertain political landscape, and to the Pivot to Asia, than to the power of the chairman. There is little evidence that Dempsey had to coerce the JCS to support the president.

Mullen's tenure shows a different pattern of civil-military relations. His position on the defense department's role in deficit reduction contradicted that of Secretary Gates and was articulated prior to Obama's support. It is unknown whether Mullen's views influenced Obama. What is clear, however, is that Mullen supported preferences because he agreed with them, not because they were the budget policies of the commander in chief. This can also be seen in the strategic shift toward Asia. When Obama entered office, he prioritized stability operations and other nontraditional activities that were seen as necessary for conflicts such as those in Iraq and Afghanistan. When the president went to the Pentagon in January 2012 to announce the new strategy, this was merely the public articulation of a shift that had been in the works for years, dating back to Mullen's tenure as chief of naval operations. Similarly, Obama was forced to shift his preferences over the war in Afghanistan and the repeal of Don't Ask, Don't Tell because of advocacy from Mullen.

Unlike Colin Powell's role in the Base Force, Mullen and Dempsey illustrate a subtler lesson for U.S. civil-military relations. During the budget battles of the 2010s, neither chairman sought to overtly exploit Obama's perceived weaknesses on national security. What is clear, however, is that Mullen and Dempsey were able to interpret the authority given to them as chairman in different ways. Dempsey disagreed with policy choices but supported them nonetheless. With respect to the budget, the available evidence suggests that Mullen disagreed with the secretary of defense and supported the president, not because he was following orders from his commander in chief, but because he agreed with him.

This period also suggests that the position of vice chairman has implications for civil-military relations. A role created by the Goldwater-Nichols Act, the vice chairman is supposed to assist the chairman with his duties, but the specific responsibilities of the position, or limits, are not defined. According to Alice Hunt Friend, this means the vice chairman is often free to define his own portfolio.[117] For both Cartwright and Winnefeld, this meant cultivating an independent relationship with the White House and, in Cartwright's case, occasionally using this to contradict the service chiefs and secretary of defense and offer his own independent advice. As a consequence, analysts of U.S. civil-military relations should pay increased attention to the independent role and power of two members of the JCS: the chairman, but also the potentially more powerful vice chairman.

8

THE CHAIRMAN, THE JOINT
CHIEFS OF STAFF, AND
CIVIL-MILITARY RELATIONS

The chairman is widely recognized as an important player in defense policy making. Although the literature on U.S. civil-military relations assumes he wields power, his particular role is often underappreciated and obscured because of a tendency to discuss the military as if it is a unitary actor, merely the sum of its individual parts. In contrast, I focus specifically on the chairman, describing the formal and informal ways he can influence civilian control of the military, and offering guidelines for predicting when his political power is maximized. Specifically, I argue that if the chairman chooses to subvert civilian control—either directly or through its gradual erosion—he is most likely to be successful if the president or secretary of defense has political vulnerabilities that can be eased by alliance with the military. More importantly, however, whether acting as a policy entrepreneur or trying to broker agreement among the services, the chairman's success is dependent on the degree to which he respects norms and policy positions agree to by the service chiefs.

The Goldwater-Nichols Act—the most important reorganization of the defense establishment since its creation by the National Security Act of 1947—was focused on the opposite outcome. The act's goal was to create a chairman who would use his authority to help civilians in the executive branch improve military policy by providing advice based on defense needs rather than service preferences. With respect to defense budgets, the act did not lead to a substantial increase in such military advice, or "jointness." It did, however, increase the need for civilian policy makers to rely on, and thus compromise with, the chairman. Moreover, as the next section shows, civilians have only themselves to blame for this outcome.

CONGRESS VERSUS THE PRESIDENT

It is not possible to understand the chairman's political agency without acknowledging the consistent and powerful role played by the service chiefs. It is the service chiefs within the structure of the Joint Chiefs of Staff (JCS) that limit the power of the chairman but also make the chairman's role so consequential for civil-military relations. The persistent power of the service chiefs is firmly rooted in the structure of American government, which divides civilians into two often competing groups: executives and legislators.

Chapters 3 and 4 showed the multiple attempts by civilians to improve military policy by changing the power and authority of the secretary of defense and the chairman. Although part of the motivation has been to strengthen civilian control, each group of civilians also has another goal: to create a decision-making process whereby their own policy preferences are more likely to win out when they conflict with those of other civilians. As a consequence, the organization of the JCS is only partially about civil-military relations. In addition, it reflects the experience of trying to manage rivalry between the services and the legacy of past battles between defense secretaries, the White House, Congress, and the military.

Since the creation of the JCS in World War II, civilians have repeatedly tried to structure decision making such that the service chiefs speak for the interests of their individual services, but also to subordinate these preferences to what is best for the overall defense effort. Rather than imposing civilian preferences on the military, the goal has been for the military to coordinate and prioritize its diverse areas of expertise and offer joint advice to civilians. But this quest to create a JCS structure that is biased in favor of jointness has met with persistent and sustained resistance from Congress. Jointness may make it easier for the executive branch to execute policy. But it is rivalry between the services that generates the information and opportunities necessary for congressional oversight of, and sometimes resistance to, the president's policy agenda. This is why Congress has consistently acted to preserve the rights of the service chiefs to give their recommendations and opinions directly to Congress and without being filtered by the secretary of defense, the White House, or even the chairman.

The organization of the JCS reflects this struggle over jointness and policy control. Presidents Truman and Eisenhower both sought to centralize authority in the JCS and Office of the Secretary of Defense (OSD). Congress, however, only agreed to more modest changes in order to preserve congressional access to independent service advice. Secretary McNamara attempted to improve and manage service advice by using systems analysis and civilians in his office as his own source of expertise. But problems with the Vietnam War eventually prompted Congress to see McNamara's leadership as marked by arrogance and disdain for service expertise. The services eventually adopted systems analysis, but more importantly, they learned to keep their disagreements internal and present only unified opinions to those empowered to make choices between them. But even when offering consensus opinions, the individual members of the JCS never shed their service identities. The result was military advice that civilians found inadequate, either because it didn't make trade-offs or because it was watered down to banal commonalities. A string of military failures eventually prompted Congress to agree to more centralized authority in an attempt to increase jointness. The resulting Goldwater-Nichols Act gave more power to the chairman, among other changes, but still left him beholden to the service chiefs.

As chapter 2 showed, subsequent to the Goldwater-Nichols Act the chairman has become the public voice of the military. Moreover, jointness and joint military advice are more frequently part of public discourse than are parochial service perspectives. But chapter 2 also offered analysis calling into question the degree to which military advice is truly joint. The persistence of essentially equal budget shares, the prioritization of service interests in the budget process, and the unwillingness to revisit the roles and missions established in 1948 all suggest that service preferences still win out even if they are disguised as joint advice. Moreover, chapters 5, 6, and 7 provided evidence that these same dynamics are still at work in budget formation, but also in resolving disputes in other policy areas including military operations and personnel policy. This is in stark contrast to the frequent assumption that jointness is now more the norm than the exception.[1]

The policy battles over downsizing after the Cold War, attempting to transform the military into a high-tech fighting force, and the repeated budget drills that were part of an effort to avoid sequestration all suggest that the JCS remains focused on building consensus between the services. At times, the chairman has used his authority to convince the service chiefs to endorse policies about which they have yet to build agreement. But there is little evidence that the chairman has increased jointness by prying apart existing consensus or forcing the services to make trade-offs that advantage some but not others. To the contrary, there is considerable evidence that any chairman who tries to do so will likely fail. As discussed in the next section, this is because regardless of previous efforts to reorganize the defense department, the service chiefs still find themselves confronted with a zero-sum game that they have strong incentives to avoid or ameliorate.

SOLVING THE ZERO-SUM GAME

Because resources are finite, it is always possible that one service's gain is another service's loss. Even when defense budgets increase, there are usually too few dollars to fund every service priority or requirement. Plus, there is always the danger that civilians will use the military expertise of one service to poke holes in the programs of another. Consensus decision making solves these problems.

Chapter 3 explained how the service chiefs learned the value of consensus during World War II. The first interactions between the army and navy chiefs and the British quickly led to the conclusion that internal divisions do not produce influential recommendations. The U.S. side had a hard time working together as well as agreeing on policy recommendations. The British, in contrast, stood together behind well-staffed proposals and, as a result, the British proposals carried the day.

The service chiefs learned that interservice division allows others to make choices between them and that their collective influence suffers when internal divisions lead to weak policy recommendations or no recommendations at all. Consensus is power. And the internal rules and norms of the JCS have consistently reinforced the value of consensus. The only exception is during the beginning of the atomic era when defense budgets were tight and decisions about the nuclear mission had overwhelming consequences for future claims to resources and missions. Since that time, consensus has been the norm. The services almost never argue with each other in public. Instead, there is a consensus that each is allowed to argue for their own priorities and to criticize the president's defense budget but not each other's claims to it.

A key component of this consensus is the presumption of equality. The tendency toward equal shares of the budget is strong and persistent, and over time the structure of the JCS has reinforced this by refusing to allow one service to dominate. Since the creation and establishment of the air force as an independent service, new technologies have not led to a significant redistribution of missions or resources. The marine corps has, over the last twenty years, come to be recognized as a separate service rather than subordinate to the navy. Marine corps generals can head combatant commands and be chairman of the JCS. But this independence has not resulted in a budget that is split between four services. Neither did the land wars and military operations of the Cold War and after permanently increase the army's budget share. And even though special operations forces and OSD have both increased their budget shares, this has not significantly altered the division of dollars between the army, navy, and air force.

The cases of the post-Goldwater-Nichols Act era that are examined here show that the consensus over budget shares remains strong. Chairman Colin Powell successfully got the service chiefs to agree to the Base Force and Bottom-Up Review because these force structures allowed defense cuts to be split more or less evenly among the services. Similarly, during the Obama administration the pain of the defense budget reductions that eventually ended in sequestration was muted because it was accompanied by a reorientation of strategy toward Asia. This strategic shift in favor of the navy and air force helped to return the services to their traditional budget shares after decades of war in Iraq and Afghanistan had boosted army and marine corps spending. In contrast are Rumsfeld's two attempts at transformation. They failed, in part, because they involved picking winners and losers among the services. Instead, the services reached a consensus that they could each claim that their established preferences were suddenly "transformative."

An equally important component of maintaining consensus is agency. Each service expects to have an equal opportunity to influence resource decisions, regardless of the process that led to them. Under Obama, Secretaries Gates and Panetta both involved the services from the beginning as they sought to make the budget reductions necessary to avoid sequestration. Powell, on the other hand, largely excluded the services and instead used the Joint Staff to develop the Base Force. But he gave the service chiefs a chance to complain, argue, and amend the results. Both Obama and Powell got the support of the service chiefs because they allowed them to exercise agency, even though in Powell's case that led to few changes. But the case of Rumsfeld and transformation shows that it is the exercise of agency, not winning, that matters. Like Powell, Rumsfeld intentionally locked out the services. In both cases, the magnitude of the changes being proposed were significant and painful. But, in contrast to Powell, who then gave the service chiefs a chance to amend what would become the Base Force, Rumsfeld exercised his prerogative as secretary of defense: he presented the chiefs with a transformation agenda they were supposed to implement. Instead, the services spoiled Rumsfeld's plans with delays and eventually co-optation.

The original JCS zero-sum game pitted the service chiefs against one another. The services solved this collective-action problem through consensus decision making and by insisting on some agency over final outcomes. But the cost has been budgets that focus on sharing resources equally among the services rather than among national security problems, and advice that is watered down to the lowest common element. An additional problem, illustrated by H. R. McMaster in his book about the JCS and Vietnam, is that sometimes the JCS do not offer advice because they cannot agree on what to say.[2] In making the chairman the principal military adviser in place of the JCS, the Goldwater-Nichols Act tried to reduce these problems by offering a replacement solution for the zero-sum game—namely, by allowing the chairman to pick winners and losers. The chairman, at least in statute, is no longer first among equals but is more important than the other JCS members both in rank and influence. The case studies, however, suggest that the chairman's ability to exercise this influence is limited because it is largely contingent on maintaining support from the service chiefs.

Consider the experiences of Chairmen Powell and Mullen. Both provided policy inputs that contradicted the preferences of the service chiefs. Powell offered a plan to reduce defense spending by 25 percent at a time when both the services and secretary of defense thought such reductions were unwise. But instead of siding with Secretary Cheney, the chiefs supported Powell's Base Force. Mullen found himself in a similar situation. The services would have preferred to exclude defense spending from any deficit-reduction plan and could have made common cause with any of several members of Congress who were vocal in their agreement. Mullen, however, argued that national security spending had to be reduced and the service chiefs went to work coming up with a plan rather than lobbying to be exempted.

The experiences of Chairmen Myers and Dempsey offer a stark contrast. Myers tried to help Rumsfeld implement his transformation agenda over the objections of hostile services. He failed. Dempsey worked with Secretaries Panetta and then Hagel to broker budget reductions in order to avoid sequestration. But there is little evidence that Dempsey played a key role or that the services needed to be persuaded to cooperate. Instead, Dempsey's role seems largely irrelevant. Moreover, there is some evidence that the service chiefs resented his leadership and that their cooperation was more a consequence of concern for an uncertain budget future than leadership from the chairman.

What explains the differences in agency enjoyed by these four chairmen?[3] Although Powell and Mullen both offered policy advice that contradicted the preferences of the service chiefs, both chairmen had a reputation of being savvy political infighters who frequently used their skills to pressure civilian leaders to follow military advice. For example, Powell strenuously argued against the limited use of military force, eventually convincing President Clinton not to undertake some missions. Mullen expressed opinions that contradicted the views of the service chiefs. The acceptance of gay men and lesbians as full-fledged members of the military and the debate over the war in Afghanistan are but two examples. But Mullen also had a reputation for consulting with the chiefs, advocating for their positions, and for not using his access to the White House to broker his own agenda. Myers and Dempsey, in contrast, were both seen as advocates for the secretary of defense. Rather than convince civilian leaders of the value of military preferences, Myers and Dempsey were faulted for the reverse: being a partisan for civilians. The experience of Vice Chairman Cartwright offers a similar lesson. Valued by the White House for giving his own personal advice, the service chiefs vetoed Cartwright's promotion to chairman because he was not seen as an advocate for their views.

The cases examined here show that the leeway the chairman has to offer advice that contradicts that of the service chiefs is contingent upon his reputation with those same service chiefs. This reputation, in turn, is dependent upon the degree to which he is seen as a team player. But the "team" that matters is not the United States or the defense department. The most important team is the JCS. It is therefore unlikely that the chairman can repeatedly provide military advice that contradicts their deeply held norms and views. Although the case studies focus on budget policy, the brief examination of other policy issues included in each chapter suggests the dynamics are the same.

There is an additional factor that contributes to the chairman's ability to break the rule about only offering consensus advice: the likelihood of external allies. In the case of the Base Force, the service chiefs had every reason to expect defense budgets would decline even further. Powell's policy option offered a way to limit both future budget reductions but also uneven cuts to the services. During Rumsfeld's attempts at transformation, ongoing military operations meant that supplemental spending could be used to fund transformation rather than cuts to service budgets. And in the battle to avoid sequestration, the service chiefs might initially have thought that Republican hawks would be able to exempt defense from budget cuts. But it soon became clear that defense hawks would be overwhelmed by Tea Party fiscal conservatives who were willing to cut defense in order to reduce the deficit.

These cases reinforce an argument made decades ago by Arnold Kanter: external allies matter.[4] But in contrast to Kanter's analysis, which showed that split decisions among the service chiefs were more likely if one had a congressional ally, today's version means the service chiefs are likely to follow the chairman's lead if they doubt they can get a better deal elsewhere.

Besides showing that logrolling and problems making trade-offs—in other words, a lack of jointness—persist even after the Goldwater-Nichols Act, there are broader and significant policy ramifications beyond redundant service capabilities or lack of coordination. As Peter Feaver has argued, the civil-military problematique is how to determine the portion of political control civilians should give up in return for an effective military.[5] My analysis shows that even with a more powerful chairman, the U.S. military still faces difficulties assessing its own needs because norms about equality between the services remain strong.[6] In creating a more powerful chairman, civilians gave up a measure of control. But, as the empirical chapters show, the chairman often uses his role to protect service preferences, to the detriment of his ability to assess requirements for national security.

LOBBYISTS AND ENTREPRENEURS

Besides showing a consistent need for the chairman to respect JCS norms, the case studies help us understand the myriad ways the chairman's role offers opportunities for political action. The notion that the chairman or the military lobby for their interests is not new. The inherently political roles of senior military officers tends, however, to be obfuscated by the prominence of Samuel Huntington's notion of objective civilian control in the study of U.S. civil-military relations.[7] Huntington's strict division between civilian and military realms of responsibility, as outlined in *The Solder and the State*, is at best simplistic, but it may also distract from understanding the many ways that a profession is required to be political in order to advance its own interests and development.[8] As Risa Brooks argues, the prominence of Huntington's concept of objective civilian control can actually enable political behavior by creating an artificial line between advice as expertise and the political consequences of using that advice, and also by discouraging debate about the differing normative implications of political versus partisan behavior.[9]

In contrast to Huntington's objective civilian control, I assume the JCS should be expected to behave like all bureaucracies and seek to project their expertise and the institutions, norms, and procedures that produce it. As Andrew Bacevich has argued, the issue of civil-military relations is a political bargaining game, something Huntington himself recognized in 1961 when he explained that the services were already well-established political organizations that acted like interest groups.[10] Increasingly, scholars of civil-military relations assume that the line between the military's political and apolitical behavior is blurry and that the framing of alternatives, the options that go unmentioned, and foot-dragging are all attempts, as Richard Kohn points out, to get around civilian control.[11] With respect to budget decisions, the distinction is even more convoluted because civilian direction is usually not as precise as orders issued for the battlefield; in other words, what constitutes disobedience is murky.[12]

The chairman adds an important new variable to the political bargaining that is increasingly assumed to be at the core of the relationship between civilian and military leaders. Most discussions of the political roles played by senior military officers focus on individual policy debates or analyze groups of military actors, such as retired officers, the combatant commanders, or popular generals.[13] My contribution is to tease out how the chairman exercises political power and the conditions under which it is maximized.

The evidence provided in chapter 2 clearly demonstrates that after the Goldwater-Nichols Act, the chairman became the main spokesperson for the military. Whereas all of the service chiefs used to interact with the White House, it is now the chairman, as principal military adviser, who maintains both a formal consultative role with the White House as well as a back channel to the National Security Council, Office of Management and Budget, and other important presidential advisers. Moreover, that back channel is independent of the service chiefs and defense secretary.

In addition to his position, the chairman also accrues power because the White House expects him to be an internal power broker who convinces the service chiefs to support the president and secretary of defense, or at least to maintain a harmonious relationship with them. Members of Congress who disagree with the president's agenda, plus strong public support for the military, mean civilians within the executive branch have incentives to avoid public disagreements with the service chiefs, chairman, or well-known senior military leaders.[14] But even within the Pentagon, there are a variety of potential problems related to cooperation. Janine Davison, for example, explains that there are differences of opinion about whether the civilian guidance to the military is adequate, an encroachment on military prerogatives, or an abdication of civilian responsibilities.[15] Additionally, implementing the president's policy agenda means convincing members of the military to work with civilians in OSD, a form of cooperation that is increasingly difficult due to the actual and perceived partisan political differences that became more obvious during the Trump administration and after.[16] Besides encouraging cooperation, the chairman can muster the Joint Staff to provide analysis or support in cases where service components are less than cooperative, or when the Pentagon's civilian staff is inadequate.

In each of the cases presented here, civilian leaders relied on the chairman to persuade or cajole the service chiefs. President Bush and Secretary Cheney assumed that Powell either had or would get the support of the chiefs as he advocated for the Base Force. Rumsfeld may have failed to get transformation, but there is plenty of evidence he assumed Shelton and Myers would rally the services to the cause. Secretaries Gates and Panetta relied heavily on Chairman Dempsey, as well as Vice Chairmen Cartwright and Winnefeld, to help implement a series of budget reductions. In each case, the secretary expected the chairman to help manage the Pentagon.

The early years of the defense department presented a different management challenge. In the 1940s and 1950s, the defense secretary was a sleuth, trying to get information from the services in support of the president's policy agenda. Open rivalry between the services was both embarrassing and a serious impediment to the president's agenda. One of the secretary's chief headaches was trying to convince the services not to appeal to Congress to redress budget choices that were not in their favor. The first secretaries of defense argued for more and more staff to help with these management challenges.

McNamara took a somewhat different tack. Although he, too, argued for more staff, the role of OSD was to generate a contending source of expertise. McNamara used this to make choices among the services. Rather than persuade, he tried to command. This tactic was also favored decades later by Secretary Rumsfeld. Both met a similar fate: the JCS refused to cooperate.

The administrations examined here show that the secretary's management problems are more likely to be solved through persuasion and teamwork than the authoritarian chain of command that is sometimes assumed in the civil-military relationship. To help broker agreement between civilian policy and military preferences, the defense secretary relies on an increasingly larger staff—OSD has grown from a few individuals under Forrestal to five thousand under Obama's last secretary of defense, Ash Carter.[17] But, as Risa Brooks, Jim Golby, and Heidi Urben have argued, this civilian staff is often under-resourced or outmaneuvered.[18] As the sequestration case suggests, civilians are more likely to get cooperation if they work with service staffs and the JCS to reach mutually acceptable solutions instead of trying to generate their own independent answers to policy problems. When it comes to budgets, the relative weakness of OSD is clear from the fact that when the services submit their lists of unfunded requirements to Congress—a process that presents a direct challenge to the president's budget request— the Pentagon's civilian leadership may ask to see the lists before they are submitted, but it seldom succeeds or even tries to change them.

But the experiences of Cheney and Gates also show another shift in budget politics. Now the secretary also has to consider the relationship between the chairman and the White House. Chairman Powell lobbied the president to accept the Base Force even though Cheney argued that Russia remained a serious competitor. Mullen made Secretary Gates's job harder because he had an independent relationship with the White House, which he used to offer policy alternatives that contradicted those of the secretary. The formal authority of the chairman and the access it provides means he is able to forge an independent relationship with the White House that can be used to upset choices made by the secretary of defense. In other words, the secretary now has to contend with policy entrepreneurs who wield military expertise the secretary may not have, and who may enjoy a better relationship with the White House.

The case studies also suggest that not every chairman embraces or maximizes their political power. Although Colin Powell raised concerns that the Goldwater-Nichols Act had created a powerful and political chairman, few of his successors have played a similarly powerful role as external power brokers or policy entrepreneurs. Mullen, perhaps, comes the closest with his willingness to assert a connection between the defense budget and deficit reduction and to do so in opposition to the view of Secretary Gates, consensus among the service chiefs, and before President Obama had reached this conclusion. But few other chairmen have chosen to play such outwardly powerful or independent roles.

Shelton offers a different model of how to exercise power. Although he made no secret of his disdain for Secretary Rumsfeld, he did not attempt to counter transformation by forging alliances with the White House or Congress. Instead, he opted for the quieter but very successful strategy of opting out.

Yet a third model can be seen in the experiences of Myers, Dempsey, and Pace. Each seemed to view their role as convincing the services to implement civilian policy directives, and not the reverse.

These different approaches to the role of chairman can't be explained by personal agreement with the policy of the president or defense secretary.

Certainly, Powell was motivated to come up with the Base Force partially because he disagreed with Secretary Cheney's view of events in the Soviet Union and then Russia and feared that the defense budget would be raided for a large peace dividend if he didn't offer an alternative. But Dempsey's experience provides a sharp contrast; Dempsey felt that the defense budget should be exempt from deficit reduction plans and disagreed with Secretary Panetta and President Obama, but he nonetheless followed the secretary's lead. Regardless of the statutory powers provided to the chairman by the Goldwater-Nichols Act, these case studies show that not all chairmen exercise power in the same way or choose to become a policy entrepreneur.

Additionally, it is important to note that the chairman's lobbying efforts and policy entrepreneurship focus on public appeals, structuring and informing debates within the White House, and either colluding with or threatening opposition to the secretary of defense. The case studies provide little evidence that the chairman sees Congress as either his constituency or a source of power to be manipulated. As stated in the Goldwater-Nichols Act: "The Chairman of the Joint Chiefs of Staff is the principal military adviser to the President, the National Security Council, and the Secretary of Defense."[19] Lobbying Congress by providing unfiltered advice and lists of unfunded "requirements," along with particularistic bonds between members and the military, remains the territory of the service chiefs.

While the case studies show that the chairman can be a powerful voice for military preferences, they also suggest that future research is needed to better understand the role of the vice chairman. In numerous instances examined here, he is relied on to play a role in organizing the services to help implement the president's agenda. James Cartwright's tenure, however, also provides evidence that the vice chairman can be a partisan for the White House, getting information from the services without the support of the service chiefs or chairman and sometimes in direct opposition to their preferences. But, similar to what happens to chairmen with an independent streak, Cartwright's experience shows that the services can impose costly sanctions on senior officers who are not seen as team players.

WHO WINS AND WHEN?

One indicator of the degree to which civilians control defense policy is who wins when military and civilian policy preferences collide.[20] During the era of interservice rivalry, the services frequently appealed to members of Congress for additional resources. Sometimes one service, usually the air force or navy, lost its battle for money or a particular weapons system to another service. Sometimes the services were able to convince Presidents Truman or Eisenhower to increase the defense budget. But the primacy of fiscal concerns among civilians meant that service desires often went unfulfilled. McNamara temporarily continued this pattern of civilian control with systems analysis. But eventually Congress tired of McNamara's seeming willingness to ignore service expertise. Growing concerns about the war in Vietnam eventually meant that McNamara stopped winning his battles with the services. After McNamara, increasing defense budgets made the question of who wins largely irrelevant. The cases examined here not only provide an important update to this story, they raise some additional concerns about civilian control.

The first case study looked at defense downsizing at the end of the Cold War. Chairman Powell designed the Base Force and the options that were adopted at the end of the Bottom-Up Review. Secretary Cheney disagreed with the Base Force and Powell engaged in a public relations campaign that convinced President Bush, and eventually Cheney, to jump on board. Under Clinton, when it became obvious that further budget cuts were likely, the results of Powell's analysis were essentially the same as the option adopted by Secretary Aspin. Although Aspin had conducted his own review, he is also on record advocating for deeper budget cuts, a position that was supported by many members of his and President Clinton's party. Further, when Aspin and Powell disagreed about strategy—Aspin favored "win-hold-win" but Powell wanted to plan for two major regional contingencies—Aspin was forced to adopt the strategy favored by Powell and the service chiefs. Similarly, whereas Aspin preferred threat-based planning, Powell won out with the "capabilities-based" approach. In case number one, it is clear that Powell scored multiple victories.

In the case of transformation, the services win, Secretary Rumsfeld loses, and the two chairmen share a split decision. Chairman Shelton won because he essentially ignored Rumsfeld's demands for transformation and watched as the services labeled their existing priorities as "transformative." Myers, in contrast, tried but failed to get the services to implement Rumsfeld's directives. Even though Rumsfeld had the backing of President Bush, and tried two different times to jump-start transformation, in the end he was unable to cancel major service programs and shift the funding. Although several major army programs were canceled, the army agreed to most of the changes and also managed to retain and reinvest these shares of the budget.

In the third case, sequestration, Chairman Mullen voiced support for reducing the defense budget to help with the federal deficit. He did so in spite of Secretary Gates arguing for stable defense budgets or at least smaller reductions. Mullen also made his endorsement during a time when Obama had yet to admit that the defense budget needed to be part of the negotiations over a future budget agreement. This was a win for Mullen, a defeat for Gates, but also a defeat for the service chiefs, who were more inclined toward the secretary's position. Once the budget negotiations required parity between defense and non-defense spending, Secretary Panetta and Chairman Dempsey worked closely with the services to get repeated agreements on smaller and smaller defense budgets. Importantly, they were also able to convince the chiefs to support President Obama's budgets and refrain from allying with members of Congress to exempt defense from the threat of sequestration. Score this a win for Panetta and Obama.

But what does it mean to win? Battles over the defense budget seldom take place in isolation. Moreover, any president must be mindful that each skirmish with Congress, or the military, has implications for future policy initiatives. Sometimes the question of who wins requires a broader perspective. For example, when the Soviet Union collapsed, there was strong support for drastic reductions in the defense budget in order to create a "peace dividend." Moreover, as Bush campaigned for reelection, he faced concerns that he had ended the Gulf War too early, and before destroying the Iraqi regime of Saddam Hussein. Powell may have exploited this to convince

Bush, and eventually Cheney, to endorse his Base Force. Similarly, Aspin and Clinton may have wanted further reductions, but they were both considered weak on national security issues. As such, criticism from the service chiefs and Powell may have created political problems beyond the defense budget. In both the Bush and Clinton administrations, allowing Powell to dictate the outcome of defense downsizing was likely a wise choice. Similarly, Obama would have certainly faced broader political problems if the service chiefs and Chairman Dempsey had balked at endorsing his budget reductions. In the case of transformation, Rumsfeld proved to be his own biggest liability. All the JCS had to do to defeat the secretary's policies was delay cooperation until Rumsfeld destroyed his own reputation with Congress and the president.

Besides complicating the politics of civilian control, my analysis of the chairman also has important implications for the quality of that control. Is civilian control in decline? One element of the answer has to do with the degree to which senior military officers dissent from civilian policy direction and the means by which this dissent is expressed. There is general agreement that active military dissent and its influence over policy outcomes has ebbed and waned since the services were brought together by the National Security Act of 1947. Presidents Truman and Eisenhower, for example, frequently found it necessary to bargain with activist service chiefs who used public dissent in an attempt to thwart numerous presidential policy initiatives.[21] Moreover, there is little disagreement that such dissent matters. Research by Jim Golby, Peter Feaver, and Kyle Dropp shows that more senior military leaders, including veterans, are speaking out against civilian policies and successfully influencing debates.[22] But, as Risa Brooks, Jim Golby, and Heidi Urben argue, public dissent doesn't capture the very real damage done to civilian control when military leaders tailor information, construct options, and engage in bureaucratic wrangling to thwart civilian policy goals, a problem they argue has increased since the end of the Cold War.[23]

There is plenty of disagreement about the degree to which this dissent and disruptive behavior erodes important norms about the role of the military in politics. The 2021 exchange in *Foreign Affairs* between Brooks, Golby,

Urben, Kori Schake, and Peter Feaver, for example, shows that the same instances of dissent can be interpreted variously as an erosion of such norms or as examples of their strength.[24] In part, these different interpretations are a function of assumptions about the causes of today's dissent: Is the military more likely to speak out because of the increased prestige given to it since the end of the Cold War, or, instead, is this dissent due to an unusually high partisan political environment? Interpretations also varying depending on expectations: Does civilian control mean the military always obeys, should only disobey in certain contexts, or that the military consistently implements policies even if it disagrees with them?[25]

A third theme in the debate over the quality of today's civilian control focuses on the role of civilians. Here there is plenty of agreement on a range of issues. Civilians too frequently seek to draw the military into what are essentially partisan not policy debates.[26] The civilian side of the Pentagon needs more training, attention, and support to compete with military staffs.[27] As Jessica Blankshain summarizes, there are numerous reasons to be concerned about the trend of appointing former military officers to national security positions that have traditionally been held by civilians.[28] When civilians defer to military authority, explains Polina Beliakova, this indicates an erosion of civilian control.[29]

But expectations for civilian activism vary. At one end of the spectrum are those who see civilian oversight and management of the military as a costly function that detracts from other policy ambitions or that is difficult because of a clash of cultures.[30] At the other extreme is the tendency to view civilian control as something available for the taking if only civilians had the courage to do so.[31]

My analysis suggests that civilian control of the military has been more problematic after the Goldwater-Nichols Act. Although the act created a powerful political agent in the chairman, the cases examined here show variation in how different chairmen have embraced or exploited their role. Powell and Mullen, for example, leveraged their office to act as policy entrepreneurs, using public advocacy and bureaucratic tactics to force presidents to give up their policy preferences in favor of ones held by senior military officers. Shelton, in contrast, demonstrates the political power of inaction;

he simply refused to help Rumsfeld implement his transformation agenda. Myers and Pace, on the other hand, actively tried to assist Rumsfeld with transformation but failed. But the variation between these chairmen is the key to the erosion of civilian control. Their political success was more likely to be limited by their relationship with the service chiefs than it was by their relationship with civilians. In other words, the greater agency for structuring the chairman's exercise of power lies with the military, not with civilians.

It is by no means clear that the JCS, on its own, would not have evolved to have a chairman that plays these external and internal brokerage roles. To the extent that the JCS is a political organization, it would be logical to do so. It is likely, however, that the Goldwater-Nichols Act accelerated this change. What is clear from the three cases presented here is that the chairman still faces a formidable foe should he choose to challenge consensus among the service chiefs or their established ways of determining budgets. The reverse, however, is more possible: the chairman can thwart the policy preferences of the president and secretary of defense.

Too often civilian control of the military in the United States is assumed to be a mandate to obey. In reality, it has always been an act of persuasion. Today the JCS and its chairman have more power and leverage, both because civilians value the political support they gain when they side with the military, but also because the senior military leadership now has multiple powerful actors to offer advice in the policy process at many levels. The result is a military that enjoys increased leverage to choose which civilian directives to follow, which to ignore, and which to co-opt. The Goldwater-Nichols Act, in combination with the evolution of the services as political institutions, has led to a power dynamic that can be the reverse of that often assumed in U.S. civil-military relations. Instead of being an agent of the president, the chairman can now lead on policy and the president may have multiple reasons to defer.

ACKNOWLEDGMENTS

This book has been a part of my life, in one way or another, for many years. As a consequence, I've incurred debts too numerous to capture here. But I'd like to acknowledge a few of the people who helped along the way. First, I owe Archie D. Barrett for introducing me to the subject of defense organization and the Goldwater-Nichols Act. He and Jim Locher were both generous with their time when I started this project. Similarly, Harvey Sapolsky has been an important source of encouragement, sage advice, and the needling necessary to make my arguments stronger.

Russel Rumbaugh is the expert in all things related to the management of the defense department, and I appreciate the very many times he was willing to engage in conversations about both grand ideas and tiny details. My dear friend and intellectual interlocutor Alice Hunt Friend was always ready to nerd out on civil-military relations. Those conversations not only improved this book, but she is responsible for rekindling my interest in this subject. Mac Owens and Risa Brooks provided critical advice and perspectives, as did two anonymous reviewers.

I have benefited from the research assistance of Jacob Poushter and Sonya Kelly and, at one time or other, the critical eyes of Eugene Gholz, Jordan

Tama, Sikina Jinnah, David Bosco, Jeff Colgan, Shoon Murray, Gordan Adams, and Tom Crosbie. The late Jim Clark kindly read the manuscript and reminded me that I had something important to say. At Columbia University Press, Kathryn Jorge made sure everything came together, and it was a pleasure to be copyedited by Ryan Perks, who not only made the manuscript read better but who productively engaged with the arguments in the book. Stephen Wesley made what is often a fraught process actually quite pleasant.

I love archival work and that is in no small part due to the assistance of the archivists and staff at the Truman, Eisenhower, and Kennedy Presidential Libraries, the National Archives and Records Administration, the Joint History and Research Office, and the History Office of the Office of the Secretary of Defense. The late Alfred Goldberg, in particular, was generous with his advice for how to locate and interpret information. To the practitioners on both sides of the civil-military equation who prefer to remain anonymous: thank you for your generosity, insights, and the occasional reminder that no matter how well I thought I understood something, sometimes I didn't.

During the life of this project, I traveled the world with Karen Gibson. Our adventures in places like Laos, Turkmenistan, Newfoundland, Morocco, our own backyards, and many places in between renewed my energy and spirits. Barry Cohen has been a dear friend throughout and helped introduce me to the pleasures of bowling in Abilene. Zia, as in all things, has been my companion, greatest supporter, and best critic.

To those I've accidentally omitted, I apologize. To the friends I've neglected, I'm sorry. And please don't burden anyone listed here with the conclusions or any errors found in this book. Those are all mine.

NOTES

1. STRUCTURE, POLITICS, AND INFLUENCE

1. Peter Baker, "How Obama Came to Plan for 'Surge' in Afghanistan," *New York Times*, December 5, 2009. Mullen later admitted he was wrong in advocating for the surge as well as nation building. See Fred Kaplan, "A Top U.S. Military Officer Finally Admits He Was Wrong About Afghanistan," *Slate*, August 23, 2021, https://slate.com/news-and -politics/2021/08/mike-mullen-afghanistan-biden-right-surge-concession.html.

2. "Dunford to Successor: In Tough Budget Times, Consider Quality Over Quantity," *Defense Daily*, May 30, 2019, https://www.defensedaily.com/dunford-successor-tough -budget-times-consider-capability-capacity/pentagon/.

3. Pace later explained that he should not have offered his personal views on the subject. Thom Shanker, "General Tries to Clarify Remarks on Gay Troops," *New York Times*, March 13, 2007.

4. Milley's call to Chinese leaders was first reported in Bob Woodward and Robert Costa, *Peril* (New York: Simon and Schuster, 2021).

5. Dareh Gregorian and Jesse Rodriguez, "Military Acted to Prevent Trump from Misus- ing Nuclear Weapons, War with China, Book Says," *NBC News*, September 14, 2021, https://www.nbcnews.com/news/military/milley-acted-prevent-trump-misusing -nuclear-weapons-war-china-book-n1279187.

6. See, for example, Peter Baker, Maggie Haberman, Katie Rogers, Zolan Kanno-Youngs, and Katie Benner, "How Trump's Idea for a Photo Op Led to Havoc in a Park," *New York Times*, September 17, 2020.

7. Robert Burns, "Milley Says He Was Wrong to Accompany Trump on Church Walk During George Floyd Protests," *Military Times*, June 11, 2020, https://www.militarytimes .com/news/your-military/2020/06/11/milley-says-he-was-wrong-to-accompany-trump -on-church-walk-during-george-floyd-protests/.

8. For the range of views, see Matthew Brown and Tom Vanden Brook, "Trump, Republicans Call Gen. Mark Milley 'Treasonous' for Calls with China," *USA Today*, September 15, 2021, https://www.usatoday.com/story/news/politics/2021/09/15/trump-rubio -accuse-general-milley-treason-over-woodward-expose/8346958002/, versus Lindsay Kornick, "Reporters and Democrats Defend Gen. Milley Contacting China's Top General with Concerns About Trump," *Fox News*, September 14, 2021, https://www.foxnews .com/media/reporters-democrats-defend-gen-milley-contacting-china-top-general.

9. For an example, see Carrie A. Lee, "Gen. Milley Reportedly Tried to Work Around Trump on Nukes. Did He Have Authority to Do This?," *Monkey Cage* (blog), *Washington Post*, September 15, 2021, https://www.washingtonpost.com/politics/2021/09/15/gen -milley-reportedly-tried-work-around-trump-nukes-did-he-have-authority-do-this /?utm_campaign=wp_monkeycage&utm_medium=social&utm_source=twitter.

10. Kori Schake, "The Deeper Problem Behind General Milley's 'Secret Phone Calls,'" *New York Times*, September 18, 2021, and Kori Schake, "The Process Is Working," *Foreign Affairs* 100, no. 5 (September/October 2021): 230–232.

11. For a summary of the key differences between Huntington and Janowitz, see Peter D. Feaver, "The Civil-Military Problematique: Huntington, Janowitz, and the Question of Civilian Control," *Armed Forces & Society* 23, no. 2 (Winter 1996): 149–178, and Risa Brooks, "Paradoxes of Professionalism: Rethinking Civil-Military Relations in the United States," *International Security* 44, no. 4 (Spring 2020): 7–44.

12. Steven L. Rearden's *Council of War: A History of the Joint Chiefs of Staff, 1942–1991* (Washington, DC: National Defense University Press, 2012), is an excellent history but does not attempt to analyze or theorize how the chairman has exercised power. Lawrence Korb's *The Joint Chiefs of Staff: The First Twenty-Five Years* (Bloomington: Indiana University Press, 1976) looks at how the service chiefs have fulfilled their formal roles rather than analyzing their political behavior. Other works, notably H. R. McMaster's *Dereliction of Duty: Johnson, McNamara, the Joint Chiefs of Staff, and the Lies that Led to Vietnam* (New York: Harper Perennial, 1998), focus on the politics of civil-military interaction but confine themselves to a specific issue or era.

13. For a summary of such concerns, see Gordon Nathaniel Lederman, *Reorganizing the Joint Chiefs of Staff: The Goldwater-Nichols Act of 1986* (Westport, CT: Greenwood Press, 1999), 57–60.

14. For concerns about the impact of both Powell and the Goldwater-Nichols Act on civilian control, see Richard H. Kohn, "The Erosion of Civilian Control of the Military in the United States Today," *U.S. Naval War College Review* 55, no. 3 (Summer 2002): 8–59; Eliot A. Cohen, "Playing Powell Politics: The General's Zest for Power," *Foreign Affairs* 74, no. 6 (November/December 1995): 102–110; and Heidi Urben and Peter D. Feaver, "The Consequential Chairman: How Colin Powell Changed Civil-Military Relations,"

Foreign Affairs, October 27, 2021, https://www.foreignaffairs.com/articles/united-states /2021-10-27/consequential-chairman.

15. Heidi Urben and Peter D. Feaver suggest that Powell's exercise of power is likely the exception rather than the norm, largely because Powell spent many years in Washington, DC, playing a role in various parts of the policy process. Urben and Feaver, "The Consequential Chairman."

16. Fred Kaplan, "Pete the Parrot Departs," *Slate*, October 5, 2007, https://slate.com/news -and-politics/2007/10/good-riddance-to-the-last-of-the-rumsfeld-generals.html.

17. Sometimes the political clout given to military advice can be inadvertent. See James Golby and Mara Karlin, "Why 'Best Military Advice' Is Bad for the Military—and Worse for Civilians," *Orbis* 62, no. 1 (Winter 2018): 137–153.

18. For a discussion of the use of military leaders to limit criticism of civilian leaders by other civilians, see Risa A. Brooks, "Militaries and Political Activity in Democracies," in *American Civil-Military Relations: The Soldier and the State in a New Era*, ed. Suzanne C. Nielsen and Don M. Snider (Baltimore, MD: Johns Hopkins University Press, 2009), 213–238.

19. The JCS also formally includes the Joint Staff and the Chairman's Action Group. But these actors are not central to my story, nor would their inclusion alter my analysis or conclusions.

20. James R. Locher III, "Has It Worked? The Goldwater-Nichols Reorganization Act," *Naval War College Review* 43, no. 4 (Autumn 2001): 95–115; James R. Locher III, "Taking Stock of Goldwater-Nichols," *Joint Forces Quarterly* 34 (Spring 2003): 10–16; Clark A. Murdock, Michele A. Flournoy, Christopher A. Williams, and Kurt M. Campbell, *Beyond Goldwater-Nichols: Defense Reform for a New Strategic Era*, Phase 1 Report (Washington, DC: Center for Strategic and International Studies, March 2004).

21. See especially Murdock et al., *Beyond Goldwater-Nichols*, Phase 1 Report, 37–45.

22. In *The Common Defense*, Sam Huntington argues that choices about military strategy or use of force are conducted in the "currency" of international relations, a context in which the president has the most power. Budgets, however, are conducted in the "currency" of domestic politics, where Congress has the advantage. See Samuel P. Huntington, *The Common Defense: Strategic Programs in National Politics* (New York: Columbia University Press, 1961), 3–5.

23. See Mackubin Thomas Owens, *US Civil-Military Relations After 9/11: Renegotiating the Civil-Military Bargain* (New York: Continuum International, 2011), especially 12–43.

24. Examples include Kohn, "The Erosion of Civilian Control," 8–59; Mackubin Thomas Owens, "Military Officers: Political Without Partisanship," *Strategic Studies Quarterly* 9, no. 3 (Fall 2015): 88–101; and Peter D. Feaver, *Armed Servants: Agency, Oversight, and Civil-Military Relations* (Cambridge, MA: Harvard University Press, 2005).

25. Amy Zegart, *Flawed by Design: The Evolution of the CIA, JCS, and NSC* (Stanford, CA: Stanford University Press, 2000), and Risa A. Brooks, *Shaping Strategy: The Civil-Military Politics of Strategic Assessment* (Princeton, NJ: Princeton University Press, 2008).

26. Carl H. Builder, *The Masks of War: American Military Styles in Strategy and Analysis* (Baltimore, MD: Johns Hopkins University Press, 1989), and Jeffrey W. Donnithorne, *Four Guardians: A Principled Agent View of American Civil-Military Relations* (Baltimore, MD: Johns Hopkins University Press, 2018). Builder's work is updated in S. Rebecca Zimmerman, Kimberly Jackson, Natasha Lander, Colin Roberts, Dan Madden, and Rebeca Orrie, *Movement and Maneuver: Culture and the Competition for Influence Among the U.S. Military Services* (Santa Monica, CA: RAND: 2019).

27. For a classic in this vein, see Nelson W. Polsby, "The Institutionalization of the U.S. House of Representatives," *American Political Science Review* 62, no. 1 (March 1968): 144–168.

28. For a discussion of the rationality behind congressional organization, see Kenneth A. Shepsle and Barry R. Weingas, eds., *Positive Theories of Congressional Institutions* (Ann Arbor: University of Michigan Press, 1995).

29. D. Roderick Kiewiet and Mathew D. McCubbins, *The Logic of Delegation: Congressional Parties and the Appropriations Process* (Chicago: University of Chicago Press, 1991).

30. For various examples of this connection, see Arnold Kanter, *Defense Politics: A Budgetary Perspective* (Chicago: University of Chicago Press, 1979); Daniel Wirls, *Irrational Security: The Politics of Defense from Reagan to Obama* (Baltimore, MD: Johns Hopkins University Press, 2010); and Harvey M. Sapolsky, Eugene Gholz, and Caitlin Talmadge, *U.S. Defense Politics: The Origins of Security Policy* (New York: Routledge, 2021).

31. Polina Beliakova, "Erosion by Deference: Civilian Control and the Military in Policymaking," *Texas National Security Review* 4, no. 3 (Summer 2021): 62–72.

32. For the role of the Chairman's Action Group, see Kevin Baron, "Inside the CAG: Dempsey's Inner Circle," *Foreign Policy*, October 12, 2012, https://foreignpolicy.com/2012/10/12/inside-the-cag-dempseys-inner-circle/.

33. The army, navy, air force, and marine corps are responsible for developing and training both equipment and personnel. But when these are used in military operations, that responsibility shifts to the combatant commanders (COCOMs). Some COCOMs are in charge of coordination for specific ongoing missions. These include transportation, special operations forces, and nuclear weapons. Others are responsible for coordination for military operations in a particular geographic area such as Africa or Europe. For more information about the evolution and composition of the COCOMs, see Andrew Feickert, *The United Command Plan and Combatant Commands: Background and Issues for Congress*, CRS Report No. R42077 (Washington, DC: Congressional Research Service, 2013), https://sgp.fas.org/crs/natsec/R42077.pdf.

34. While recognizing the different sources of power, the literature on civil-military relations tends to homogenize the civilians in the relationship, and especially those in the defense department. For a deep dive into the variations among civilian preferences, powers, and relations with military actors, including differences between the secretary of defense, other political appointees, and career bureaucrats, see Alice Hunt Friend, *Mightier than the Sword: Civilians in Civil-Military Relations* (Stanford, CA: Stanford University Press, forthcoming).

35. For example, Deborah Avant's *Political Institutions and Military Change: Lessons from Peripheral Wars* (Ithaca, NY: Cornell University Press, 1994) explains how the executive-legislative relationship has implications for civil-military relations and specifically limited war.

36. See, for example, Paul Y. Hammond, *Organizing for Defense: The American Military Establishment in the Twentieth Century* (Princeton, NJ: Princeton University Press, 1961), and Nathaniel Gregory, *The Role of Congress in the Department of Defense Reorganization Act of 1958* (Washington, DC: Congressional Research Service, June 2, 1975).

37. The history and intent of the Goldwater-Nichols Act has been analyzed by others, but that literature tends to focus on what happened rather than analyzing the implications in the years since passage of the act. For histories of passage of the act, see James R. Locher III, *Victory on the Potomac: The Goldwater-Nichols Act Unifies the Pentagon* (College Station: Texas A&M University Press, 2004), and Gordon Lederman, *Reorganizing the Joint Chiefs of Staff: The Goldwater-Nichols Act of 1986* (Westport, CT: Praeger, 1999). The Center for Strategic and International Studies conducted an assessment of whether the Goldwater-Nichols Act achieved its goals, but it focused more on policy outcomes rather than the policy process that led to these outcomes or on civil-military relations. For the conclusions of the study, see Murdock et al., *Beyond Goldwater-Nichols*, Phase 1 Report, and Clark A. Murdock, Michele A. Flournoy, Kurt M. Campbell, Pierre A. Chao, Julianne Smith, Anne A. Witkowsky, and Christine E. Wormuth, *Beyond Goldwater-Nichols: U.S. Government and Defense Reform for a New Strategic Era*, Phase 2 Report (Washington, DC: Center for Strategic and International Studies, July 2005).

38. Feaver, *Armed Servants*.

39. Huntington, *The Common Defense*.

40. Warner R. Schilling, Paul Y. Hammond, and Glenn H. Snyder, *Strategy, Politics and Defense Budgets* (New York: Columbia University Press, 1962).

41. Brooks, *Shaping Strategy*; and Owens, *US Civil-Military Relations After 9/11*.

42. Donnithorne, *Four Guardians*.

43. Risa Brooks, Jim Golby, and Heidi Urben, "Crisis of Command," *Foreign Affairs* 100, no. 3 (May/June 2021): 63–75.

44. Schake, "The Process Is Working"; Peter D. Feaver, "A Stormy but Durable Marriage," *Foreign Affairs* 100, no. 5 (September/October 2021): 232–235; and Risa Brooks, Jim Golby, and Heidi Urben, "Brooks, Golby, and Urben Reply," *Foreign Affairs* 100, no. 5 (September/October 2021): 235–238.

2. THE CHAIRMAN AND JOINTNESS

1. The term "Joint Chiefs of Staff" came into use in 1942.

2. This section extends analysis originally presented in Sharon K. Weiner, "Military Advice for Political Purpose," in *Mission Creep: The Militarization of U.S. Foreign Policy?*,

ed. Gordon Adams and Shoon Murray (Washington, DC: Georgetown University Press, 2014), 192–209.

3. I count comments by service chiefs, not articles in the newspaper. In other words, an article that provides comments by three service chiefs would be counted as three different comments.

4. Support for the military seems to be based on allegiance to the institution, not support for military preferences. See Kori Schake and Jim Mattis, eds., *Warriors & Citizens: American Views of Our Military* (Stanford, CA: Hoover Institution Press, 2016). For a summary of other reasons behind high public support for the military, see Heidi Urben and James Golby, "Five Pitfalls that Could Squander the American Public's Confidence in the Military," in *Reconsidering American Civil-Military Relations*, ed. Lionel Beehner, Risa Brooks, and Daniel Maurer (New York: Oxford University Press, 2021), 137–142.

5. Jim Golby, Kyle Dropp, and Peter D. Feaver, *Listening to the Generals: How Military Advice Affects Public Support for the Use of Force* (Washington, DC: Center for a New American Security, April 2013); Jim Golby, Kyle Dropp, and Peter Feaver, "Elite Military Cues and Public Opinion About the Use of Military Force," *Armed Forces & Society* 44, no. 1 (January 2018): 44–71; and Stefano Recchia, *Reassuring the Reluctant Warriors: U.S. Civil-Military Relations and Multilateral Intervention* (Ithaca, NY: Cornell University Press, 2015).

6. Prior to the Spanish-American War, the army and navy operated autonomously. The Spanish-American War, however, required the first real coordination when the navy was asked to take the army to Cuba and land there for an invasion. After the war, Congress raised concerns about inadequacies in planning for the operation but also about waste due to unnecessary duplication in purchasing supplies for the war effort.

7. For the most comprehensive analysis of problems with service cooperation, see U.S. Senate, Committee on Armed Services, *Defense Organization: The Need for Change*, 99th Cong., 1st sess. (1985), S. Prt. 99-86. Often referred to as the Locher Report after the Senate staffer who directed the study, the report was intended to provide rigorous analysis and documentation in support of the congressional reform efforts that culminated in the Goldwater-Nichols Act. Other discussions of these problems include Archie D. Barrett, *Reappraising Defense Organization* (Washington, DC: National Defense University Press, 1983); Barry M. Blechman and William J. Lynn, eds., *Toward a More Effective Defense: Report of the Defense Organization Project* (Cambridge, MA: Ballinger, 1985); and Robert J. Art, Vincent Davis, and Samuel P. Huntington, eds., *Reorganizing America's Defense: Leadership in War and Peace* (Washington, DC: Pergamon-Brassey's, 1985).

8. For multiple illustrations of the influence of service identity on priorities for strategy and weapons, see Carl H. Builder, *The Masks of War* (Baltimore, MD: Johns Hopkins University Press, 1989).

9. For example, operations in the Middle East primarily fell to the European Command until the 1980s, when Central Command was created. For a history of the organization

of the unified combatant commands, see Office of the Chairman of the Joint Chiefs of Staff, Joint History Office, *The History of the Unified Command Plan 1946–1993* (Washington, DC: U.S. Government Printing Office, 1995). World War II also saw the creation of the Strategic Air Command, the first of what would become specified or functional commands, each of which focuses on control of a particular type of military capability.

10. This problem is compounded by the fact that strategy is often so ambiguous it does not translate clearly into precise force requirements. Policy makers have incentives to be vague about strategy. There is also an argument that it is difficult or perhaps even impossible for countries to articulate meaningful strategies because of future uncertainties. See, for example, Richard K. Betts, *American Force: Dangers, Delusions, and Dilemmas in National Security* (New York: Columbia University Press, 2012), 232–271.

11. Historically, the JCS has been composed of the heads of the army, navy, and air force. The commandant of the U.S. Marine Corps was officially represented on the JCS by the chief of naval operations until 1952, when he was made an equal member of the JCS on those occasions when issues effecting the marine corps are considered. In 1978, the commandant became a permanent member of the JCS with the right to participate on all issues.

12. As quoted in U.S. Senate, *Defense Organization*, 5.

13. The incentive for the services to collude has long been recognized. See, for example, Samuel P. Huntington, "Interservice Competition and the Political Roles of the Armed Services," *American Political Science Review* 55, no. 1 (March 1961): 40–52.

14. See, for example, R. Russell Rumbaugh, "The Best Man for the Job? Combatant Commanders and the Politics of Jointness," *Joint Forces Quarterly* 75, no. 4 (October 2014): 91–97.

15. See, for example, Jeffrey G. Barlow, *Revolt of the Admirals: The Fight for Naval Aviation, 1945–1950* (Washington, DC: Naval Historical Center, 1995).

16. Similarly, the services each have an equal share of combatant commander positions. Prior to the Goldwater-Nichols Act, individual combatant command positions were usually filled by only one service. For example, Pacific Command was always led by a navy admiral. After the act, commands were supposed to be filled by the most appropriate joint officer, regardless of service. Yet there is evidence to suggest that such command positions are instead split evenly among the services. The leaders of combatant commands now come from multiple services, with no one service "owning" a particular command. But the positions rotate among the services, with all services having essentially equal shares of these leadership positions. This suggests that the selection of combatant commanders is the result of a service compromise intended to treat all services equally, as opposed to jointness. See Rumbaugh, "The Best Man for the Job?," 91–97.

17. Total defense spending in this figure excludes spending for defense agencies and other activities that fall outside of the army, navy, or air force.

18. Kevin N. Lewis, "The Discipline Gap and Other Reasons for Humility and Realism in Defense Planning," in *New Challenges for Defense Planning: Rethinking How Much Is Enough*, ed. Paul K. Davis (Santa Monica, CA: RAND, 1994), 114–118; Kevin N.

Lewis, *The U.S. Air Force Budget and Posture Over Time* (Santa Monica, CA: RAND, report number R-3807-AF, February 1990), 9–15; and Jim Cooper and Russell Rumbaugh, "Real Acquisition Reform," *Joint Forces Quarterly* 55, no. 4 (2009): 59–65.

19. A similar conclusion is reached by the CSIS study *Beyond Goldwater-Nichols*, which finds that service interests tend to win out over joint interests in the defense budget process. See Clark A. Murdock, Michele A. Flournoy, Christopher A. Williams, and Kurt M. Campbell, *Beyond Goldwater-Nichols: Defense Reform for a New Strategic Era*, Phase 1 Report (Washington, DC: Center for Strategic and International Studies, March 2004). See also Clark A. Murdock and Richard W. Weitz, "Beyond Goldwater-Nichols: New Proposals for Defense Reform," *Joint Forces Quarterly* 38, no. 3 (2005): 38.

20. Put into place during the tenure of Secretary of Defense Robert McNamara, the name of the process has changed periodically but the purpose of PPBS remains the same. Under Rumsfeld, the name was changed to the Planning, Programming, Budgeting and Execution System.

21. One exception would be the relatively small but growing part of the budget for special operations forces (SOF). Because the services have never embraced special forces as key to their mission, the SOF community has become adept at arguing for resources in other ways. See Alice Hunt Friend, "Creating Requirements: Military Capabilities, Civilian Preferences, and Civil-Military Relations" (PhD diss., American University, September 2019).

22. During the 1980s, these were called commanders in chief. Beginning in 1984, they were allowed to submit prioritized lists of requirements—Integrated Priority Lists—that were intended to inform JCS advice.

23. The degree to which the National Security Strategy and the National Military Strategy are produced in cooperation depends upon each administration and its organization of the National Security Council (NSC) and the NSC-led policy development process.

24. See, for example, testimony by Michael G. Vickers, U.S. Senate, Committee on Armed Services, *Improving the Pentagon's Development of Policy, Strategy, and Plans: Hearings Before the Senate Committee on Armed Services*, 114th Cong., 1st sess. (Dec. 8, 2015), and Kathleen J. McInnis, *Goldwater-Nichols at 30: Defense Reform and Issues for Congress*," CRS Report No. R44474 (Washington, DC: Congressional Research Service, 2016), 24, 29–30, https://crsreports.congress.gov/product/pdf/R/R44474/11.

25. Jerry L. McCaffery and Lawrence R Jones, "Reform of Program Budgeting in the Department of Defense," *International Public Management Review* 6, no. 2 (2005): 141–176. Reportedly, in 2014 the Obama-era Pentagon considered major revisions to PPBS in order to provide guidance to the services earlier in the POM process.

26. This timing problem is largely due to a disconnect between the eighteen-month service POM process, which corresponds to the PPBS cycle, and the twelve-month budget process, which determines when the Defense Planning Guidance is issued.

27. Richard M. Meinhart, "Vice Chairmen of the Joint Chiefs of Staff and Leadership of the Joint Requirements Oversight Council," *Joint Forces Quarterly* 56, no. 1 (January 2010): 147.

28. Erik W. Hansen, "Goldwater-Nichols—Failing to Go the Distance" (Strategy Research Project, U.S. Army War College, March 15, 2008), 23–24; Fred Gregory and Scott Maley, "Requirement Portfolios and the Joint Warfighter," *Army AL&T Magazine*, July–September 2012, 116–118; and Patrick Wills, "Joint Capabilities Integration and Development System (JCIDS) Changes" (presentation, Defense Acquisition University, October 2012; slides in the author's possession). According to the U.S. Government Accountability Office (GAO), until 2011, JROC meetings included a variety of service participants who frequently provided input about service perspectives on new capabilities. After 2011, however, meetings were limited to key stakeholders, but GAO reported a year later that it was unable to assess whether this change had made a difference. See U.S. Government Accountability Office, *Defense Management: Guidance and Progress Measures Are Needed to Realize Benefits from Changes in DOD's Joint Requirements Process*, GAO-12-339 (Washington, DC: Government Accountability Office, February 2012), 12.

29. Hansen, "Goldwater-Nichols," 24.

30. Jason Sherman, "Consolidated CoComs' Wish List Set to Influence FY-14 Budget," *Inside the Pentagon* 28, no. 14 (April 5, 2012): 1, 12–13.

31. Hansen, "Goldwater-Nichols," 23–24.

32. See, for example, Christopher Lamb, "Cross-Functional Teams in Defense Reform: Help or Hindrance?," *Strategic Forum* 298 (August 2016): 1–16. Especially notable is Wilson Brissett, "School of JROC," *Air Force Magazine* 100, no. 3 (March 2017): 54, which describes a JROC that is focused on consensus and the streamlining of decision making.

33. Wills, "Joint Capabilities Integration."

34. U.S. Government Accountability Office, *Defense Acquisitions: DOD's Requirements Determination Process Has Not Been Effective in Prioritizing Joint Capabilities*, GAO-08-1060 (Washington, DC: Government Accountability Office, September 2008).

35. U.S. Government Accountability Office, *Defense Management*, 2–3, 14–15. GAO also found that of the JCIDs proposals it reviewed, 70 percent came from the services with little joint involvement, and all were approved, often going forward in the absence of complete information about critical issues.

36. Christopher J. Castelli, "Cartwright Seeks Independent Look at Acquisition Requirements Process," *Inside Missile Defense* 17, no. 1 (June 1, 2011): 6–8.

37. This was also the conclusion of the CSIS *Beyond Goldwater-Nichols* study. See Murdock et al., *Beyond Goldwater-Nichols*, 37. The services have changed their own internal PPBS processes, but these changes seem intended to help each service better defend its priorities against joint actors, not to incorporate joint input into service resource decisions. See Leslie Lewis, Roger Allen Brown, and C. Robert Roll, *Service Responses to the Emergence of Joint Decisionmaking* (Santa Monica, CA: RAND, 2001).

38. Cooper and Rumbaugh, "Real Acquisition Reform," 61. For a similar assessment, see Business Executives for National Security (BENS), *Framing the Problem of PPBS* (Washington, DC: BENS Tail-to-Tooth Commission Report, January 2000), 21.

39. BENS, *Framing the Problem of PPBS*.

40. In 1993, the chairman led a study (*Chairman of the Joint Chiefs of Staff Report on the Roles, Missions, and Functions of the U.S. Armed Forces*), and in 1995 Congress mandated the Commission on the Roles and Missions of the Armed Forces. For a more recent discussion, see U.S. Senate, Senate Armed Services Committee, *Revisiting the Roles and Missions of the Armed Forces: Hearings Before the Senate Armed Services Committee*, 114th Cong., 1st sess. (Nov. 5, 2015).

41. Murdock et al., *Beyond Goldwater-Nichols*, 15, criticizes the chairman for his inability to make significant changes to service roles and missions.

42. See, for example, U.S. Government Accountability Office, *Unmanned Aerial Systems: Actions Needed to Improve DOD Pilot Training*," GAO-15-461 (Washington, DC: Government Accountability Office, May 2015); Thomas P. Ehrhard, "Unmanned Aerial Vehicles in the United States Armed Services: A Comparative Study of Weapon System Innovation" (PhD diss., John Hopkins University, June 2000); and Sandra I. Erwin, "Mid Air Collision: A Never-Ending Feud Over Roles and Missions," *National Defense* 91, no. 643 (June 2007): 32–35.

3. THE ORIGINS OF NORMS FOR THE JOINT CHIEFS OF STAFF

1. For example, in the 1930s, powerful bureaus in the army were those of the judge advocate general, inspector general, quartermaster, ordnance department, and the signal corps. See James E. Hewes Jr., *From Root to McNamara: Army Organization and Administration, 1900–1963* (Washington, DC: Center for Military History, U.S. Army, 1975), 3.

2. See D. W. Brogan, "The United States: Civilian and Military Power," in *Soldiers and Government: Nine Studies in Civil-Military Relations*, ed. Michael Howard (Westport, CT: Greenwood Press, 1959), 177, and, Hewes, *From Root to McNamara*, chap. 1.

3. The Dodge Commission, appointed by President McKinley to investigate problems in the Spanish-American War, concluded that the independence of the bureaus created delays and inefficiencies, but that part of the problem also stemmed from congressional micromanagement and detailed reporting requirements. See U.S. Congress, *Report of the Commission Appointed by the President to Investigate the Conduct of the War Department in the War with Spain*, vols. 1–8, 56th Cong., 1st sess., Document No. 221 (Washington, DC: U.S. Government Printing Office, 1900).

4. The Army Reorganization Act of 1903 created a general staff headed by a chief of staff. For details of the act and its changes, see Paul Y. Hammond, *Organizing for Defense: The American Military Establishment in the Twentieth Century* (Princeton, NJ: Princeton University Press, 1961), 10–12.

5. Hewes, *From Root to McNamara*, 97.

6. For a discussion on the navy's efforts at internal reform prior to World War II, see Paul Y. Hammond, *Organizing for Defense: The American Military Establishment in the 20th Century* (Princeton, NJ: Princeton University Press, 1961), chap. 3.

7. Demetrios Caraley, *The Politics of Military Unification* (New York: Columbia University Press, 1966), 14–16.

8. On the appropriations committees, the norm was to defer to subcommittee decision making and expertise. Thus, the key players for defense were the military and naval affairs subcommittees, not the entire appropriations committees. For authorization, the Committee on Military Affairs and the Committee on Naval Affairs were, in practice, separate. But, from the turn of the century until 1946 when these committees were merged into the Armed Services Committee in each body of Congress, the membership overlapped to a small extent and they regularly trespassed on each other's jurisdiction, although there was little effort to oversee army and navy matters together. See Elias Huzar, *The Purse and the Sword: Control of the Army by Congress Through Military Appropriations, 1933–1950* (Ithaca, NY: Cornell University Press, 1950), 27–29, 40–46. There appear to have been few complaints about these turf violations. See Huzar, 44–45.

9. With respect to appropriations, the House subcommittees conducted a much more detailed review than the Senate, which acted as an appellate court for those who had been denied funds in the House. This division of labor was a product of the sequencing of appropriations bills, which were considered first in the House and then given to the Senate.

10. Prior to 1951, yearly peacetime authorizations were typically less than 3 percent of the amount appropriated. Indeed, in studies of the role of Congress in defense spending before the 1960s, the role of the authorizing committees is seldom mentioned.

11. In *The Decline and Resurgence of Congress* (Washington, DC: Brookings Institution, 1981), James L. Sundquist chronicles and explains shifts in congressional power throughout U.S. history. For his discussion of the turn of the century, see 25–35.

12. Before the Bureau of the Budget was created in 1921, these requests went to the secretary of the Treasury.

13. Although the Budget and Accounting Act of 1921 required that no department, including the services, ask for more money than was contained in the president's original budget, the services often worked around this by informally providing information to members of Congress. Members would then formally invite the bureau chiefs to testify about these budget disagreements. See Huzar, *The Purse and the Sword*, 125–126.

14. Huzar, 47–52.

15. Samuel P. Huntington, *The Common Defense: Strategic Programs in National Politics* (New York: Columbia University Press, 1961), 129–135.

16. Huzar, *The Purse and the Sword*, 141.

17. Elias Huzar in *The Purse and the Sword*, his study of Congress and army appropriations, explains that members of Congress frequently asked service witnesses questions that were designed to tap into differences of opinion. Huzar explains that, although the services were afraid of retribution from the president and the Bureau of the Budget, they were also aware that "in the competition for appropriations the meek do not inherit the earth." Huzar, 128.

18. The service chiefs originally met as the Combined Chiefs of Staff, but during World War II, this came to be referred to as the JCS.

19. Roosevelt never formally specified duties for the JCS because he wanted them to be free to assume whatever responsibilities were required for the war effort. See Joint Secretariat, Historical Division, *Organizational Development of the Joint Chiefs of Staff, 1942–1989* (Washington, DC: Joint Chiefs of Staff, November 1989), 3.

20. Ray S. Cline, *Washington Command Post: The Operations Division* (Washington, DC: Department of the Army, 1951), 236, and Hammond, *Organizing for Defense*, 161–162.

21. Unification—Memorandum, "Keeping the Nation Strong," Box 17, Subject File: 1916–1960, Harry S. Truman Presidential Library.

22. Hammond, *Organizing for Defense*, 161–175. Hammond bases this conclusion on those reached by officers involved in the war, House and Senate committees that investigated the conduct of the war, and the army's own assessment of the war effort.

23. Caraley, *The Politics of Military Unification*, 20.

24. See Congressional Quarterly, *Congress and the Nation, 1945–1964*, vol. 1, *The 80th and 88th Congresses* (Washington, DC: Congressional Quarterly Service, 1965).

25. The act also contained provisions that let the navy retain its own air assets and that prevented the army from absorbing the marine corps.

26. The National Security Act of 1947 as printed in Alice C. Cole, Alfred Goldberg, Samuel A. Tucker, and Rudolph A. Winnacker, *The Department of Defense: Documents on Establishment and Organization, 1944–1978* (Washington, DC: Historical Office, Office of the Secretary of Defense, 1978), 36.

27. Steven L. Rearden, *The Formative Years: 1947–1950* (Washington, DC: Historical Office, Office of the Secretary of Defense, 1984), 136–137.

28. Originally, the first section of the law had been about the National Military Establishment (NME), but Congress, reasoning that it would "put first things first," changed the order of Titles I and II, putting the provisions for national security coordination before those establishing the NME. See R. Earl McClendon, *Unification of the Armed Forces: Administrative and Legislative Developments, 1945–1949* (Maxwell Air Force Base, AL: Air University Documentary Research Study, April 1952), 45.

29. See especially chap. 4 in Amy B. Zegart, *Flawed by Design: The Evolution of the CIA, JCS, and NSC* (Stanford, CA: Stanford University Press, 1999).

30. Hammond, *Organizing for Defense*, 237.

31. For a discussion of the Newport Agreement, see Rearden, *The Formative Years*, 401–402.

32. Doris M. Condit, *The Test of War, 1950–1953* (Washington, DC: Historical Office, Office of the Secretary of Defense, 1988), 521–522.

33. Rearden, *The Formative Years*, 132–141.

34. For details, see Condit, *The Test of War*, 520.

35. Condit, 520.

36. Huntington, *The Common Defense*, 384–385.

37. Walter Millis, *The Forrestal Diaries* (New York: Viking Press, 1951), 448–449.

38. Rearden, *The Formative Years*, 32. Forrestal used the War Council to develop a closer working relationship with the services and as a forum for discussing major policy issues. See Rearden, *The Formative Years*, 34.

39. For the fiscal year 1950 budget, Truman gave the JCS a ceiling of $15 billion and the chiefs returned a budget request of $30 billion. Forrestal, with the help of a group of officers called the McNarney Board, was able to get the JCS request down to $23 billion. As a bargaining ploy, Forrestal asked the JCS to develop two options, an "unhealthy" budget and a larger one, both of which would be presented to Truman. Forrestal hoped that the president would realize that $15 billion was too low and a compromise could be reach between the two figures. The chiefs, however, feared that the lower budget would be accepted. They divided the $15 billion by giving one-third to each service. This is the budget that Truman accepted.

40. Forrestal had not been Truman's first choice; indeed, he had annoyed Truman because he headed the navy's push against unification. Also, Forrestal repeatedly expressed opinions on political matters that Truman considered outside the jurisdiction of the defense secretary.

41. Hammond, *Organizing for Defense*, 245. For example, Secretary Johnson used dissent among the JCS in support of his decision to cancel the navy's proposed "supercarrier." In response, the navy challenged the air force's B-36 bomber, which could serve a similar role in strategic bombing. This prompted a fierce battle between the navy, air force, and Johnson, which paralyzed the JCS and interservice relations on most other issues. See Rearden, *The Formative Years*, 410–422.

42. Rearden, *The Formative Years*, 50.

43. C. W. Borklund, *The Department of Defense* (New York: Frederick A. Praeger, 1968), 121.

44. Borklund, 212.

45. Hammond, *Organizing for Defense*, 238.

46. Rearden, *The Formative Years*, 73.

47. Forrestal suggested either selecting one of the three service chiefs as the chairman or appointing a fourth person for the job. See Cole et al., *The Department of Defense*, 65. Originally, Forrestal had wanted a military chief of staff, but the Truman administration was concerned that this might be seen as a threat to civilian control. See Michael J. Hogan, *A Cross of Iron: Harry S. Truman and the Origins of the National Security State, 1945–1954* (Cambridge: Cambridge University Press, 1998), 201–202.

48. There were other problems identified by Forrestal, but these four were his main concerns. See U.S. National Military Establishment, *First Report of the Secretary of Defense* (Washington, DC: U.S. Government Printing Office, 1948), as printed in Cole et al., *The Department of Defense*, 63–65.

49. For the text of the Eberstadt report, see Cole et al., *The Department of Defense*, 65–75.

50. Creating a comptroller had been recommended by the Eberstadt subcommittee of the Hoover Commission. The amendments did not create a deputy secretary of defense because Congress had approved legislation to do so in February 1949.

51. The National Security Act had allowed them to make recommendations to the president and director of the budget.

52. Hewes, *From Root to McNamara*, 275–278.

53. Charles Wilson as quoted in Congressional Quarterly, *Congress and the Nation, 1945–1964*, 292.

54. Specifically, Senator Stuart Symington (D-MO) and his committee on airpower challenged the National Intelligence Estimates on Soviet missile developments. See Peter J. Roman, *Eisenhower and the Missile Gap* (Ithaca, NY: Cornell University Press, 1995), 36, 43–44.

55. Roman, 131.

56. The National Defense Education Act provided aid to improve U.S. education in the sciences.

57. Congressional Quarterly, *Congress and the Nation, 1945–1964*, 298.

58. Congressional concern for national security in the wake of Soviet developments, plus concern about money wasted due to interservice rivalry over missile technology, can be seen in Edward A. Kolodziej, *The Uncommon Defense and Congress, 1945–1963* (Columbus: Ohio State University Press, 1966), 255, and Nathaniel Gregory, *The Role of Congress in the Department of Defense Reorganization Act of 1958* (Washington, DC: Congressional Research Service, June 2, 1975), 3–4.

59. U.S. Senate, Committee on Armed Services, Subcommittee on the Air Force, *Airpower*, 85th Cong., 1st sess. (1957), S. Doc. 29, at 96.

60. Congress did, however, repeatedly limit plans for peaceful nuclear developments in the United States, including by reducing development of nuclear reactors in the United States in the mid-1950s.

61. Huntington, *The Common Defense*, 412–415.

62. Huntington, 412.

63. Huntington, 414.

64. Huntington chronicles the development of multiple intermediate missile programs in *The Common Defense*. In 1955, the secretary of defense announced his intention to decide between the air force's Thor and the army's Jupiter intermediate range ballistic missile programs, which, according to one military officer quoted by Huntington, were "about as alike as the Ford and the Chevrolet." No decision was made between the programs, however, and three years later both were put into production. Huntington estimates that producing both missiles cost $200 million over what would have been necessary to produce only one. Spending for ballistic missiles jumped from $631 million in fiscal year 1955 to $1.3 billion in fiscal year 1957. Huntington lists other duplicate programs that proceeded in tandem, including the air defense control systems being developed by both the army and air force, army and air force programs for antiaircraft missiles, and army and marine corps units being developed for counterinsurgency. See Huntington, 400, 414–415, and Congressional Quarterly, *Congress and the Nation, 1945–1964*, 291, 298.

65. Gregory, *The Role of Congress*, 3n.

66. Both Glenn Snyder and Samuel Huntington conclude that the New Look was more of an evolutionary change from the policies of Truman than a radical departure. Snyder explains that the new strategy was advertised as a major change, but that in reality, the most significant change was an increased reliance on nuclear weapons in more contingencies. Although the New Look also shifted budgets toward the air force and away from the other services, Snyder points out that Truman had also planned on increases in

offensive airpower. See Glenn H. Snyder, "The 'New Look' of 1953," in *Strategy, Politics and Defense Budgets*, ed. Warner R. Schilling, Paul Y. Hammond, and Glenn H. Snyder (New York: Columbia University Press, 1962), 492–503, and Huntington, *The Common Defense*, 85–88.

67. Eisenhower intended to involve the JCS in the determination of budget ceilings in the New Look. However, the JCS were aware of the economic assumptions that went into determining budgets and, even though they were told to determine their own defense budget, they were well aware of what the ceiling would be. For a discussion of the New Look and its formulation, see Snyder, "The 'New Look' of 1953." For Eisenhower's frustrations with the JCS, see David Jablonsky, *War by Land, Sea, and Air* (New Haven, CT: Yale University Press, 2010), 241–257.

68. Robert J. Watson, *The Joint Chiefs of Staff and National Policy, 1953–1954*, vol. 5 of the *History of the Joint Chiefs of Staff* (Washington, DC: Joint Chiefs of Staff Historical Division, 1986), 107.

69. Snyder, "The 'New Look' of 1953," 410–412. Former chairman Maxwell Taylor argued that Eisenhower saw the JCS as part of his administration, rather than merely the representatives of the military. Eisenhower expected them to accept public responsibility for the actions of the administration, regardless of their views or recommendations, and they were to avoid disunity in front of Congress or the public. Taylor goes on to point out that the new JCS were appointed for no specific term, thus implying that dissent might result in dismissal. See Maxwell D. Taylor, *The Uncertain Trumpet* (New York: Harper and Brothers, 1959), 18–20.

70. Eisenhower's emphasis on unanimity extended to prohibiting testimony on matters that had not been resolved. See Douglas Kinnard, *The Secretary of Defense* (Lexington: University of Kentucky Press, 1980), 63.

71. Wilson served as defense secretary from the beginning of the Eisenhower administration until October 1957. McElroy then took over and held office until December 1959. Eisenhower's third defense secretary, Thomas Gates, who served from December 1959 through January 1961, held office after the Reorganization Act of 1958.

72. Borklund, *The Department of Defense*, 123–124.

73. Kinnard, *The Secretary of Defense*, 54.

74. For the complete text of Reorganization Plan No. 6, see U.S. House of Representatives, Committee on Government Operations, *Hearings on H. J. Res. 264: Reorganization Plan No. 6 of 1953 (Department of Defense)*, 83rd Cong., 1st sess. (June 17–19, 20, 1953).

75. Defense Secretaries Marshall and Lovett did make a few organizational changes during the war. These included integrating some functions in the areas of supply management, military housing, technology information, and use of commercial transportation. For details, see Condit, *The Test of War*, 515. The text of Reorganization Plan No. 6 was based on recommendations made by Secretary Lovett as he was leaving office at the end of the Truman administration.

76. Under previous arrangements, the JCS itself determined who was to serve as executive agent for each command. This allowed important functions to be assigned independent

of the authority of the secretary, confused lines of command and responsibility, and weak-ened civilian control. It also resulted in military chiefs being assigned administrative responsibilities that should have belonged to the service secretaries. See Historical Divi-sion, Joint Secretariat, Joint Chiefs of Staff, "Role and Functions of the Joint Chiefs of Staff: A Chronology," Washington, DC, January 1987, 77.

77. The position of chairman was created in amendments to the National Security Act in 1949.

78. Eisenhower had asked Congress for greater authority to reorganize the executive branch, but this was denied, and he was given the same restrictions that had been applied to Tru-man when he made changes in 1949. See "Reorganization Bill Passes," *Congressional Quarterly Weekly Report* 11, no. 6 (1953): 185.

79. In the House, the plan was considered by the Government Operations Committee, whose chair, Clare Hoffman (R-MI), had also led House consideration of the National Secu-rity Act. Hoffman's committee recommended, by a vote of 14–12, that the House approve all of the plan except for those provisions dealing with the chairman. These, the com-mittee explained, might lead to militarism or a "single military commander with a super-staff." The House Committee on Rules denied a rule for floor consideration of the mea-sure, and therefore it could not be debated. In response, the Government Operations Committee approved, by a vote of 16–14, a bill that served to reject all of Eisenhower's reorganization plan. House approval of the committee's actions, however, was defeated by a vote of 108–235. The House therefore refused to reject Eisenhower's plan, and when the Senate took no action on the measure, it became law.

80. John C. Ries, *The Management of Defense: Organization and Control of the U.S. Armed Ser-vices* (Baltimore, MD: Johns Hopkins University Press, 1964), 167- 169.

81. General Ridgeway as quoted in Ries, 168–9.

82. Ries, 167.

83. The Defense Reorganization Act also made changes to the defense support agencies, increased the number of assistant defense secretaries, as well as other changes that are not directly relevant to the power of the JCS. For the text of the law, see "Department of Defense Reorganization Act of 1958–6 August 1958 (72 Stat. 514)," as printed in Cole et al., *The Department of Defense*, 188–230.

84. The secretary was also made responsible for eliminating duplication. See Cole et al., 198–201.

85. The 1958 law removed the service secretaries from the chain of command and replaced them with the service chiefs. The reasoning behind this change was that the chain of command ran through too many officials to be useful in emergencies or to enable quick reaction time.

86. "Defense Reorganization Comment," *Congressional Quarterly Weekly Report* 16, no. 23 (1958): 717–718.

87. One debate was whether to refer to collective service perspectives as "joint," "integrated," or "unified." Eisenhower had preferred one of the last two words so as to differentiate between integrated advice and simply the sum of all the individual service perspectives. The president went so far as to suggest that the JCS be renamed the "Military Chiefs of

Staff for Defense." The JCS, however, complained that replacing "joint" would involve huge amounts of time rewriting plans, orders, directives, and military texts, and was therefore not worth the effort. See Historical Division, Joint Secretariat, *Role and Functions of the Joint Chiefs of Staff*, 115–116, and Memorandum of Conference with the President by John S.D. Eisenhower, December 23, 1958, in folder for JCS-(5), Jan–Feb 1959, Box 4, Files of the White House Office, 3, Dwight D. Eisenhower Presidential Library.

88. Alfred Goldberg, *A Brief History of the Organization of the Department of Defense* (Washington, DC: Office of the Secretary of Defense Historical Office, January 1995), 41.

89. These issues revolved around the idea that the services objected to putting the JCS within OSD because they felt doing so would obscure their independent status and require them to answer to lower staffers within OSD. OSD was concerned that leaving the JCS outside of it would suggest that the military was beyond civilian control. See Goldberg, "A Brief History of the Organization of the Department of Defense," 41. See also Memorandum for the Secretary of Defense, December 19, 1958, from JCS Chairman N. F. Twining, Subject: Organizational Position of the Joint Chiefs of Staff, Files of the Office of the Secretary of Defense, Washington, DC; Memo for Mr. Dechert and Mr. Winnacker, dated December 10, 1958, from Brig. Gen. Robert H. Warren, USAF, Military Assistant to the Deputy Secretary of Defense, Files of the Office of the Secretary of Defense, Washington, DC; and Memorandum for Mr. Quarles, dated December 10, 1958, from Dr. Winnacker, Office of the Secretary of Defense, Subject: The Place of the JCS in the National Security Organization, Files of the Office of the Secretary of Defense, Washington, DC. Eisenhower claimed the whole debate was so insignificant it amounted to "straining at a gnat." Memorandum of Conference with the President by John S.D. Eisenhower, December 23, 1958, in folder for JCS-(S), Jan–Feb 1959, Box 4, 2, Files of the White House Office, Dwight D. Eisenhower Presidential Library.

90. Management and Organization Needs in the Department of Defense, September 23, 1959, in folder for Defense Reorganization (I), Misc., Box 1, Files of Ann Whitman, Dwight D. Eisenhower Presidential Library.

91. Ries, *The Management of Defense*, 193–198.

4. CREATING A STRONGER CHAIRMAN

1. For a more detailed explanation of these, and McNamara's utilization of them, see Alain Enthoven and K. Wayne Smith, *How Much Is Enough? Shaping the Defense Program 1961–1969* (New York: Harper & Row, 1971), and William W. Kaufman, *The McNamara Strategy* (New York: Harper & Row, 1964).

2. Paul Y. Hammond, "A Functional Analysis of Defense Department Decision-Making in the McNamara Administration," *American Political Science Review* 62, no. 1 (1968): 57.

3. Clark A. Murdock, *Defense Policy Formation: A Comparative Analysis of the McNamara Era* (Albany: State University of New York Press, 1974), 77–86.

4. For the rationale behind this shift, see David Novick, *A New Approach to the Military Budget*, RM-1759, RAND Project Memorandum, June 12, 1956, and David Novick, *Efficiency and Economy in Government Through New Budgeting and Accounting Procedures* (Santa Monica, CA: RAND, report number R-254, RAND, February 1954).

5. Stephen Enke, ed., *Defense Management* (Englewood Cliffs, NJ: Prentice-Hall, 1967), 7.

6. For details, see H. R. McMaster, *Dereliction of Duty: Lyndon Johnson, Robert McNamara, the Joint Chiefs of Staff, and the Lies that Led to Vietnam* (New York: Harper Perennial, 1997).

7. Edward J. Drea, *McNamara, Clifford, and the Burdens of Vietnam 1965–1969*, vol. 6 of the Secretaries of Defense Historical Series (Washington, DC: Historical Office, Office of the Secretary of Defense, 2011), 12. This shift was partly enabled by the exit of Generals Maxwell Taylor and Curtis LeMay, two divisive members of the JCS. But as chairman, Wheeler also refused to bring split decisions to the secretary of defense and instead let the chiefs know that meetings would continue until they reached an agreement. Lawrence Korb, *The Joint Chiefs of Staff: The First Twenty-Five Years* (Bloomington: Indiana University Press, 1976), 116.

8. U.S. Senate, Committee on Appropriations, Subcommittee on Department of Defense, *Department of Defense Appropriations for Fiscal Year 1965, Part 1: Procurement Programs Requiring Annual Authorization; Research, Development, Test, and Evaluation Programs*, 88th Cong., 2nd sess. (1964), 6, and U.S. House of Representatives, Committee on Appropriations, *Department of Defense Appropriations for 1965, Part 4: Secretary of Defense, Chairman, Joint Chiefs of Staff, Overall Financial Statements, Service Secretaries and Chiefs of Staff*, 88th Cong., 2nd sess. (1964), 678.

9. Jon Wayne Fuller, *Congress and the Defense Budget: A Study of the McNamara Years* (Ph.D diss., Princeton University, 1972), 151–152.

10. Drea, *McNamara, Clifford, and the Burdens of Vietnam*, 12. Moreover, the most contentious issues were about budgets, not the ongoing war in Vietnam. See also Arnold Kanter, *Defense Politics: A Budgetary Perspective* (Chicago: University of Chicago Press, 1979), 26.

11. For a description of these stages in the 1980s, see "Joint Staff Process," Files of Archie D. Barrett; and Mark Perry, *Four Stars* (Boston: Houghton Mifflin, 1989), 38–39.

12. William J. Lynn, "The Wars Within: The Joint Military Structure and Its Critics," in *Reorganizing America's Defense: Leadership in War and Peace*, ed. Robert J. Art, Vincent Davis, and Samuel P. Huntington (Washington, DC: Pergamon-Brassey's, 1985), 181–201, and William J. Lynn and Barry R. Posen, "The Case for JCS Reform," *International Security* 10, no. 3 (Winter 1985–86): 69–97.

13. Edward A. Kolodziej, *The Uncommon Defense and Congress, 1945–1963* (Norman: Ohio State University Press, 1966), 351. McNamara also reduced the power of the services by taking some common functions such as defense intelligence, research, and supply issues out of the individual services and giving them to the Joint Staff. See James E. Hewes Jr., *From Root to McNamara: Army Organization and Administration 1900–1963* (Washington, DC: Center for Military History, U.S. Army, 1975), 311–312.

14. Lawrence J. Korb, *The Fall and Rise of the Pentagon: American Defense Policies in the 1970s* (Westport, CT: Greenwood Press, 1979), 86–87. Korb also points out that, within one year, the first group of service secretaries McNamara appointed had all resigned.

15. Aaron Wildavsky, *The New Politics of the Budgetary Process* (Glenview, IL: Scott, Foresman and Company, 1988), 365–366.

16. Wildavsky, 366.

17. Enthoven and Smith, *How Much Is Enough*, 41.

18. Korb, *The Joint Chiefs of Staff*, 120.

19. Kolodziej, *The Uncommon Defense*, 361.

20. For example, see the exchange between the service chiefs and members of the House Armed Services Committee in McMaster, *Dereliction of Duty*, 310–311.

21. In the fiscal year 1970 defense authorization bill, the House Armed Services Committee included a provision to abolish the Office of Systems Analysis. The office was saved by the Senate, which blocked the provision.

22. For a history of these disputes, see Fuller, *Congress and the Defense Budget*, 330–437, and Congressional Quarterly, *Congress and the Nation, 1965–1968*, vol. 2, *The 89th and 90th Congresses* (Washington, DC: Congressional Quarterly Service, 1969), 827–830, 832–833, 840–867.

23. Arends, as quoted in Fuller, *Congress and the Defense Budget*, 268.

24. Members of Congress did this in two ways: they asked questions in hearings, and they used informal contacts as a source of information about service points of view. With respect to the latter, McNamara asked the committees to funnel their contacts through his office. Congress refused because it saw these relations as essential sources of information. See Fuller, 211–212.

25. Fullers' account of congressional defense politics under McNamara explains that this alliance between a service and the committees against McNamara became the norm. See Fuller, 419–425.

26. David C. Morrison, "Chaos on Capitol Hill," *National Journal*, September 27, 1986, 2303.

27. Morrison, 2305.

28. Although the Goldwater-Nichols Act was passed in 1986, it was actually the culmination of twenty years of executive studies, independent panels, and congressional hearings devoted to solving problems with a lack of jointness in the military. For this history and the legislative battles that came before the act, see James R. Locher III, *Victory on the Potomac: The Goldwater-Nichols Act Unifies the Pentagon* (College Station: Texas A&M University Press, 2002).

29. U.S. Senate, Committee on Armed Services, *Reorganization of the Department of Defense: Hearings Before the Committee on Armed Services*, 99th Cong., 1st sess. (Oct. 16, Nov. 14, 19, 20, 21, Dec. 4–6, 11, 12, 1985).

30. "Aspin Concept Papers—Improving Joint Officer Capabilities," February 4, 1986, Files of Archie D. Barrett.

31. Desert One had brought criticism that the military lacked useful or up-to-date contingency plans for certain eventualities. James Locher explains that he favored contingency

planning guidance because of his belief that there was inadequate review by OSD of non-nuclear contingency plans. He wanted this guidance to be provided in writing because it would be directed toward military officers who were located in operational command headquarters that were far from the Pentagon. See U.S. Senate, Committee on Armed Services, *Defense Organization: The Need for Change*, 99th Cong., 1st sess. (1985), S. Prt. 99-86, at 239.

32. The service secretaries had been identified as potential allies for the defense secretary to use in managing the military. To enable this, the House Armed Services Committee had favored partial integration of the civilian and military staffs within each service. This would have reduced the size of the bureaucracy in each service and made the services' civilian and military staffs more dependent upon each other, thereby increasing their cooperation. This, in turn, would increase the service secretaries' access to information and ability to manage the service. The Senate Armed Services Committee saw staff integration as more a means of reducing the size of the bureaucracy, not necessarily as a way of increasing the management abilities of the defense secretary. It balked at the degree to which the House wanted to integrate these staffs and instead insisted only on partial integration. Archie Barrett of the House Armed Services Committee laments that the "major concession of the entire conference on the House side" was to give up total consolidation of the military department staffs and accept the Senate's approach of combining only seven specific functions. See "Military Department Headquarters Reorganization," Files of Archie D. Barrett. For the rationale behind this staff consolidation, see Archie D. Barrett, *Reappraising Defense Organization* (Washington, DC: National Defense University Press, 1983), and "Aspin Concept Papers—Military Departments Reorganization," Files of Archie D. Barrett.

33. The law also changed the relationship of the service secretaries and their staffs to the defense secretary and specified that the undersecretary of defense for policy help the defense secretary prepare guidance for the chairman to use in the preparation of contingency plans.

34. President Reagan, Secretary Weinberger, and the services all favored continuing to allow the defense secretary more liberal reorganization authority. The Senate Armed Services Committee, however, was concerned that this would be used to work around congressional intent and therefore asked for repeal of the provision. James Locher, interview with author, April 2, 1996.

35. Goldwater-Nichols ignored some suggestions for reforming OSD. Several studies highlighted the office's tendency to micromanage rather than delegate management responsibilities or concentrate on the larger issues of planning, policy formation, and oversight. These studies include the Blue Ribbon Defense Panel from 1970, the Commission on Government Procurement from 1973, a U.S. General Accounting Office study from 1976, an internal OSD review from 1975, and the Defense Manpower Commission, in addition to U.S. Senate, *Defense Organization: The Need for Change*, and Barrett, *Reappraising Defense Organization*.

36. The intent behind this change was to increase jointness by reducing the need for the chairman to rely on the staffs of the services. Goldwater-Nichols also increased the size of the Joint Staff to 1,627 persons. The Senate Armed Services Committee had favored a limit of 1,617 while the House wanted the old limit of 400.

37. The House Armed Services Committee version of the bill had required the chairman to pass along all dissenting advice. The Senate, which originally had no similar provision, preferred that the chairman be given some discretion such that trivial or inconsequential advice could be omitted. The solution was to give the chairman some discretion but to express the intent of the committees, by using the bill's Statement of Managers Language, that this did not alter the chairman's responsibility to submit dissenting views or provide him with substantive discretion in information civilians.

38. While these tasks clearly fell within the job description of the chairman, in the past they had been done in a vague and imprecise manner. Although this was often due to a lack of direction and similar ambiguity from civilians, Goldwater-Nichols assumed that if such requirements were made, they would increase the quality of the results. The Senate and House Armed Services Committees both came to conference with a list of things for which they wanted the chairman to be responsible. The final recitation contained in the law was a combination of their two lists, with some minor changes in wording and emphasis.

39. Specifically, the law gave the president authority to reappoint the chairman to a third two-year term, an extension over past practice. The law also specifies that if the chairman is unable to serve out a term, his successor can finish the unexpired term and then also be reappointed to two full terms after that. To allow the president to appoint his own chairman, the law requires the chairman's term to begin on October 1 of an odd-numbered year. The House and Senate Armed Services Committees had major arguments over how long the chairman would serve and when the new terms would start.

40. The rationale behind creating a vice chairman was to increase the abilities of the chairman by giving him a deputy. This provision was endorsed by the services and provoked little dissent. The problem was the role the vice chairman should play. The Senate Armed Services Committee preferred making the vice chairman a member of the JCS, as a symbol of his equality with the service chiefs. The House Armed Services Committee, however, felt this would detract from the idea that the vice chairman was to be subordinate to the chairman and that it would result in the vice chairman offering an independent opinion along with the rest of the JCS members. There was also the danger that the vice chairman might come to represent his service in JCS deliberations. After lengthy debate on the issue, the vice chairman was not included in JCS membership but was still expected to make an "extremely important contribution" to the work of the JCS and the chairman. As for the services, they, too, wanted a vice chairman but preferred that officer not act as director of the JCS in the absence of the chairman. Instead, they preferred the current practice of rotating that position among the members of the JCS. Both the House and Senate Armed Services Committees saw this as an excuse for the services to downplay joint issues when the chairman was absent. See "Vice Chairman as a Member

of JCS," Files of Archie D. Barrett; U.S. House of Representatives, *Goldwater-Nichols Department of Defense Reorganization Act of 1986: Conference Report*, 99th Cong., 2nd sess. (1986), H. R. Rep. 99-824, at 110–111.

41. News Release, House Armed Services Committee, "House-Senate Conference Wraps Up Defense Reorganization Bill," September 11, 1986, 2, Files of Archie D. Barrett.

42. Because the combatant commanders are not in the Pentagon on a daily basis, their views were often underrepresented in the decision making that goes into budgets, strategy, contingency plans, and other matters. The services, however, were present and forcefully argued for their own preferences. Making the chairman the spokesman for the combatant commanders was intended to create more of a balance between combatant commander and service inputs. See "Aspin Concept Papers—Strengthening the CINCs," January 22, 1986, Files of Archie D. Barrett. Originally, the House Armed Services Committee had envisioned creating a Joint Commanders Council composed of all the combatant commanders and the chairman. This council would provide advice to the president and defense secretary as requested and would establish a routine means of communicating advice between the combatant commanders and the chairman. The idea, however, was abandoned. See Memorandum to: Chairman Aspin, From: Archie D. Barrett, Subject: The CINCs Bill, November 7, 1985, Files of Archie D. Barrett.

43. This last bit was controversial because it seemed to imply that the chairman rather than the defense secretary was responsible for the combatant commanders.

44. Specifically, the law states that the service secretaries are to assign all forces under their jurisdiction to the combatant commanders. The defense secretary is also allowed to make specific assignments. The combatant commanders were prohibited, however, from being given service forces that were used to carry out certain organizational and administrative functions. The goal of these changes was to clearly establish the right of the combatant commanders to control operational forces without allowing this to serve as an excuse for eliminating the services or allowing the combatant commanders to govern their organization and administration.

45. Examples would be for joint training exercises and regional contingencies. These budgets proved very controversial. The House Armed Services Committee wanted more funding for them. But the Senate Armed Services Committee was uncertain as to whether they were needed, and it was also concerned that they would create new bureaucracies at the combatant commander level. See "CINC Budgets," "Examples Where CINC Budgets Would Make a Difference," and "CINC Budget Issues," all from the Files of Archie D. Barrett. See also Major James A. Coggin, and John B. Nerger, "Funding the Sinews of War: The CMCs," *Armed Forces Journal International*, October 1987, 96–104.

46. The explosion at the marine barracks in Beirut in October 1983 had raised problems about the chain of command. Specifically, communications between Washington and the field, and including each of the services, were thought to be too long and convoluted. The Goldwater-Nichols Act specified that the chain of command was to run from the president to the defense secretary and then directly to the combatant commander, thus

bypassing all the intervening service commands. The president was allowed to alter the chain of command and to pass it through the chairman to facilitate communication and other command functions. One of the more controversial elements of the conference between the House and Senate Armed Services Committees was determining exactly how much authority the combatant commanders should get and how to ensure that the chairman would not be given command in place of the defense secretary. See Barrett, *Reappraising Defense Organization*; News Release, House Armed Services Committee, "House-Senate Conference Wraps Up Defense Reorganization Bill," September 11, 1986, Files of Archie D. Barrett; and U.S. House of Representatives, *Goldwater-Nichols Department of Defense Reorganization Act of 1986: Conference Report*, 115–129.

47. This part of the Goldwater-Nichols Act was quite specific. It established an occupational category within the military for the management of officers who are trained in and oriented toward joint matters. Called the "joint specialty," such officers would provide staff for the chairman and the combatant commanders. The law included very detailed provisions to ensure that officers had sufficient joint military education, training, and experience, that large numbers of them then go to joint assignments, and that they be promoted at rates equal to that of officers with only service experience. One thousand critical joint duty assignments were to be identified and thereafter filled only with officers having the joint specialty. All officers promoted to the rank of general or admiral were required to have specified amounts of joint education and experience, with further prerequisites for advancing to combatant commander or chairman. Finally, a transition period was specified during which the services were given firm deadlines for achieving these results. See "Aspin Concept Papers—Improving Joint Officer Capabilities," February 4, 1986, Files of Archie D. Barrett.

5. LEAVING THE COLD WAR BEHIND

This chapter is derived, in part, from a previously published article: Sharon K. Weiner, "The Politics of Resource Allocation in the Post-Cold War Pentagon," *Security Studies* 5, no. 4 (Summer 1996): 125–142. It is available online at https://www.tandfonline.com/doi/abs/10.1080/09636419608429290.

1. See, for example, testimony by Colin Powell, U.S. House of Representatives, *Hearings on the National Defense Authorization Act for FY 93: H. R. 5006 and Oversight of Previously Authorized Programs*, 102nd Cong., 2nd sess. (Feb. 6, 20, 26, Mar. 4, 1992); testimony by Richard B. Cheney, U.S. Senate, Committee on Armed Services, *Department of Defense Authorization for Appropriations for Fiscal Years 1992 and 1993: Hearings Before the Committee on Armed Services*, 102nd Cong., 1st sess. (Feb. 21, 1991); and Les Aspin, *The Bottom-Up Review: Forces for a New Era* (Washington, DC: Office of the Secretary of Defense, September 1, 1993).

2. For examples, see Stephen Alexis Cain, "Analysis of the FY 1992–93 Defense Budget Request," Defense Budget Project, Washington, DC, February 7, 1991; Andrew F.

Krepinevich, "The Bottom-Up Review: An Assessment," Defense Budget Project, Washington, DC, February 1994; and Andrew J. Bacevich, *American Empire: The Realities and Consequences of U.S. Diplomacy* (Cambridge, MA: Harvard University Press, 2002), 135.

3. This summary of the Base Force draws upon interviews conducted in the summer of 1991 with participants in the Base Force process on the Joint Staff, Office of the Secretary of Defense, National Security Council, and service and congressional staffs, as well as Lorna Jaffe, *The Development of the Base Force: 1989–1992* (Washington, DC: Joint History Office, Office of the Chairman of the Joint Chiefs of Staff, July 1993).

4. Originally, the Budget Enforcement Act set individual limits for defense as well as international and domestic discretionary spending. But, starting in fiscal year 1994, these were merged into one overall spending cap, with savings in one category used to offset increases in another.

5. The Budget Enforcement Act targets for defense were $289 billion in fiscal year (FY) 1991, $292 billion in FY 1992, and $292 billion in FY 1993 (all budget authority), whereas in FY 1990, the defense budget for FY 1991 was projected to be $332 billion. See Office of the Assistant Secretary of Defense (Comptroller), National Defense Budget Estimates for 1990/1991, March 1989.

6. Jaffee, *The Development of the Base Force*, 8–9.

7. See Jaffe, 9.

8. This analysis is based upon interviews conducted with staff of the J5 and J8 Joint Staff directorates, as well as within OSD, during January and March 1996.

9. Jaffee, *The Development of the Base Force*, 10.

10. Jaffee, 21–22.

11. Steven L. Rearden, *Council of War: A History of the Joint Chiefs of Staff, 1942–1991* (Washington, DC: U.S. Government Printing Office, 2012), 483.

12. Jaffee, *The Development of the Base Force*, 123.

13. Richard Halloran, "Cheney Criticizes Cuts in Military," *New York Times*, August 24, 1989, 20.

14. Jaffee, *The Development of the Base Force*, 39–41.

15. According to Powell, Cheney called him into his office and in a tense meeting asked the chairman whether or not he backed the president. See Colin Powell with Joseph E. Persico, *My American Journey* (New York: Random House, 1995), 455.

16. See, for example, Halloran, "Cheney Criticizes Cuts in Military."

17. President George H. W. Bush, Speech to the Aspen Institute Symposium, August 2, 1990, as printed in U.S. House of Representatives, *Subcommittee of the Committee on Appropriations, Department of Defense Appropriations for 1992: Hearings Before a Subcommittee of the Committee on Appropriations*, 102nd Cong., 1st sess. (1991), at 245.

18. This summary of the Bottom-Up Review is based on interviews conducted during January, July, and August 1993 and August 1994 with individuals in the Joint Staff, Office of the Secretary of Defense, Headquarters of the U.S. Army, National Defense University, and congressional staffers, as well as Les Aspin, *The Report on the Bottom-Up Review*

(Washington, DC: Office of the Secretary of Defense, October 1993). Input was also provided by Raoul Henri Alcala, Patrick J. Garrity, and Derek Johnson.

19. Les Aspin, *An Approach to Sizing American Conventional Forces for the Post-Soviet Era* (Washington, DC: House Armed Services Committee, January 24, 1992).

20. Prior to assuming the position of secretary of defense, Aspin had been a member of Congress and chair of the House Armed Services Committee. From this position, he criticized the Base Force, claiming it was not based on a bottom-up review and exceeded defense needs.

21. Jaffee, *The Development of the Base Force*, 22.

22. Jaffee, 12.

23. Jaffee, 19.

24. An article in the Washington popular press at the time explains that the Base Force "meant preserving the largest base force he [Powell] could get away with to satisfy, on the one hand, calls in Congress for a peace dividend and, on the other, the chief's reluctance to cut *anything*." Jon Meacham, "How Colin Powell Plans the Game," *Washington Monthly*, December 1994, 37. Emphasis in the original.

25. Jaffee, *The Development of the Base Force*, 34.

26. Jaffee, 39.

27. Unattributed quote in Don M. Snider, *Strategy, Forces and Budgets: Dominant Influences in Executive Decision Making, Post-Cold War, 1989–91* (Carlisle Barracks, PA: Strategic Studies Institute, U.S. Army War College, 1993), 18n44.

28. Unattributed quote in Snider, 18n45.

29. Aspin endorsed option C in his confirmation hearing for the position of secretary of defense. U.S. Senate, Committee on Armed Services, *Nominations Before the Senate Armed Services Committee*, 103rd Cong., 1st sess. (Jan. 7, 1993), at 43, 69, 82. See also Chairman Les Aspin, "An Approach to Sizing American Conventional Forces for the Post-Soviet Era, Four Illustrative Options," House Armed Services Committee, February 25, 1992.

30. Eric V. Larson, David T. Orletsky, and Kristin Leuschner, "The Bottom-Up Review: Redefining Post-Cold War Strategy and Forces," chap. 3 in *Defense Planning in a Decade of Change: Lessons from the Base Force, Bottom-Up Review, and Quadrennial Defense Review* (Santa Monica, CA: RAND, 2001), 36.

31. Larson, Orletsky, Leuschner, 24, 29, 30, 54, 56–57.

32. Robert S. Litwak, *Rogue States and U.S. Foreign Policy: Containment After the Cold War* (Washington, DC: Woodrow Wilson Center Press, 2000), 30.

33. F. G. Hoffman, "Strategic Concepts and Marine Corps Force Structure in the 21st Century," *Marine Corps Gazette*, December 1993, 71.

34. For a more contemporary critique of capabilities-based planning, see Sharon Burke, "The Pentagoner: The Long Slow Death of Capabilities-Based Planning," *Foreign Policy*, January 5, 2015, https://foreignpolicy.com/2015/01/05/the-pentagoner-the-long-slow-death-of-capabilities-based-planning/.

35. Larson, Orletsky, and Leuschner, 57, 73.

36. Larson, Orletsky, and Leuschner, 73–74.

37. John Lancaster, "Military Reshaping Plan Is Short of Clinton Goals," *Washington Post*, February 13, 1993, A4.

38. Powell with Persico, *My American Journey*, 447.

39. "Voters Polled Favor Powell Over Quayle for No. 2 Spot," *Wall Street Journal*, March 1, 1991, A10.

40. For a brief summary of serious but also trivial conflicts, see Bruce B. Auster, "Pentagon Culture Clash," *U.S. News & World Report*, July 12, 1993, 32.

41. Steven. V. Roberts and Bruce B. Auster, "Colin Powell Superstar." *U.S. News & World Report*, September 20, 1993, 7.

42. Barton Gellman, "Powell-Nunn Secret Deal Collapsed," *Washington Post*, January 29, 1993, A1.

43. See, for example, Powell's exchanges with the head of U.S. Southern Command and later U.S. Forces Command. In both cases, Powell overruled their objections and showed little concern about appeasing them. See Jaffee, *The Development of the Base Force*, 22.

44. Ronald H. Cole, *Operation Just Cause: The Planning and Execution of Joint Operations in Panama, February 1988–January 1990* (Washington, DC: Joint History Office, Office of the Chairman of the Joint Chiefs of Staff, 1995), 29.

45. For the evolution of the Powell Doctrine, see Walter LaFeber, "The Rise and Fall of Colin Powell and the Powell Doctrine," *Political Science Quarterly* 124, no. 1 (Spring 2009): 71–93.

46. Cole, *Operation Just Cause*, 2–3.

47. H. Norman Schwarzkopf, *It Doesn't Take a Hero* (New York: Bantam Books, 1992), 297.

48. James Mann, *Rise of the Vulcans: The History of Bush's War Cabinet* (New York: Viking, 2004), 184.

49. For a detailed discussion about the lack of cooperation, see Michael R. Gordon and Bernard E. Trainor, *The General's War: The Inside Story of the Conflict in the Gulf* (Boston: Little Brown and Company, 1995).

50. John M. Broder, "Air Force Chief Fired by Cheney: Military: Gen. Dugan Used 'Poor Judgment' in Discussing Possible Iraq Targets, the Defense Secretary Says," *Los Angeles Times*, September 18, 1990.

51. Some argue that the marine corps was so zealous in pursuing its part of the land campaign that its success hindered the ability of the United States to destroy more of Iraqi's Republican Guard elite military forces. See Gordon and Trainor, *The General's War*, part 2.

52. See, for example, Jon Western, "Sources of Humanitarian Intervention: Beliefs, Information, and Advocacy in the U.S. Decisions on Somalia and Bosnia," *International Security* 26, no. 4 (Spring 2002): 121, 125.

53. James L. Woods, "U.S. Government Decisionmaking Processes During Humanitarian Operations in Somalia," in *Learning from Somalia: The Lessons of Armed Humanitarian Intervention*, ed. Walter Clarke and Jeffrey Herbst (Boulder, CO: Westview, 1997), 157.

54. Western, "Sources of Humanitarian Intervention," 112–142.

55. Michael R. Gordon, "Powell Delivers a Resounding No on Using Limited Force in Bosnia," *New York Times*, September 28, 1992, A01.

56. Colin L. Powell, "U.S. Forces: Challenges Ahead," *Foreign Affairs* 71, no. 5 (Winter 1992): 32–45.

57. Western, "Sources of Humanitarian Intervention," 113, 136.

58. Earlier interagency discussions found the JCS opposing State Department and National Security Council proposals for an expanded mission focused on nation building. See Robert B. Oakley, "An Envoy's Perspective," *Joint Forces Quarterly* 2 (Autumn 1993): 45. See also Michael F. Beech, *"Mission Creep": A Case Study in U.S. Involvement in Somalia* (Fort Leavenworth, KS: School of Advanced Military Studies, United States Army Command and General Staff College, 1996), 10.

59. John R. Bolton, "Wrong Turn in Somalia," *Foreign Affairs* 73, no. 1 (January/February 1994): 60.

60. Some argue this shift was an intentional embrace of nation building by Clinton. Others argue that the problematic handover of the mission to UN forces had already inherently involved U.S. troops in a broader mission beyond humanitarian assistance. For these different views, see Woods, "U.S. Government Decisionmaking Processes During Humanitarian Operations in Somalia," and Walter Clarke and Jeffrey Herbst, "Somalia and the Future of Humanitarian Intervention," *Foreign Affairs* 75, no. 2 (March/April 1996): 70–85.

61. Beech, *"Mission Creep,"* 31–32.

62. Beech, 35.

63. "Gallup Presidential Election Trial-Heat Trends, 1936–2008," Gallup, accessed March 14, 2022, https://news.gallup.com/poll/110548/gallup-presidential-election-trial-heat-trends.aspx.

64. Rearden, *Council of War*, 483.

65. "Who's in Charge of the Military?," editorial, *New York Times*, January 26, 1993; and Richard H. Kohn, "Out of Control: The Crisis in Civil-Military Relations," *National Interest* 35 (Spring 1994): 3–17.

66. See, for example, Meacham, "How Colin Powell Plans the Game," 33–42.

6. TRANSFORMATION

1. Some argue that Bush deserves credit for the idea of transformation and that Rumsfeld embraced it because it was his job as secretary of defense and not because he initially thought it was a crucial shift in strategy. See Charles A. Stevenson, *Warriors and Politicians: US Civil-Military Relations Under Stress* (London: Routledge, 2006), 177–180.

2. For the official word on transformation, See Department of Defense, "Transformation Planning Guidance," April 2003, https://www.hsdl.org/?abstract&did=446256.

3. For a colorful illustration, see Dale R. Herspring, "Rumsfeld as Secretary of Defense," in *The George W. Bush Defense Program*, ed. Stephen J. Cimbala (Washington, DC: Potomac Books, 2010), 80.

4. Stevenson, *Warriors and Politicians*, 180. The practice of submitting UFR lists began in 1995 when House Armed Services Committee chairman Floyd Spence asked the service

chiefs how they would spend an additional $1.5–$2 billion. See U.S. House of Representatives, Committee on National Security, *Hearings on National Defense Authorization Act for FY 1996: H. R. 1530 and Oversight of Previously Authorized Programs*, 104th Cong., 1st sess. (Feb. 8, 22, 23, 28, Mar. 2, 8, 22, May 3, Aug. 2, 1995), at 406. Since that time, a senior member of the committee has sent a written request to the service chiefs for their unfunded requirements.

5. Thomas E. Ricks, "Rumsfeld Outlines Defense Overhaul; Reorganization May Alter, Kill Weapons Systems," *Washington Post*, March 23, 2001, A1.

6. U.S. Government Accountability Office, *Quadrennial Defense Review: Future Reviews Can Benefit from Better Analysis and Changes in Timing and Scope*, GAO-03-13 (Washington, DC: Government Accountability Office, November 2002), 6.

7. Tom Bowman, "Pentagon Faces Transformation: A Secretive Review, Fashioned by a Small Team at the Pentagon, Could Mean Radical Changes for U.S. Forces," *Baltimore Sun*, March 13, 2001, 1A, and Bradley Graham, *By His Own Rules: The Ambitions, Successes, and Ultimate Failures of Donald Rumsfeld* (New York: Public Affairs, 2009), 224–225.

8. Greg Jaffe, "Rumsfeld Aides Seek Deep Personnel Cuts in Armed Forces to Pay for New Weaponry," *Wall Street Journal*, August 8, 2001, A3.

9. Thomas K. Adams, *The Army After Next: The First Postindustrial Army* (Stanford, CA: Stanford University Press, 2008), 104.

10. See, for example, the account in Graham, *By His Own Rules*, 245.

11. Graham, 245.

12. Thomas E. Ricks, "Rumsfeld on High Wire of Defense Reform," *Washington Post*, May 20, 2001, A01.

13. See "Democratic Control of Senate May Change Defense Spending Number," *Defense Daily*, May 25, 2001, 1.

14. Graham, *By His Own Rules*, 246–247.

15. Bob Woodward, *State of Denial: Bush at War, Part III* (New York: Simon and Schuster, 2006), 38.

16. Graham, *By His Own Rules*, 246.

17. Graham, 247.

18. U.S. Government Accountability Office, *Quadrennial Defense Review*, 10.

19. Jaffe, "Rumsfeld Aides Seek Deep Personnel Cuts," A3, and Melinda Myers, "Myers Picked for Joint Chiefs," *Milwaukee Journal Sentinel*, August 25, 2001, A3.

20. Jaffe, "Rumsfeld Aides Seek Deep Personnel Cuts," A3.

21. Carolyn Khorneck, "Rumsfeld Pushes Base Closings, Cuts in B-1 Force," *Orlando Sentinel*, July 17, 2001, A4.

22. "The Rumsfeld Death Watch," *Slate*, August 7, 2001, https://slate.com/news-and-politics/2001/08/the-rumsfeld-death-watch.html.

23. Paul Richter, "Pentagon Is Likely to Abandon Cold War's Two-Front Strategy," *Los Angeles Times*, April 15, 2001, A16.

24. See Peter J. Boyer, "The New War Machine," *New Yorker*, June 30, 2003, 55–71, and Vernon Loeb and Thomas E. Ricks, "Rumsfeld's Style, Goals Strain Ties in Pentagon," *Washington Post*, October 16, 2002, A01.

25. Andrew Feickert, *The Army's Future Combat System (FCS): Background and Issues for Congress*, CRS Report No. RL32888 (Washington, DC: Congressional Research Service, 2006), 12, https://www.everycrsreport.com/files/20090803_RL32888_f0fe8ba4f7d 3ecfc371efff2d1b9f2a439f34ddf.pdf.

26. Matthew Moten, "A Broken Dialogue: Rumsfeld, Shinseki, and Civil-Military Tension," in *American Civil-Military Relations: The Soldier and the State in a New Era*, ed. Suzanne C. Nielsen and Don M. Snider (Baltimore, MD: Johns Hopkins University Press, 2009), 49. Also, Shinseki disagreed with the notion that ground troops would be less crucial in future wars. Plus, he was concerned that cuts to the army would be used to buy new weapons for the other services. See Thomas K. Adams, *The Army After Next*, 97–98.

27. Thomas E. Ricks, "Rumsfeld Warned Not to Cut Size of Army; 82 Lawmakers Sign Letter to Pentagon," *Washington Post*, August 3, 2001, A8.

28. Rumsfeld undercut Shinseki's authority by announcing Shinseki's replacement more than a year before the chief's term was to end.

29. Graham, *By His Own Rules*, 250–251.

30. See Graham, 251–252.

31. Donald Rumsfeld, "The National Security Threat Posed by Military Bureaucratic Inefficiency and Waste," as delivered on September 10, 2011, https://asbl.com/documents /Donald_Rumsfeld_Speech_About_Bureaucratic_Waste.pdf.

32. Hugh Shelton, with Ronald Levinson and Malcolm McConnell, *Without Hesitation: The Odyssey of an American Warrior* (New York: St. Martin's Press, 2010), 401, 418, 420. See pages 407–408 for a particularly colorful illustration of Shelton's disdain for Rumsfeld.

33. Bob Woodward, *Bush at War* (New York: Simon and Schuster, 2002), 24.

34. Shelton, *Without Hesitation*, 426.

35. See, for example, Andrew Scutro, "Was Clark too Strong or Rumsfeld?—Personality Clash Cost Admiral Top Job Woodward Writes," *Navy Times*, October 30, 2006, 11.

36. Lloyd Grove, "General Hugh Shelton on Clinton, Rumsfeld, and McCain," *Daily Beast*, October 14, 2010, https://www.thedailybeast.com/general-hugh-shelton-on-clinton -rumsfeld-and-mccain.

37. For example, several key members of Congress cooperated with Rumsfeld to significantly increase spending for special operations forces. See Robert D. Kaplan, "What Rumsfeld Got Right," *The Atlantic*, July–August 2008, https://www.theatlantic.com/magazine /archive/2008/07/what-rumsfeld-got-right/306870/.

38. Donald H. Rumsfeld, "Transforming the Military," *Foreign Affairs* 81, no. 3 (May–June 2002): 20–32.

39. Remarks by the President and Secretary Rumsfeld in Announcement of Chairman and Vice-Chairman of the Joint Chiefs of Staff, Crawford Community Center, Crawford,

TX, August 24, 2001, https://georgewbush-whitehouse.archives.gov/news/releases/2001/08/20010824.html.

40. "Rumsfeld Dumps Crusader, Defends Decision," CNN, May 9, 2002, https://www.cnn.com/2002/ALLPOLITICS/05/08/rumsfeld.crusader/index.html.

41. "Army Cancels Comanche Helicopter, Will Shift Money Into Other Aviation Programs," CNN, February 23, 2004, https://www.cnn.com/2004/US/02/23/helicopter.cancel/.

42. U.S. Department of Defense, "Transformation Planning Guidance," 3, 6–7.

43. Mark G. Czelusta, "Business as Usual: An Assessment of Donald Rumsfeld's Transformation Vision and Transformation's Prospects for the Future" (Occasional Paper Series No. 18, George C. Marshall European Center for Security Studies, June 2008), 25.

44. Jason Sherman, "Rumsfeld Officially Kicks Off 2005 QDR, Issues New 'National Defense Strategy,'" *Inside Defense*, March 8, 2005, and Adams, *The Army After Next*, 202.

45. David Ignatius, "Grand Vision vs. Patchwork," *Washington Post*, October 7, 2005, A23.

46. "Mr. Rumsfeld's Flawed Vision," *Washington Post*, February 13, 2006, A20.

47. David M. Walker, "DOD Transformation: Challenges and Opportunities" (presentation at the Army War College, February 12, 2007, U.S. Government Accountability Office, GAO 07-500CG), 29.

48. Walker, 32.

49. Based on Office of the Under Secretary of Defense (Comptroller), "National Defense Budget Estimates for FY 2017," Department of Defense, March 2016, 22, https://comptroller.defense.gov/Portals/45/Documents/defbudget/fy2017/FY17_Green_Book.pdf.

50. According to analysis by the Congressional Budget Office, prior to 2000, these additions to the base budget typically accounted for about 2 percent of all defense department appropriations. By 2007–2008, they had grown to 28 percent of all defense appropriations, and this figure began to include items that traditionally were part of the base budget. Congressional Budget Office, *Funding for Overseas Contingency Operations and Its Impact on Defense Spending*, CBO Publication 54219 (Washington, DC: Congressional Budget Office, 2018), 3, https://www.cbo.gov/system/files/2018-10/54219-oco_spending.pdf.

51. Adams, *The Army After Next*, 250.

52. See, for example, Jim Garamone, "Myers: Changing Military Culture Key to Transformation," Armed Forces Press Service, October 7, 2004.

53. Loeb and Ricks, "Rumsfeld's Style, Goals Strain Ties in Pentagon," A01.

54. Shelton, *Without Hesitation*, 408–409.

55. Michael R. Gordon and General Bernard E. Trainor, *Cobra II: The Inside Story of the Invasion and Occupation of Iraq* (New York: Pantheon Books, 2006), 17.

56. See especially Risa A. Brooks, *The Civil-Military Politics of Strategic Assessment* (Princeton, NJ: Princeton University Press, 2008), 226–255.

57. For details about the flaws in U.S. reconstruction and stability efforts in Iraq, including the Rumsfeld team's contempt for and failure to consult the service chiefs, see Bob Woodward, *Plan of Attack* (New York: Simon and Schuster, 2004); Gordon and Trainor, *Cobra II*; and Thomas E. Ricks, *Fiasco: The American Military Adventure in Iraq* (New York: Penguin Press, 2006).

58. In his autobiography, Shelton argues that Franks lacked the skills to critique Rumsfeld's postwar plans, and also that his ego discouraged him from consulting the service chiefs. See Shelton, *Without Hesitation*, 447, 480–483. Franks, for his part, found the service chiefs too parochial and with a tendency to interfere because of bureaucratic self-interest. See Gordon and Trainor, *Cobra II*, 46–48.

59. Eric Schmitt, "Army Chief Raises Estimate of G.I.'s Needed in Postwar Iraq," *New York Times*, February 25, 2003.

60. Boyer, "The New War Machine," 55–71.

61. Thomas E. Ricks, "Rumsfeld Rebuked by Retired Generals," *Washington Post*, April 13, 2006, A01.

62. Paul D. Eaton, "For His Failures, Rumsfeld Must Go," *New York Times*, March 19, 2006, https://www.nytimes.com/2006/03/19/opinion/a-topdown-review-for-the-pentagon.html.

63. "A Conversation with General Richard B. Myers, Chairman of the Joint Chiefs of Staff," *National Guard* 57, no. 8 (September 2003): 32–36.

64. See, for examples, Loeb and Ricks, "Rumsfeld's Style," A01, and Graham, *By His Own Rules*, 563.

65. Andrew Cockburn, *Rumsfeld: His Rise, Fall, and Catastrophic Legacy* (New York: Scribner, 2007), 111.

66. Woodward, *State of Denial*, 404.

67. See, for example, Fred Kaplan, "Pete the Parrot Departs: Good Riddance to the Last of the Rumsfeld Generals," *Slate*, October 5, 2007, https://slate.com/news-and-politics/2007/10/good-riddance-to-the-last-of-the-rumsfeld-generals.html.

68. Office of the Under Secretary of Defense (Comptroller), *National Defense Estimates for FY 2007* (Washington, DC: Office of the Under Secretary of Defense [Comptroller], Department of Defense, 2006), 213, https://comptroller.defense.gov/Portals/45/Documents/defbudget/Docs/fy2007_greenbook.pdf.

69. Shelton, *With Hesitation*, 408. Emphasis in the original.

7. SEQUESTRATION

1. For a chronicle of Obama's shift, see Jeffrey Goldberg, "The Obama Doctrine," *The Atlantic*, April 2016, https://www.theatlantic.com/magazine/archive/2016/04/the-obama-doctrine/471525/.

2. Senator Barack Obama, "Remarks in Grand Rapids, Michigan, October 2, 2008," American Presidency Project, accessed April 19, 2022, https://www.presidency.ucsb.edu/documents/remarks-grand-rapids-michigan-2.

3. See Theda Skocpol and Vanessa Williamson, *The Tea Party and the Remaking of Republican Conservatism* (Oxford: Oxford University Press, 2013), especially chap. 5.

4. Concern about the deficit brought together such unlikely allies as Ron Paul and Barney Frank. In July 2009, they co-wrote a letter to their colleagues asking them to support

significant cuts in military spending as a way to reduce the deficit. Congressman Barney Frank and Congressman Ron Paul, "Why We Must Reduce Military Spending," *The Hill*, July 6, 2010, https://thehill.com/blogs/congress-blog/economy-a-budget/107229 -why-we-must-reduce-military-spending-reps-barney-frank-and-ron-paul.

5. The federal budget is divided into categories or "functions" rather than agencies or departments. For an explanation of this budget classification system, see Christopher T. Mann, "Defense Primer: The National Defense Budget Function (050)," Congressional Research Service, March 17, 2017, https://crsreports.congress.gov/product/pdf/IF/IF10618/2.

6. The Budget Control Act caps applied only to the Department of Defense's base budget and not funding for ongoing military operations, such as those in Iraq and Afghanistan, that were covered as part of Overseas Contingency Operations (OCO). After 9/11, funding for these wars came in the form of supplemental spending bills, enacted at various times throughout the fiscal year. Obama introduced the OCO budget and the process of requesting funding for the wars as part of the regular budget process. Over time, however, the OCO budget expanded to include funding for a variety of items that are arguably of tangential or no relevance to ongoing military operations. See Congressional Budget Office, *Funding for Overseas Contingency Operations and Its Impact on Defense Spending*, CBO Publication No. 54219 (Washington, DC: Congressional Budget Office, 2018), https://www.cbo.gov/publication/54219.

7. See Mann, "Defense Primer," 2.

8. Bob Woodward, *The Price of Politics* (New York: Simon and Schuster, 2013), 339.

9. Brendan W. McGarry, *The Defense Budget and the Budget Control Act: Frequently Asked Questions*, CRS Report No. R44039 (Washington, DC: Congressional Research Service, 2018), 7, https://sgp.fas.org/crs/natsec/R44039.pdf.

10. See Laura Meckler, "U.S. News: Prospect of Defense Cuts Tests GOP," *Wall Street Journal*, August 3, 2011, A2.

11. Using the more expansive "security" category for the Budget Control Act would help protect the military budget from absorbing the brunt of any spending reduction. This was included in the agreement because the act's negotiators, and especially those from the White House, were increasingly frantic to reach an agreement to raise the debt ceiling before August 2, 2011, to avoid a government default. See Woodward, *The Price of Politics*, 349–352.

12. Charles Hoskinson, "More Defense Cuts? Kyl's Out," *Politico*, September 8, 2011, https://www.politico.com/story/2011/09/more-defense-cuts-kyls-out-063005.

13. Reihan Salam, "The United States Doesn't Spend Enough on Its Military," *Slate*, November 12, 2015, https://slate.com/news-and-politics/2015/11/military-spending-the-case -for-spending-more-not-less.html.

14. See Michelle D. Christensen, "Submission of the President's Budget in Transition Years," CRS Report No. RS20752 (Washington, DC: Congressional Research Service, 2012), https://sgp.fas.org/crs/misc/RS20752.pdf.

15. Robert M. Gates, *Duty: Memoirs of a Secretary at War* (New York: Knopf, 2014), 313.

16. Gates, 146.

17. Gates, 142.
18. DOD Press Operations, "Secretary of Defense Testimony, Defense Budget Recommendation Statement" (Arlington, VA), April 6, 2009, and Department of Defense, "Sec. Gates Announces Efficiencies Initiatives," News Release no. 706–10, August 9, 2010, http://archive.defense.gov/Releases/Release.aspx?ReleaseID=13782.
19. Gates, *Duty*, 315–316.
20. Gates, 316.
21. The amount of UFRs continued to decline in FY 2011 and FY 2012. See Todd Harrison, *Analysis of the FY 2012 Defense Budget* (Washington, DC: Center for Strategic and Budgetary Assessments, 2011), 5, https://csbaonline.org/uploads/documents/2011.07.16-FY-2012-Defense-Budget.pdf.
22. Gates, *Duty*, 271–272.
23. Gates, 455–456.
24. Gates, 303–304.
25. Department of Defense, "Sec. Gates Announces Efficiencies Initiatives."
26. Gates, *Duty*, 465.
27. Department of Defense, "Sec. Gates Announces Efficiencies Initiatives."
28. Philip Ewing, "Gates Details Pentagon Cuts," *Politico*, January 6, 2011, https://www.politico.com/story/2011/01/gates-details-pentagon-cuts-047158. When the budget was submitted, the Pentagon claimed it found $178 billion in savings.
29. Gates, *Duty*, 462–463.
30. Gates had wanted to cancel these programs because he felt they were ill-suited for future wars. He had proposed cutting these programs prior to the efficiencies initiatives.
31. See Harrison, *Analysis of the FY 2012 Defense Budget*, 6. Harrison also points out that the budget was announced prior to the decision to begin withdrawal of surge forces in Afghanistan. See also Ewing, "Gates Details Pentagon Cuts."
32. The navy got increased funding for aircraft-based drones and the air force got funding for a new long-range bomber.
33. Gates, *Duty*, 547–548.
34. Robert Gates, "Speech to the American Enterprise Institute, Delivered 24 May 2011," American Rhetoric Online Speech Bank, accessed March 17, 2022, http://www.americanrhetoric.com/speeches/robertgatesamericanenterpriseinstitute.htm.
35. For examples, see Defense Secretary Leon Panetta and Joint Chiefs Chairman Admiral Mike Mullen, "Defense Department News Conference," C-SPAN, August 4, 2011, https://www.c-span.org/video/?300900-2/defense-department-news-conference, and Leon Panetta, *Worthy Fights: A Memoir of Leadership in War and Peace* (New York: Penguin, 2015), 372–375.
36. Panetta, *Worthy Fights*, 375.
37. Department of Defense, "DOD New Briefing with Secretary Panetta and Adm. Mullen From the Pentagon."
38. See Scott Wilson and Greg Jaffee, "A Strong Defense for Obama," *Washington Post*, January 8, 2012, A1.

39. See Wilson and Jaffe, A1.

40. For the new plan, see Department of Defense, *Sustaining U.S. Global Leadership: Priorities for 21st Century Defense* (Washington, DC: Department of Defense, 2012).

41. Department of Defense press briefing announcing the Defense Strategic Guidance, as quoted in Catherine Dale and Pat Towell, *In Brief: Assessing the January 2012 Defense Strategic Guidance (DSG)*, CRS Report No. R42146 (Washington, DC: Congressional Research Service, 2013), 1, https://sgp.fas.org/crs/natsec/R42146.pdf.

42. Department of Defense press briefing announcing the Defense Strategic Guidance as quoted in Dale and Towell, 5.

43. Kevin Baron, "Quick Take; Dempsey Says Military Not Planning for Sequester," *National Journal Daily P.M. Update*, December 9, 2011.

44. Thom Shanker, "No 'Plan B' for Pentagon in Case of Big Budget Cut," *New York Times*, November 30, 2012, A26.

45. Marcus Weisgerber, "Panetta: Impasse Would Mean Severe Cuts in Operations," *Military Times*, January 10, 2013.

46. See, for example, Yochi J. Dreazen, "The Pentagon's War of Words and Numbers," *National Journal*, November 17, 2011. Panetta, in his autobiography, notes that among cabinet officials he felt he was the sole one speaking out against sequestration, when in fact none supported it. Panetta, *Worthy Fights*, 375.

47. Panetta, *Worthy Fights*, 375.

48. Department of Defense, *Summary of Performance and Financial Information Report, Fiscal Year 2013* (Washington, DC: Office of the Under Secretary of Defense [Comptroller]/Chief Financial Officer, 2014), https://comptroller.defense.gov/Portals/45/documents/citizensreport/fy2013/2013_report.pdf.

49. Mattea Kramer, "Sequestration's Impact of Military Spending, 2013–2014," National Priorities Project, March 4, 2014, https://www.nationalpriorities.org/analysis/2014/sequestration-impact-on-military-spending-2013-2014/.

50. Ernesto Londono, "Pentagons' Proposed Budget about the Same as Last Year," *Washington Post*, April 10, 2013, https://www.washingtonpost.com/world/national-security/pentagons-proposed-budget-about-same-as-last-year/2013/04/10/4a57fdd8-a224-11e2-82bc-511538ae90a4_story.html.

51. Craig Whitlock, "Budget Cutting Spurs Hagel to Order Pentagon Review of Year-Old Strategy," *Washington Post*, March 19, 2013, A11.

52. Christopher J. Castelli, "Carter: Strategic Review Progressing, But Bolder Thinking Still Needed," *Inside the Pentagon*, May 9, 2013.

53. "Hagel's Strategic Budget Review," *Air Force Times*, June 10, 2013, 3, and Secretary of Defense Chuck Hagel, "Statement on Strategic Choices and Management Review," RealClear Defense, July 31, 2013, https://www.realcleardefense.com/articles/2013/07/31/statement_on_strategic_choices_and_management_review_106730.html.

54. Secretary Hagel, "Statement on Strategic Choices and Management Review."

55. This concern about future budgets prompted criticism from some Republicans in Congress. The QDR is supposed to offer proposals that are unconstrained by current

budgets. Whereas Republicans hoped to use the QDR as an excuse to call for increased defense spending, the QDR denied this by arguing that the strategy could be executed under current budgets, but not under sequestration.

56. For more specific decisions, see Stephanie Gaskell, "Pentagon's Post-War Budget Marks End of War Era," *Defense One*, February 24, 2014, https://www.defenseone.com /business/2014/02/pentagons-post-war-budget-marks-end-war-era/79288/.

57. Some argued that the FY 2015 budget was not sufficient to execute the choices made in the QDR and that funding over the next five years would actually fall $200–$300 billion short over the Future Years Defense Program's five-year period. See, for example, Todd Harrison, *Analysis of the FY 2015 Defense Budget* (Washington, DC: Center for Strategic and Budgetary Assessments, 2014), 3, https://csbaonline.org/uploads/documents /ANALYSIS-OF-THE-FY-2015-DEFENSE-BUDGET.pdf.

58. CNN Wire Staff, "Mullen: Debt Is Top National Security Threat," CNN, August 27, 2010, http://www.cnn.com/2010/US/08/27/debt.security.mullen/index.html.

59. Mullen met Obama just after he was elected president. Obama told him there was an economic crisis he would have to deal with, and Mullen said he understood that defense would not be exempt from cuts. Bob Woodward, *Obama's Wars* (New York: Simon and Schuster, 2010), 34.

60. Thom Shanker and Christopher Drew, "Obama Puts Deficit Ball Back in Pentagon's Court," *New York Times*, April 15, 2011, A20.

61. See U.S. Senate, Committee on Armed Services, "Joint Chiefs of Staff Chair Nomination," C-SPAN, July 26, 2011, https://www.c-span.org/video/?300711-1/joint-chiefs-staff -chair-nomination.

62. Panetta, *Worthy Fights*, 375.

63. Christopher J. Castelli, "Cuts to Ground Forces Loom Large in Strategic-Choices Review," *Inside the Pentagon*, October 27, 2011.

64. Castelli.

65. Christopher J. Castelli, "DOD Proposes Shrinking Ground Forces, Shunning Stability Ops," *Inside the Pentagon*, January 5, 2012.

66. Department of Defense, "Press Briefing by Secretary Hagel and Adm. Winnefeld from the Pentagon," U.S. Department of Defense Information/FIND, July 31, 2013.

67. For a summary of the SCMR results, see Department of Defense, "Press Briefing by Secretary Hagel and Adm. Winnefeld," July 31, 2013.

68. Jason Sherman, "Struggling to Find Efficiencies in POM Outyears, Army Proposes 'IOUs,'" *Inside the Pentagon's Inside the Army*, August 9, 2010.

69. Kate Brannen, "Services United Against Further Defense Cuts," *Federal Times*, October 24, 2011, 10.

70. Brannen, 10.

71. See, for example, Carlo Munoz, "Amos Takes Marine Corps Case Directly to Panetta," *Breaking Defense*, September 15, 2011.

72. William H. McMichael, " 'Hard Choices' Looming, JCS Chairman says," *Navy Times*, March 2, 2009, 24.

73. U.S. House of Representatives, Committee on Armed Services, *Hearing on National Defense Authorization Act for Fiscal Year 2009 and Oversight of Previously Authorized Programs: Budget Request from the Department of Defense*, 110th Cong., 2nd sess. (Feb. 6, 2008).

74. Christopher J. Castelli, "Mullen: Divide Defense Department Budget Differently," *Inside the Pentagon's Inside the Army*, September 26, 2011.

75. Marcus Weisgerber and Zachary Fryer-Biggs, "Pentagon Punts on Major Program Cuts," *Defense News*, January 30, 2012.

76. I thank Russell Rumbaugh for this idea.

77. According to the Congressional Budget Office, personnel account for about one-quarter of the military budget, and one of the biggest factors in the increasing cost of personnel is health care. See Congressional Budget Office, *Costs of Military Pay and Benefits in the Defense Budget*, CBO Publication No. 4234 (Washington, DC: Congressional Budget Office, 2012), https://www.cbo.gov/sites/default/files/112th-congress-2011-2012/reports/11-14-12-militarycompo.pdf.

78. Based on analysis from "Table 2-1: Base Budget, War Funding and Supplementals by Military Department, by Public Law Title," in Office of the Under Secretary of Defense (Comptroller), *National Defense Budget Estimates for FY 2017* (Washington, DC: Department of Defense, 2016), 24–32, https://comptroller.defense.gov/Portals/45/Documents/defbudget/fy2016/FY16_Green_Book.pdf.

79. Brannen, "Services United Against Further Defense Cuts."

80. Hillary Clinton, "America's Pacific Century," *Foreign Policy*, October 11, 2011.

81. For details, see Benjamin M. Jensen and Eric Y. Shibya, "The Military Rebalance as Retcon," in *Origins and Evolution of the U.S. Rebalance Toward Asia*, ed. Hugo Meijer (New York: Palgrave Macmillan, 2015), 89–97.

82. Sydney J. Freedberg Jr., "Amos & Dempsey: Don't Just Stop Sequester, Save the Ground Force," *Breaking Defense*, November 18, 2013.

83. Gates, *Duty*, 315.

84. Initially, although the vice chairman outranked the service chiefs, he was not an official member of the JCS and could vote only when acting as chairman. In 1992, however, Congress made the vice chairman a full member of the JCS.

85. For details, see Woodward, *Obama's Wars*, 235–237, 295.

86. Vago Muradian, "No Decision Yet on Top U.S. Military Jobs," *Defense News*, May 23, 2011, 4, and Bob Woodward, *Obama's Wars*, especially 234–238.

87. Obama's preference for Cartwright was clearly expressed more than two years before Mullen's retirement. According to Gates, prior to Mullen's reappointment for a second term, the president told him privately that he wanted Cartwright to take over in two years when Mullen retired. Gates, *Duty*, 350.

88. Mallie Jane Kim, "Is Gen. Martin Dempsey the Right Choice for Joint Chiefs Chair?," *U.S. News & World Report*, May 31, 2001; Gates, *Duty*, 537.

89. Department of Defense, "Sec. Gates Announces Efficiencies Initiatives."

90. "VCJCS: DoD Efficiency Drill an Opportunity for Further 'Rebalancing,'" *Defense Daily*, December 9, 2010.

91. "Pentagon Officials Debate Future of B-Model Joint Strike Fighter," *Defense Daily*, December 3, 2010.

92. "Cartwright Addresses Drawdowns, Budget with Reporters," GlobalDefence.net, July 15, 2011, https://www.globaldefence.net/archiv/defence-news/cartwright-addresses -drawdowns-budget-with-reporters, and Andrew Tilghman, "Top DoD Official: Budget Cuts Will Bring Huge Changes," *Air Force Times*, July 25, 2011, 23.

93. For his criticism of service culture and its deleterious effect on force planning, see Chuck Paone, "JCS Vice Chairman: Break Service Barriers," U.S. Fed News Service, June 20, 2008.

94. Admiral James Winnefeld, Remarks at the Association of the U.S. Army General Bernard Rogers Lecture Series, Arlington, VA, September 18, 2013.

95. McKiernan was forced into retirement. Although Gates had recommended his replacement, the move was widely thought to reflect a shift in strategy toward Afghanistan, as well as concern over McKiernan's lack of progress in stabilizing the country. See Elisabeth Bumiller and Thom Shanker, "Commander's Ouster Is Tied to Shift in Afghan War," *New York Times*, May 11, 2009, and Simon Tisdall, "The Curious Sacking of Gen McKiernan," *The Guardian*, May 12, 2009.

96. Woodward, *Obama's Wars*, 94–95.

97. Gates, *Duty*, 354.

98. Woodward, *Obama's Wars*, 235–237.

99. Gates, *Duty*, 378–381.

100. For details, see Gates, 373.

101. U.S. Senate, Armed Services Committee, "Military Nominations Hearing," C-SPAN, June 2, 2009, https://www.c-span.org/video/?286758-1/military-nominations-hearing.

102. Woodward, *Obama's Wars*, 193.

103. Bob Woodward, "McChrystal: More Forces on 'Mission Failure,' " *Washington Post*, September 21, 2009.

104. Michael Hastings, "The Runaway General," *Rolling Stone*, June 22, 2010.

105. Michael Gerson, "In Afghanistan, No Choice but to Try," *Washington Post*, September 4, 2009.

106. Woodward, *Obama's Wars*, 159, and Kate Ackley, "Lindsey Graham: Don't Rumsfeld Afghanistan," *Roll Call*, August 9, 2009.

107. U.S. Senate, Armed Services Committee, "Joint Chiefs of Staff Chairman Nomination," C-SPAN, September 15, 2009, https://www.c-span.org/video/?288911-1/joint-chiefs-staff -chairman-nomination.

108. For examples, see Renee Montage and Steve Inskeep, "Violence Shatters Afghan Sense Of Security," *Morning Edition*, NPR, August 5, 2009, https://www.npr.org/programs /morning-edition/2009/08/05/111387260/, and "U.S. Military Says Its Force in Afghanistan is Insufficient," *New York Times*, August 23, 2009, https://www.nytimes.com/2009 /08/24/world/asia/24military.html.

109. Woodward, *Obama's Wars*, 123, 142–143, 195, 197, 258, 278. See also David E. Sanger, *Confront and Conceal: Obama's Secret Wars and Surprising Use of American Power* (New York: Crown Publishers, 2012), 32, and, Gates, *Duty*, 338, 350, 367–368.

110. Gates, *Duty*, 377.
111. Woodward, *Obama's Wars*, 196, and, Gates, *Duty*, 377–378.
112. Gates, *Duty*, 383.
113. Woodward, *Obama's Wars*, 257–260.
114. Woodward, 295.
115. See testimony by Chairman Mike Mullen, U.S. Senate, Armed Services Committee, *Department of Defense Authorization for Appropriations for Fiscal Year 2011*, 111th Cong., 2nd sess. (Feb. 2, 2010).
116. Woodward, *Obama's Wars*, 235.
117. Conversation with Alice Friend Hunt in February 2016.

8. THE CHAIRMAN, THE JOINT CHIEFS OF STAFF, AND CIVIL-MILITARY RELATIONS

1. For examples, see John Shanahan and Laura Junor, "We Need a Goldwater-Nichols Act for Emerging Technology," *Defense One*, December 16, 2020, https://www.defenseone .com/ideas/2020/12/we-need-goldwater-nichols-act-emerging-technology/170794/; John Wright, "Solving Japan's Joint Operations Problem," *The Diplomat*, January 31, 2018, https://thediplomat.com/2018/01/solving-japans-joint-operations-problem/; Colin Clark, "Carter to Reshape US Military: Goldwater-Nichols II," *Breaking Defense*, April 5, 2016, https://breakingdefense.com/2016/04/carter-to-reshape-us-military-goldwater-nichols -ii/; and U.S. Senate, Committee on Armed Services, *30 Years of Goldwater–Nichols Reform: Hearing Before the Committee on Armed Services*, 114th Cong., 1st sess. (Nov. 10, 2015). For a more nuanced view of the progress toward jointness, see Don M. Snider, "Jointness, Defense Transformation, and the Need for a New Joint Warfare Profession," *Parameters* 33, no. 3 (2003): 16–30.
2. H. R. McMaster, *Dereliction of Duty: Johnson, McNamara, the Joint Chiefs of Staff, and the Lies that Led to Vietnam* (New York: Harper, 1998).
3. Although the case studies show that chairmen vary in the degree to which they assert agency or entrepreneurship in the policy process, my goal has been to explain the circumstances under which they are either more or less successful in achieving their goals. The point is not to determine why a particular chairman chooses to be more or less politically active in his relations with the White House or service chiefs.
4. Arnold Kanter, *Defense Politics: A Budgetary Perspective* (Chicago: University of Chicago Press, 1970).
5. Peter D. Feaver, "The Civil-Military Problematique: Huntington, Janowitz, and the Question of Civilian Control," *Armed Forces & Society* 23, no. 2 (Winter 1996): 149–178.
6. Besides the norm of equality, service choices about national security are often heavily influenced by their organizational culture and experiences. Although I find evidence to support the influence of organizational culture, I do not examine it specifically. For the prevalence of organizational culture in service decision making, see Carl H. Builder, *The*

Masks of War: American Military Styles in Strategy and Analysis (Baltimore, MD: Johns Hopkins University Press, 1989), and the discussion in Mackubin Thomas Owens, "What Military Officers Need to Know About Civil-Military Relations," *Naval War College Review* 65, no. 2 (Spring 2021): 16–17.

7. For a discussion of the central role Huntington's construct plays in U.S. civil-military relations, see Risa A. Brooks, "Integrating the Civil-Military Relations Subfield," *Annual Review of Political Science* 22 (2019): 386–388.

8. For a critique of the Huntington approach and its influence on civil-military relations, see Risa Brooks, "Paradoxes of Professionalism: Rethinking Civil-Military Relations in the United States, *International Security* 44, no. 4 (2022): 7–44.

9. Brooks, especially 17–21. Jim Golby also argues that the focus on objective control can serve to absolve the military from adjusting its advice as political conditions change. See Jim Golby, "Improving Advice and Earning Autonomy: Building Trust in the Strategic Dialogue," *Strategy Bridge*, October 3, 2017, https://thestrategybridge.org/the-bridge/2017/10/3 /improving-advice-and-earning-autonomy-building-trust-in-the-strategic-dialogue.

10. Andrew Bacevich, *The New American Militarism* (New York: Oxford University Press, 2013), and Samuel P. Huntington, *The Common Defense: Strategic Programs in National Politics* (New York: Columbia University Press, 1961), 384–385. For details about this bargaining relationship, see MacKubin Thomas Owens, *U.S. Civil-Military Relations After 9/11: Renegotiating the Civil-Military Bargain* (New York: Continuum, 2011).

11. Richard H. Kohn, "The Erosion of Civilian Control of the Military in the United States Today," *U.S. Naval War College Review* 55, no. 3 (Summer 2002): 15–16.

12. For a review of debates over disobedience and civilian control, see Lindsay Cohn, Max Margulies, and Michael A. Robinson, "What Discord Follows: The Divisive Debate Over Military Disobedience," *War on the Rocks*, August 2, 2019, https://warontherocks .com/2019/08/what-discord-follows-the-divisive-debate-over-military-disobedience/.

13. For a few examples, see James Golby, Kyle Dropp, and Peter Feaver, *Military Campaigns: Veterans' Endorsements and Presidential Elections* (Washington, DC: Center for a New American Security, 2012), https://s3.us-east-1.amazonaws.com/files.cnas.org/documents /CNAS_MilitaryCampaigns_GolbyDroppFeaver.pdf?mtime=20160906081631&focal =none; Carrie A. Lee, "Dear Civ-Mil Community: The (Retired) Generals Are Speaking & We Should Listen," *Duck of Minerva* (blog), June 3, 2020, https://www.duckofminerva .com/2020/06/dear-civ-mil-community-the-retired-generals-are-speaking-we-should -listen.html; James Golby and Mara Karlin, "Why 'Best Military Advice' Is Bad for the Military—and Worse for Civilians," *Orbis* 62, no. 1 (2018): 137–153; and Richard H. Kohn, "On Resignation," *Armed Forces & Society*, 43, no. 1 (January 2017): 41–52.

14. See, for example, James Fallows, "The tragedy of the American Military," *The Atlantic*, January–February 2015.

15. Janine Davidson, "Civil-Military Friction and Presidential Decision Making: Explaining the Broken Dialogue," *Presidential Studies Quarterly* 43, no. 1 (March 2013): 129–145.

16. The gap Richard Kohn noted in 1994 (see Richard H. Kohn, "Out of Control: The Crisis in Civil-Military Relations," *National Interest* 35 [Spring 1994]: 3–17) is increasingly seen

as a difference, not in general political preferences, but in partisan affiliation. See Hugh Liebert and James Golby, "Midlife Crisis? The All-Volunteer Force at 40," *Armed Forces & Society* 43, no. 1 (January 2017): 115–138.

17. Scott Maucione, "Pentagon Staff Size Takes More Flack from Experts," Federal News Network, December 8, 2015, https://federalnewsnetwork.com/defense/2015/12/pentagon -staff-size-takes-slack-experts/.

18. For concerns that the Office of the Secretary of Defense lags behind its military counterparts, see Risa Brooks, Jim Golby, Heidi Urben, "Crisis of Command: America's Broken Civil-Military Relationship Imperils National Security," *Foreign Affairs* 100, no. 3 (May–June 2021): 63–75.

19. Goldwater-Nichols Department of Defense Reorganization Act of 1986, Public L. No. 99-433, 100 Stat. 992 (1986).

20. In using policy victory as a proxy for the quality of civil-military relations, I acknowledge that it fails to capture important aspects of the relationship. Alice Hunt Friend, for examples, argues that increasingly civilian preferences are actually derived from or adopted in their entirety from military preferences, and thus it is misleading to consider civilian policy victories as distinct from military ones. See Alice Hunt Friend, "Creating Requirements: Emerging Military Capabilities, Civilian Preferences, and Civil-Military Relations" (PhD diss., American University, 2020). Peter Feaver's principal-agent framework suggests that winning a particular policy battle isn't sufficient because the costs of monitoring and punishment also influence civilian incentives to challenge the military. See Peter D. Feaver, *Armed Servants: Agency, Oversight, and Civil-Military Relations* (Cambridge, MA: Harvard University Press, 2005). Rebecca Schiff's *The Military and Domestic Politics: A Concordance Theory of Civil-Military Relations* (London: Routledge: 2008) makes the case that civilian control is less important than agreement between civilians and the military over a variety of policy issues, including the proper role the military should assume in the policy process. Lindsay Cohn's discussion of civilian control offers multiple reasons why policy victory does not encapsulate the ability of civilians to control the military. See Lindsay P. Cohn, "It Wasn't in My Contract: Security Privatization and Civilian Control," *Armed Forces & Society* 37, no. 3 (July 2011): 381–398.

21. For a summary of such dissent, see Andrew J. Bacevich, "Elusive Bargain: The Pattern of U.S. Civil-Military Relations Since World War II," in *The Long War: A New History of U.S. National Security Policy since World War II*, ed. Andrew J. Bacevich (New York: Columbia University Press, 2007), 207–264.

22. James Golby, Peter Feaver, and Kyle Dropp, "Elite Military Cues and Public Opinion About the Use of Military Force," *Armed Forces & Society* 44, no. 1 (January 2018): 44–71; Peter D. Feaver, "Civil-Military Relations and Policy: A Sampling of a New Wave of Scholarship," *Journal of Strategic Studies* 40, nos. 1–2 (2017): 325–342; Jim Golby, Kyle Dropp, and Peter Feaver, *Listening to the Generals: How Military Advice Affects Public Support for the Use of Force* (Washington, DC: Center for a New American Security, 2013), https://s3.us-east-1.amazonaws.com/files.cnas.org/documents/CNAS-Generals

-report-updated.pdf?mtime=20160906081306&focal=none; and Golby, Dropp, and Feaver, *Military Campaigns.*

23. Brooks, Golby, and Urben, "Crisis of Command," 63–75.

24. Kori Schake, "The Process Is Working," *Foreign Affairs* 100 no. 5 (September–October 2021): 230–232; Peter D. Feaver, "A Stormy but Durable Marriage," *Foreign Affairs* 100, no. 5 (September–October 2021): 232–235; and, Risa Brooks, Jim Golby, and Heidi Urben, "Brooks, Golby, and Urben Reply," *Foreign Affairs* 100, no. 5 (September–October 2021): 235–238.

25. Don Snider, for example, argues that if civilian policy directives violate what he describes as a narrow range of moral responsibilities to protect the state, military officers should dissent—indeed, they have a duty to, based on their professional obligations. Don M. Snider, "Dissent, Resignation, and the Moral Agency of Senior Military Professionals," *Armed Forces & Society* 43, no. 1 (January 2017): 5–16.

26. Brooks, Golby, Urben, Schake, and Feaver all agree on this point. See their exchange in *Foreign Affairs* 100, no. 5 (September–October 2021): 230–238.

27. Brooks, Golby, and Urben, "Crisis of Command," 63–75, and Feaver, "A Stormy but Durable Marriage," 232–235.

28. See Jessica Blankshain, "Trump's Generals: Mattis, McMaster, and Kelly," part of a broader discussion on this topic in "Policy Roundtable: Civil-Military Relations Now and Tomorrow," chaired by Celeste Ward Gventer, *Texas National Security Review,* March 27, 2018, https://tnsr.org/roundtable/policy-roundtable-civil-military-relations-now-tomorrow/#essay2.

29. Polina Beliakova, "Erosion by Deference: Civilian Control and the Military in Policymaking," *Texas National Security Review* 4, no. 3 (Summer 2021): 56–57.

30. Brooks, Golby, and Urben, "Crisis of Command," 63–75, discusses the political costs of ignoring military advice. Others focus on misunderstandings that arise from different cultures. "Best military advice," for example, can be interpreted by civilians as a veiled threat, which they ignore at their peril. See Golby and Karlin, "Why 'Best Military Advice' Is Bad," 137–153, and also Peter D. Feaver and Richard H. Kohn, "Civil-Military Relations in the United States: What Senior Leaders Need to Know (and Usually Don't)," *Strategic Studies Quarterly* 15, no. 2 (Summer 2021): 12–37. Similarly, military "requirements" are often misunderstood as necessities rather than choices. See Mark Cancian, "Bad Idea: Using the Phrase 'Military Requirements,'" *Defense 360,* December 6, 2018, https://defense360.csis.org/bad-idea-using-the-phrase-military-requirements/.

31. For examples of this argument see Schake, "The Process Is Working," and Eliot A. Cohen, *Supreme Command: Soldiers, Statesmen, and Leadership in Wartime* (New York: Free Press, 2002).

INDEX

Italicized page numbers indicate figures; those with a *t* indicate tables.